THE POLITICS OF DISCIPLESHIP

THE CHURCH AND POSTMODERN CULTURE

James K. A. Smith, series editor
www.churchandpomo.org

The Church and Postmodern Culture series features high-profile theorists in continental philosophy and contemporary theology writing for a broad, nonspecialist audience interested in the impact of postmodern theory on the faith and practice of the church.

Also available in the series

James K. A. Smith, *Who's Afraid of Postmodernism? Taking Derrida, Lyotard, and Foucault to Church*

John D. Caputo, *What Would Jesus Deconstruct? The Good News of Postmodernism for the Church*

Carl Raschke, *GloboChrist: The Great Commission Takes a Postmodern Turn*

Merold Westphal, *Whose Community? Which Interpretation? Philosophical Hermeneutics for the Church*

THE POLITICS OF DISCIPLESHIP

Becoming Postmaterial Citizens

GRAHAM WARD

a division of Baker Publishing Group
Grand Rapids, Michigan

Published by Baker Academic
a division of Baker Publishing Group
P.O. Box 6287, Grand Rapids, MI 49516-6287
www.bakeracademic.com

Printed in the United States of America

Library of Congress Cataloging-in-Publication Data

Ward, Graham S.
The politics of discipleship : becoming postmaterial citizens / Graham Ward.
p. cm. — (The church and postmodern culture)
Includes index.
ISBN 978-0-8010-3158-8 (pbk.)
1. Christianity and politics. 2. Church and the world. 3. Postmodernism—Religious aspects—Christianity. I. Title.
BR115.P7W35 2009
261—dc22 2009008075

For Rachel and Yazeed

and

in picem memoriam

Marcella Althaus-Reid and Paul Fletcher

"Since the theology of the world is . . . a theology of emerging political and social order, this theology of the world must be a *political theology*."

Johannes B. Metz

Contents

Series Preface

Current discussions in the church—from emergent "postmodern" congregations to mainline "missional" congregations—are increasingly grappling with philosophical and theoretical questions related to postmodernity. In fact, it could be argued that developments in postmodern theory (especially questions of "post-foundationalist" epistemologies) have contributed to the breakdown of former barriers between evangelical, mainline, and Catholic faith communities. Postliberalism—a related "effect" of postmodernism—has engendered a new, confessional ecumenism wherein we find nondenominational evangelical congregations, mainline Protestant churches, and Catholic parishes all wrestling with the challenges of postmodernism and drawing on the culture of postmodernity as an opportunity for rethinking the shape of our churches.

This context presents an exciting opportunity for contemporary philosophy and critical theory to "hit the ground," so to speak, by allowing high-level work in postmodern theory to serve the church's practice—including all the kinds of congregations and communions noted above. The goal of this series is to bring together high-profile theorists in continental philosophy and contemporary theology to write for a broad, nonspecialist audience interested in the impact of postmodern theory on the faith and practice of the church. Each book in the series will, from different angles and with different questions, undertake to answer questions such as What does postmodern theory have to say about the shape of the church? How should concrete, in-the-pew and on-the-ground religious practices be impacted by postmodernism? What should the church look like in postmodernity? What has Paris to do with Jerusalem?

The series is ecumenical not only with respect to its ecclesial destinations but also with respect to the facets of continental philosophy and theory that are represented. A wide variety of theoretical commitments will be included, ranging from deconstruction to Radical Orthodoxy, including voices from Badiou to Žižek and the usual suspects in between (Nietzsche, Heidegger, Levinas, Derrida, Foucault, Irigaray, Rorty, and others). Insofar as postmodernism occasions a retrieval of ancient sources, these contemporary sources will be brought into dialogue with Augustine, Irenaeus, Aquinas, and other resources. Drawing on the wisdom of established scholars in the field, the series will provide accessible introductions to postmodern thought with the specific aim of exploring its impact on ecclesial practice. The books are offered, one might say, as French lessons for the church.

Series Editor's Foreword

James K. A. Smith

What do we do *now*? This might be the first question of discipleship. It is the question asked by the disciples at the foot of the cross: The Messiah is dead. *What do we do now?* It is the question asked by the same disciples after the resurrection: He's alive! *What do we do now?* And it is the question asked by these same Jesus followers after the ascension: The King has left us. *What do we do now?*

If this is the first question of discipleship, it is also a perennial question of discipleship. If, as Kierkegaard suggests, every generation is contemporaneous with the Messiah—if every follower is a contemporary of the Teacher—then this question will be constantly asked anew. But in order to answer the question, we need to understand this "now"; we need to grapple with the present. I have long appreciated the work of Graham Ward because I have always sensed that he is asking this basic question: "What time is it?" Theology, for Ward, is not an arcane game consumed with systematizing timeless truths; rather, it is the concrete and contemporary task of trying to faithfully discern "the times."

This is why the best theology (indeed, just the sort of theology Ward undertakes in this book) will be a kind of ethnography—a "thick description" of our present, attentive to the layers and the complexity of those institutions and practices that constitute our globalized world. *The Politics of Discipleship* is concerned with postmodernity, not as a matter of epistemological debates about foundationalism, but rather in terms of the phenomena we regularly encounter on CNN: the crisis of democracy, the effects of globalization, the resurgence of religion in global politics, the global expansion of materialism and consumerism, and more. In the face of these shifting realities, we find ourselves asking the disciples' question: What do we do *now*? Ward's theology of thick description is as attentive to "the world" as it is to "the church." Indeed, he's out to complicate the distinction. But *The Politics of Discipleship* also offers an unabashedly theological reading of our present, asking "What time is it?" in order to help us more wisely ask, "What do we do *now*?"

However, Ward reproves those who might be looking for easy direction: "My account of Christian political discipleship," he cautions, "will not inform you how Jesus wants you to vote. . . . I am not going to tell you that Jesus loves democracy, or that Jesus and Che Guevara shared the same political vision, or that the Christian gospel advocates the political need for hierarchy and dictatorship" (262). You will not find here "Seven Easy Steps to Political Discipleship" or any other formula coined for the fundraising brochures of a Christian Political Action Committee. This is not a manifesto for either the Religious Right or the Religious Left (even though he clearly advocates a Christian socialism). Instead, what Ward offers is an ecclesiology: an account of the body of Christ as a body politic.

So rather than remaining fixated on issues of knowledge or epistemology, Ward's postmodern ecclesiology is, perhaps surprisingly, a matter of metaphysics. I say "surprisingly" only because the postmodern has long been associated with what's been called "the end of metaphysics." In contrast to the clunky, solid stabilities of modernity and the metaphysical "stuff" of medieval scholasticism, postmodernism has trafficked in flow and flux. Postmodernity has been identified with the surface and the simulacrum, the fluid and flashy, the "virtual" as opposed to "the real." Thus all that is solid melts into thin air, and metaphysics evaporates with it. Postmodernity, on this account, spells the end of metaphysics and the advent of the virtual.

But this melting of solidity was precisely what Marx suggested was the outcome of capitalism, and it's hard to imagine anything more "modern" than capitalism. So in a strange way, the postmodern allergy to "metaphysics" betrays its very modern provenance, which is why Frederic Jameson could famously describe postmodernism as "the cultural logic of late capitalism." Ward notes the same: "there is no doubt," he concludes, "that the favored language of postmodernity—'flux,' 'flows,' [etc.]—and the move toward soft understandings of the subject as agent and of power as diffuse are at best not going to be effective resistors to laissez-faire capitalism and at worst help foster a culture in which such capitalism can have its greatest impact" (75). In other words, much of postmodernism turns out to be hypermodernism, providing fuel for late (globalized) capitalism. Thus the irony: the "materialism" of consumer capitalism actually eviscerates the material, thins it out to nothingness. So "the end of metaphysics" is everything capitalism could have hoped for.

This is why Ward sees an imperative to redeem metaphysics. A properly postmodern theology, he argues, will spell the end of "the end of metaphysics." And here Ward's theological ethnography gives us new eyes to see our present. For in the midst of our disenchanted, commodified world, we find ciphers of transcendence and the desire for enchantment. In analyses of Harry Potter, the *Lord of the Rings*, marketing, and other cultural phenomena, Ward discerns a disenchantment with disenchantment. "What is culturally evident," he notes, "is that although certain philosophers of both the analytical and the Continental traditions speak loudly about the postmetaphysical, contemporary living is shot through with metaphysical themes, desires, and dreams. One might even write of a renaissance of the metaphysical" (152).

This presents an occasion and a catalyst not only for Christian theology but more importantly for Christian mission—the church sent to the world for the world, seeking to enact a re-enchantment of the political while at the same time *materializing* the political. In contrast to the depoliticization, dematerialization, and commodification that characterizes late modern culture, the Christian gospel announces a theology of creation, embodiment, and resurrection that revalues the material. Thus Christianity is a more-thorough materialism than the faux-materialism of a commodified world of consumption and disposal.

So what do we do now? Ward helps us imagine the shape of political discipleship: "The politics of Christian discipleship is about first unmasking the theological and metaphysical sources of current mythologies and revealing the distortions and perversions of their current secularized forms. Then we need to reread and rewrite the Christian tradition back into contemporary culture" (165). This is not merely an intellectual program or a vision for a new Christian empire; rather, it is a mission pursued in "the micropractices of Christian living" (166). At stake here is *action*. To ask "What do we *do* now?" is to consider the shape of our action. And thus at the heart of this book is Ward's stunning and rigorous answer to the question: "What is it for the Christian to act" (181)? What follows is a phenomenology of Christian action that locates our doing not only within the practices of the church but also, and more importantly, within the Spirit's divine action in the world (192). Christian "action," then, is "a *praxis* that participates in a divine *poiēsis* that has soteriological and eschatological import." And "the church is this body of action" (201). In other words, this is *our* doing. The church *is* our action. Or as Ward puts it: "The church is only what this body of Christians do" (202). *The Politics of Discipleship* is nothing short of a call to action.

Proviso

The majority of academics have been trained to write books as doctoral students. And doctoral supervisors hammer home to these students that the question at the forefront of their minds should be: "What am I arguing?" or, "What is my thesis?" But I sense that when someone sets out to write an academic book, there is one question that is more foundational: "What am I trying to do with my argument, my thesis?" And this question, in its turn, provokes others: "What superior perspective do I believe I have achieved through my research, such that my argument should change the way things are by making an original contribution? What other voices have I silenced or with some intellectual integrity struggled with, or what ignorances am I concealing such that I can claim some superiority?" In the preparation of this book, such questions would not go away—and they have made the writing of it so much more difficult. Let me explain.

In *Cities of God* (2000) I attempted to map out a new terrain, the postmodern city, and construct an engaged systematic theology that might emerge within such a terrain. By an "engaged systematic theology" I mean a logically coherent account of the faith that is continually reflecting on the situation in which the writing takes place, the global city. So I began with descriptions of the postmodern city and slowly wove into those descriptions, and from those descriptions emerged, an interpretation of the ontological scandal of the body of Christ both in the Eucharistic liturgy and in the Gospel narratives of Jesus of Nazareth. The aim was to construct a theological anthropology and a theology of desire on the basis of which a doctrine of the church and a doctrine of God might be developed. I then returned in the final chapter to the culture of the contemporary city and the theologian's task.

But the plot started to unravel toward the end because, in the face of that postmodern city and its culture, and particularly the new poverties it was generating, I kept asking myself, "What is my theology trying to achieve?" And I could answer this question only in terms of critiquing contemporary perspectives that appeared to me inadequate—even collaborating with a process of dehumanization—while announcing the need for a vision of an alternative account of Christian living according to a traditional analogical worldview.

In doing this I was adding my voice and work to what the church was already proclaiming. But I was left feeling unsatisfied. The theology was just not engaged enough. Paramount was, as Marx put it, not just to interpret the world but also to change it. I wanted to develop a systematic theology that transformed the way we see and experience the contemporary city. For this city, like Christian theology, is invested heavily in the body, desire, and presence; it aspires to angelic knowledge and appearances.

A second volume was already beginning to shape itself as *Cities of God* was being published. This would engage more with how the city saw itself. But the questions the first volume raised would not go away, and they needed to be answered before I could again embark on the culture of the postmodern city and a theological response to it. Three questions came to the fore: From what place does theology speak? How do cultures change? And what is the relationship between cultural transformation and religious practices such as the writing of theology? These questions formed the basis of what was now to be the second volume in that city project, titled *Cultural Transformation and Religious Practice* (2005). In answering these questions and providing an account of Christian practices of hope that constructively critiqued the cultures within which these practices were working, I knowingly left behind both the rich texture of civic living and any particular theological doctrine—although ecclesiology was very much the undertow of my argument. I explored philosophically more fundamental questions about the ways cultures are produced and reproduced and the transformative role theological discourse and Christian praxis might play in that production and reproduction. And in this way I could answer for myself that question "What am I trying to do with my theological arguments?" And the answer was: change the cultural imaginary.

In coming to write *The Politics of Discipleship*, I gradually realized it was going to be the final part of what began with *Cities of God*. I could not develop the politics of discipleship without returning to the city and its cultural dynamics. I needed, then, to uncover some of the prominent aspects of the cultural imaginary of the contemporary city—that is, the dominant discourses and activities whereby people living in the city make sense of their experience; the imagined possibilities that shape their understanding of themselves and inform their moral, political, and religious beliefs. What I am attempting here, then, is to develop a Christian theological imaginary that might modify and transform aspects of that civic imaginary that is so antithetical to Christian living today. I hold no superior position from which I can prescribe a Christian politics or a Christian polity—to either the secular world (which does not ask for it) or the church (which has been engaged in state politics for almost two millennia and has likewise not asked for my prescriptions). In fact, I am far from sure there is either a Christian politics or a Christian polity as such. I am simply offering a "description"—a description of major aspects of the contemporary world that have shaped what people believe about themselves and their present cultural conditions. It is a description with a difference, for it explores the operations of the church in this cultural imaginary—its traditions, its liturgies, its symbols and stories, its current practices and future hopes. It is a description of social and cultural interactions, the pasts and projected futures and the dreams and ideologies that inform them. It is not an attempt to make the church more political or make individual believers more political (although it does describe an increasing and worrying tendency toward depoliticization, a tendency that it wishes to counter). It is rather an attempt to describe what is already taking place—that is, the politics of being a disciple, or what I term "political discipleship." And it is a description that aims at fostering other descriptions of these social and cultural interactions—including interactions with other faiths. It is offered not in the hope that it will enable the church and individual believers to recognize their political nature; the people I know in the church tend to be more politically aware and engaged than most people I know in other social groups. It is a description offering a potential framework for what is already beginning to emerge in ethnographic and congregational studies of the church, which enable us to have thicker accounts of the practices of faith and the social and cultural interactions within which they are enmeshed in the contemporary global city. That is all. The most rewarding comments about this description would be that it was useful, it was insightful, it enabled me, the reader, to recognize and name something of the world in which I live and the role my faith plays in it.

Acknowledgments

Without Jamie Smith inviting me for a drink at the Granta in Cambridge, this book would never have been written, because it was there at a table overlooking the pool with a pint of lager that we first discussed the possibilities of a contribution to his series. Without many lengthy conversations with Michael Hoelzl, with whom I edited two books and translated a third, I would not have seen how, the more I wrote, I was constructing the last part of my City Project. Without the superb and intelligent copyediting team at Baker Academic, this book would have laid itself open to several significant errors. I owe a debt of immense gratitude to all three parties.

Introduction

> In [Nazi] Germany they first came for the Communists, and I didn't speak up because I wasn't a Communist. Then they came for the Jews, and I didn't speak up because I wasn't a Jew. Then they came for the trade unionists, and I didn't speak up because I wasn't a trade unionist. Then they came for the Catholics, and I didn't speak up because I was a Protestant. Then they came for me—and by that time no one was left to speak.
>
> attributed to Pastor Martin Niemöller

On the Need for Impoliteness

This is a political book. It is not a polite book. The time for polite books is over, with little prospect, at present, of returning. I began the writing of this book surrounded by sheets of a morning newspaper. A war between Israel and Lebanon was in a tense state of suspension. A Jewish nation, to which many British Jews each year are returning, occupied, with the help of a predominantly Christian superpower, the southern lands of a nation divided between Christians and Muslims. Israel had just blitzed and scorched the Muslim parts of Lebanon's major cities, attempting to root out the Islamic militants of Hezbollah. There were photographs of the devastated areas of Beirut, taken from apartments in the Christian quarters. Many Muslims from those areas sought refuge among their Christian neighbors. This event, and others that have followed it, announces that this is not a time when theologians—Christian, Jewish, or Islamic—can be polite.

It is not just that the time demands impoliteness. This book cannot be polite for two other reasons. First, it is proclaiming a politics from only one of these theological standpoints. I cannot speak as a Jew or a Muslim. But it is we who believe that must speak, even if impolitely, because our faiths and our communities are tearing and being torn apart. And it matters not one iota that I am not an Israeli or a Lebanese, an Afghan or an Iraqi. For religion is once more dominating the public sphere in every country of the world, and the torture of a Jew in Paris, the bombing of Muslim children in Qaan (in southern Lebanon), the raping and shooting of a Christian in Iraq affect the faith communities everywhere to which we each belong. As believers in, and worshipers of, God, we inhabit diasporas that make our identities international. And each of us recognizes that the evils of this world, which are multiple, are of humankind's own making. It is human beings who wage war, who press the buttons that release the bombs, who plan murderous attacks on subways (such as London's Underground) and aircraft. What we also recognize is that ideas, stories, and mythologies count, that these acts of atrocity are committed in the name of ideas, stories, and mythologies that are held to be more precious than the world itself and all its inhabitants. We theologians of all faiths have to write our political and impolite books because we are the perpetrators and purveyors of these traditions. And if we are to reach any common understanding of ourselves, one another, and the threats and possibilities that pervade the cultures in which we are situated, it is only by being impolite and listening to one another's impoliteness.

This is the second reason this book cannot be polite. Not only does it not issue from some neutral space; it does not issue into any neutral space either. The sacred space is a contested space. This book invites and encourages contestation, and I will argue that only such contestation can reverse the accelerated trend toward depoliticization.

This study is about the Christian worldview as I see and understand it in the context of the political and economic changes happening all around us—changes that are informing the wars we fight, the values we are espousing, and the cultures we are producing. This study seeks to take a religious stand against the materialism engulfing the West. It does not take such a stand alone. In the contestation about religious truth, resistances can also be found in other faith traditions. They can be found too in the pursuit of postmaterialist, metaphysical values, in other purely human endeavors: in those concerning climate change, in nongovernmental organizations (NGOs) working on migration issues and engaged in countries where material resources are scarce, and in new philosophies of well-being that wish to nurture the spiritual (as distinct from the religious), to name but a few.

The cultural location for the changes we are experiencing is the global city, and understanding the cultural aspects of these changes is fundamental, for it is here that ideas, stories, and mythologies do battle before the wars are declared between nations or the explosives are strapped around the bodies of extremists. I say this even though, professionally, I have little expertise in either politics or economics. But part of the impoliteness of this writing is that regardless of such expertise, the issues are too important for theologians to leave them to the politicians and the economists. We have to speak up and speak out. The Australian film director Peter Jackson decided to transpose lines from Tolkien's *Fellowship of the Ring* to preface his movie adaptation. A voice-over by Cate Blanchett as Galadriel informs us, "The world is changed. I feel it in the water; I feel it in the earth; I smell it in the air. Much that once was is lost and none now liveth that remember it." Production on the movie began in October 1999, ten years after the end of the cold war, and the film opened in December 2001, three months after 9/11. Both Tolkein's and Jackson's trilogy are composed of ideas, stories, and mythologies, but their contemporary resonance in the social psyche is undeniable. The resonance can be quantified, if quantification is required, by their overwhelming commercial success. The world is changing. And we have to understand how even if we get lost in the thickets when we try to sort out the complexities of why. The world is changing, and religion is one of the drivers of this change. The spirit of new capitalism is another. These changes shape us and therefore shape our futures. This book analyzes these changes and their religious import so that we theologians—Christian, Jewish, and Islamic—might make better peacemakers. And the only way

I see of doing this is to keep from evading the issues. I can present only the Christian perspective. This is why I am engaged in what a fellow theologian and friend of mine would call "indecent theology."[1] But theology is always indecent because transcendence in a secular world is always scandalous.

The Church and the World

Before we embark on an exploration of the changes, I must clarify the structure of this book and the understanding of the political that informs its thesis. The division of the book into two sections dramatically titled "The World" and "The Church," respectively, should not be taken to indicate two opposed realms of activity. The church is hardwired into the world; that is where it works out its vision and its mission, however that vision and that mission are interpreted. Whatever action the church undertakes, whatever proclamations it makes, is located in the world's times and spaces, its histories, its societies, its cultures, its languages, and its ideologies. But insofar as the church is a public and material manifestation of that which transcends the world—the operations of God in Christ with respect to redemption—the church's actions and speech address the world from a point beyond it.[2] The church speaks and acts *in the name of*. And so the politics of Christian living in the world both reflects and critiques the values, emphases, and trajectories of its histories, its societies, its cultures, its languages, and its ideologies. It is this complex position of being *within* and yet struggling to address the world from *beyond* that the division of this book into two sections expresses.

The church's address to the world issues from a struggle, an internal struggle to discern the truth of its own vision and its mission. There is no voice from above, not even in the Christian Scripture, no voice that descends unmediated from some empyrean realm. Christians can accept that God is not silent, that Christ remains head of his church, and that the Holy Spirit guides this church into all truth. But they also have to accept that it handles

1. Marcella Althaus-Reid, *Indecent Theology* (London: Routledge, 2000).

2. See the opening question, "From what place does theology speak?" in Graham Ward, *Cultural Transformation and Religious Practice* (Cambridge: Cambridge University Press, 2005), 12–60.

interpretations and conflicts among them. It has to make judgments, but there is a provisional nature about these judgments, for only when Christ judges all things will the relationship between these judgments and the truth of the church's vision and mission become evident. The precariousness of all earthly judgment is terrifying; it is a scandalous aspect of acting in faith that we must never understate. This necessary trafficking in interpretations and judgments is inseparable from the more universal trafficking in interpretations and judgments that goes on in the world. The church and the world are not, then, discrete entities. This fact gives rise to the church's ongoing struggle of faith seeking understanding. And this ongoing struggle is the substance of the church's political life.

The struggle to discern the truth as well as the cultural politics of the church's embeddedness in the world is rendered more complex by the recognition that neither the church nor the world is a homogeneous whole. There has never been a time when the church was one. The centralizing of the church around Rome and the papacy was a historical move emerging between the third and fifth centuries in an already divided and contested Christendom. "Each one of you says, 'I belong to Paul,' or 'I belong to Apollos,' or 'I belong to Cephas,' or 'I belong to Christ,'" as Paul attests in one of his early epistles (1 Cor. 1:12). There never has been a Christendom in terms of a universal kingdom of Christ. While the Roman medieval church was extending both its powers and its territorial domain from the eleventh century to the sixteenth, it became increasingly aware of its own smallness. Not only did it encounter the imperial ambitions of the Ottoman Turks; it was aware that Islam created a cultural shield that separated the Christian West from the huge and mainly uncharted empire of the Mongols. The danger, as the church understood, was that the Mongols would be converted to Islam (which is what happened), further isolating globally the Christian enclave. As the voyages of discovery began and flourished in the fifteenth century, not only were other parts of the world that had not heard of Christ mapped, but also other forms of worship, other forms of piety, and other gods were encountered. The domestic heresies of the Waldensians and the Albigensians and the hybrid Christianities of the forced conversions of Jews and Muslims were mirrored and multiplied as the world grew larger. The intense missionizing, first by the Franciscans and the Dominicans and then by the Jesuits, was in part a response to the recognition of the new understanding of global space and of how small the church was within such a space; the church divided between East and West, whose papal power base waxed and waned as the political climate changed. Even before the Reformation's splintering, Christendom was an ideology only partially realized and internally contested. The church, then, is always to come. It is a promise rooted in New Testament teaching, a promise that forms the horizon within which churches seek to be and become more fully the church.

As the church increasingly had to recognize its territorial limitations, the world too changed. Since the exploration of space and the photographs beamed back by Sputnik and Explorer in the late 1950s, we are accustomed to pictures of our planet taken from beyond it. We have an external perspective of Earth that hitherto was unavailable. This perspective no doubt informs our understanding now of "the world," for we take "world" not as the name of a global mass of land and sea but as an imaginative conception of such a global mass. We conceive of "the world"; it is a creation. The conception, then, of the world changes both historically and culturally, for there is no reason to think that the way the world is conceived in Cambodia or Kabul, Cape Town or Canberra, is the same. The world is always conceived from a certain standpoint in time and culture. Much of the work of twentieth-century philosophy on difference and otherness has drawn attention to the fact that the world as conceived by a white professional male is not quite the same world as conceived by one who is marginalized (by gender, race, class, religion, or disability). As conceptions of the world were changed by the early Portuguese and Spanish explorers, so conceptions of the world have changed through the philosophies of difference. The reevaluation of difference and alterity has, however, been competing with the rapid development of global trading and telecommunications, with globalization. The Live 8 concert of 2005 provided a rich illustration of the globalized worldview in its celebration of what the presenters called our "intradependence"; all nations are integrated within a complex system that is social, political, ecological, and economic. Our understandings and images of the world today, then, are complex; they are not easily homogenized.

And so "the church" names an unfinished project, and "the world" names a certain conception of our global living constituted from a specific standpoint.[3] This makes manifest that the naming of this set of institutional variables, church or world, is itself political. By "political" I mean an act that entails power—that is, an act the effect of which is (a) subjection (an act that puts things into a hierarchy that favors the individual or institution that is acting), (b) liberation (an act that deconstructs the hierarchy that is involved in subjection), or (c) maintenance of the status quo. Power in this sense is not an entity as such although it can be measured as other material forms of power are conventionally measured in watts, the force of gravity, or the strength of horses. Power in its political sense can be measured by what supports and invests in it—money or an electorate, for example. It is this support and investment that render such power material and its operations visible. Political power is a social operation with respect to relations between people and the institutions to which these people belong (whether they are conscious of it or not). These relations and institutions can subject people, liberate them, or sustain them. And they might do all three across a period of time; or all three at any single time across a spectrum of different peoples. A British Conservative government, for example, can cut income taxes that *free* me to employ my money elsewhere or to *sustain* a standard of living that I have become accustomed to and that rising prices have recently affected. But the same political action might also *subject* me and other people receiving benefits who were neither freed up nor sustained by the tax cuts, because cuts in public service that become necessary to offset the tax reductions mean that waiting lists at hospitals increase and education and the police are starved of resources for effectively adding to the quality of national life. The church too is a political player; the power with which it is invested and that it then deploys *subjects* people to its doctrinal rule, *sustains* them through the ups and downs of life, and preaches *freedom* from sin and judgment (the liberties of Christ). Furthermore, as only one player on the world stage (and even then not universally a main player), the church too is subjected, freed, or sustained by other political players.

3. For a more extensive analysis of standpoint and the way in which it is related to, but not synonymous with, a subject position, see Ward, *Cultural Transformation*, 79–89, 96–116.

Micro- and Macropolitics

A further distinction in political power returns us to the politics of naming: that between micropolitics and macropolitics (even if later we have to submit this distinction to a number of complexities). The church, for example, is a vast network of interrelations composing what Paul terms a body or a building. These interrelations all pass through and exist in Christ because of their relation *with* him (see chap. 6, below). The internal connectedness of the church has a diaspora connectedness with respect to the world, for its members are, in highly individual and individuating ways, affiliated with other social institutions. A distinction can be made between the way members *participate* in Christ and the way they *relate* to specific societies and cultures, histories, and geographies. It is not a neat distinction because a relationship with something requires a degree of participation in it. But with respect to the church, my metaphysical and theological participation in the body of Christ is ontologically prior to the relations I may build up with other members of that body. There is no prior participation, however, when I decide to affiliate myself with a political party or a group of ecoactivists or take up employment in an institution. Furthermore, in these other affiliations or relations, my participation may be minimal; for example, I pay my subscriptions but do not actively engage in campaigning at election time or in promoting awareness of environmental issues or in institutional management. The difference between participation and relation reflects a hierarchy of theological importance, involvement, and incorporation for individual Christians and the world in which they live. Nevertheless, these members of the church buy this washing powder or instant coffee rather than that, support this after-school activity rather than that, belong to this gym or this train-spotting club or this country club rather than that. In other words, the church is composed of social beings embedded within, by relating to, certain cultural situations. And these people make choices (and prioritize regarding these choices) that determine the degree of their participation.

Choices entail investments—of time, energy, status, and money. These investments support (and foster the development of) some objects, institutions, values, and practices while neglecting others. The investments that accompany such choices are transferrals or bestowals of power of different kinds. Put simply, in contemporary Western society, power can take four forms: social, economic, biological, and cultural.[4] Money is an economic mode of power; time, a social mode of power; energy, a biological mode of power; and status, a cultural or symbolic mode of power. In advanced capitalist societies, all modes of power can be translated into economic power. They need not, however, be so translated. An accountant may inform me that the time I invest in painting the walls of my home would take up so many hours in which I could otherwise earn so much money. And so, economically, it may be cheaper to employ someone to do the painting for me. In so doing, I would also sustain my energy level, which could be invested elsewhere. Nevertheless, because I enjoy the relaxation of painting, I may decide that the translation of my time and energy into money is inappropriate for this activity. The point here is that all social relations entail certain transferrals or bestowals of power that *can* be—but do not necessarily have to be—translated into economic power. It is these transferrals or bestowals that compose the micropolitics of everyday life. Here are two examples. By buying Gap jeans, I expand, on a microlevel, the economic power base of a certain international corporation. By not buying Levi jeans, however, I withdraw, on a microlevel, an economic power that may affect (if a significant number of other people are also withdrawing their support), on a macrolevel, the future of Levi jeans, the employment of a worker, or the location of a manufacturing output. By bestowing my time and energy on helping, as a volunteer, to staff a drop-in center for the homeless or the drug-dependent, I am expanding the social power base, on a microlevel, of an organization assisting with problems at a macrolevel in society. By not giving my time and energy to helping my local branch of Greenpeace, however, I am withdrawing, on a microlevel, my social power. If I happen to be the queen of England or the archbishop of Canterbury, then the choices of where I invest my social, biological, and economic power are obviously greatly enhanced by my cultural and symbolic status.

4. To some extent, this description combines, in the typology and in the analysis that follows, Pierre Bourdieu's work on different modes of capital and Michel Foucault's examination of biopower and governmentality. For a more detailed account of the value of Bourdieu's and Foucault's methodological tools, see Ward, *Cultural Transformation*.

It is a truism that no one can do everything. Another is that no one is without power of some kind. And a third is that in every society the distribution of these modes of power is uneven (and will always be so). Hence it can be misleading to view individuals as situated in grids or fields of power relations, for these spatial images flatten hierarchical differences.[5] The possession and subsequent transferal or bestowal of power are the basis of social and cultural difference. Indeed, differences and hierarchies (which arise when differences are unevenly valued) are themselves produced through the interweave constituted by these relational transactions of power. And it is these differences that constitute the priorities and hierarchies implicated in micropolitics.

Macropolitics is the operation of power when we treat not individuals but governments, dominant practices that shape our behavior, and monolithic value systems that are constituted and reproduced through the social affiliations of individuals. Macropolitics requires a legitimate/legitimated authority for the exercising of power. For example, it is macropolitics when the French government imposes a curfew and state of emergency on certain sections of Paris during a time of riot. In November 2005, the action of cordoning off an area where Algerian youths were in revolt involved not simply a number of state institutions—the police, the judiciary, and the president's office—it made visible certain dominant practices that educate us into being "good" citizens of a liberal democracy and certain dominant values informing that liberal democracy.[6] That the Algerians were Muslims, for example, was rarely mentioned in the newspapers. They were treated as

5. Bourdieu speaks of fields of cultural production, but he recognizes that the field is composed of certain dominant and marginal positions. See his essay "The Field of Cultural Production," in *The Field of Cultural Production*, ed. Randal Johnson (New York: Columbia University Press, 1993), 29–73. Foucault speaks of "grids of intelligibility" composed of certain discourses, but he recognizes that in any episteme some discourses dominate the way specific phenomena, such as the body or punishment, are interpreted. See *History of Sexuality*, vol.1, *An Introduction*, trans. Robert Hurley (New York: Random House, 1990), 93.

6. The Marxist Louis Althusser called these practices state apparatuses that governed a citizen's behavior and value system; the church, the school, the law courts, and the military all have their ways of training or disciplining or instilling citizens with certain views of how to live that they believe are correct or right or normative. See his essay "Ideology and Ideological State Apparatuses: Notes Towards an Investigation" in *Lenin and Philosophy and Other Essays*, trans. Ben Brewster (New York: Monthly

youths who were disrupting the peace-making neutrality of a state governed by the liberal value of *laïcité*; they were youths breaking the law.

Macropolitical engagement is framed by a legitimated authority to act; it has a recognized mandate to executive power. The engagement is not so much concerned with the individuals involved as with their appointed offices and the institutions they represent and on whose behalf they have the legal right to make decisions. This is social power having a legal, constitutional, and nationally accepted source of authorization. Secular legitimations are arrived at through hereditary rights, the force of a preemptive coup, or a common consent framed in published laws, constitutions, public codes of practice, and institutional policies. In Matthew's Gospel, when Jesus had scourged the temple of its trading, he was confronted by the chief priests and the elders, who asked, "By what authority are you doing these things, and who gave you this authority?" (Matt. 21:23). Other than themselves, the only legitimate sources of authority to act in such a provocative way in Jerusalem at that time were either the puppet king, Herod Antipas, the governor of Galilee and Peraea, or the Roman procurator, Pontius Pilate. Jesus was asked to name the legitimating source for his action. Had he said Herod or Pilate, he would have been engaged in macropolitics.[7] As it was, Jesus raised for the chief priests and the elders a metaquestion concerning two sources of authority—human and divine. He would raise the same question in a more dramatic way when facing Pilate himself (see chap. 7, below). And it was probably not until the conversion of Constantine that Christianity shifted from the micropolitical to the macropolitical.

Macropolitics requires an authority to execute power on a grand level—for example, being in charge of a police force that can impose peace, having the state capacity to declare war, or being able to order a military force into action—but it too operates through the four forms of power mentioned above: social, biological, symbolic or cultural, and economic. Every national investment

Review Press, 2001), 127–86. Foucault later called these practices "technologies" that figured, for those subjected to them, their sense of themselves.

7. There were illegitimate authorizations to act. Scholars have identified two groups: the Zealots and the Sicarii, who sought by violent means to stir up anti-imperial hatred. But illegitimate power bases operate at the margins of the power structures operating in any given social order; they lack the legal structures necessary for macropolitics.

in international diplomatic relations is a national investment to increase its stock of social power; every government intervention for maintaining and improving the nation's health is an exercise of its biological power; every city of international prestige (and its ability to generate income through tourism) deploys its cultural power (e.g., Florence, Istanbul, Jerusalem);[8] and both UN economic sanctions and the international power of the euro are forms of economic power.

Why is this distinction between micro- and macropolitics important? First, it provides us with a tool to examine the composition and structure of various social engagements, for it aims to give an account of the church in terms of its political operations and obligations (at both micro- and macrolevels). That is, it is concerned with how the church is the church with respect to the world (its institutions, its making of meaning, its values, and its practices) within which its members are located. Second, there has been a discernable shift in politics since 1989, at the end of the cold war, that impacts the church directly. In this shift there has been a new visibility of religion evident in the public sphere (see chap. 3, below). This shift has affected prevailing trends in political activism—the publicity and media space given to certain forms of politicking. Since 1989, western European, North American, and Australasian societies have moved from culture wars to the clash of civilizations, from an active commitment to micropolitics to a more passive witness to macropolitics (chap. 1 will examine this in terms of "postdemocracy"). We might monitor this move in the international scholar Judith Butler. Her groundbreaking work in the early 1990s catapulted gender studies in the direction of queer theory,[9] but her more recent work has developed beyond gender politics (which is a micropolitics) into mainline political theory.[10]

8. On global cities floating free of national ties, see Graham Ward, *Cities of God* (London: Routledge, 2000), 238–41.

9. Judith Butler, *Gender Trouble: Feminism and the Subversion of Identity* (New York: Routledge, 1990); Butler, *Bodies That Matter: On the Discursive Limits of Sex* (New York: Routledge, 1993).

10. Judith Butler, *The Psychic Life of Power: Theories of Subjection* (Stanford, CA: Stanford University Press, 1997); Butler, *Excitable Speech: The Politics of the Performative* (New York: Routledge, 1997); Butler, *Precarious Life: The Power of Mourning and Violence* (London: Verso, 2004); Judith Butler, Ernesto Laclau, and Slavoj Žižek, *Contingency, Hegemony, Universality: Contemporary Dialogues on the Left* (London: Verso, 2000).

We begin, then, with the world, sketching the contemporary conditions that prevail politically, economically, socially, and culturally. It is within the context of this world that I will define the operations of the church and the nature of political discipleship as it pursues a postmaterialist agenda. By "postmaterialist" I do not mean that the church is antimaterialist but rather that the church is critical of a purely material understanding of objects, activities, and values. We will discover that a postmaterialist agenda is also being pursued elsewhere, and we will have to investigate the similarities and differences of each approach to the postmaterialist. The three chapters of section 1 are devoted to the examination of three dominant trends in contemporary European, North American, and Australasian society and their consequences. These trends are political, economic, and cultural: the crisis of democracy, globalization, and the new visibility of religion. They are situated within two further developments that cut across the political, the economic, and the cultural: postmateriality and postmodernity. This study begins by isolating the three trends in order to treat each of them in detail and depth. But the extent to which they are interconnected and inseparable from the developments of postmaterialism and postmodernity will become increasingly apparent. This grid of trends I understand as sketching the cultural imaginary of the contemporary city. The four chapters that compose section 2 are devoted to examining three possible ecclesial responses based on what I call the eschatological remainder: practices of hope, a metaphysics of embodiment, and the recognition of a kingdom that is being established. Each of these responses constitutes something of the Christian imaginary as it might intersect with the secular cultural imaginary. To return to the theme of impoliteness: in the relationship between these two sections, the overriding concern is to establish a new tradition of theological disputation (the church is already gauging the temperature of the times, assessing both its limitations and opportunities and developing its operational strategies). This study offers a description of where we are and, on that basis, advocates the need to stop being so polite. The description is necessary. Once Christians understand more of what is taking place, once they have a map of political engagement, they will be better equipped both to recognize the nature of the discipleship that is demanded of them and to see what it is they have to contest. Forget tea and cucumber sandwiches with the vicar; there is a genuine struggle here.

SECTION 1

THE WORLD

1

Democracy

Crisis and Transformation

> The domination of "capital" behind the scenes is still no form, though it can undermine an existing political form and make it an empty façade. Should it succeed, it will have "depoliticized" the state completely.[1]

Washington

The complexities, ambiguities, and downright paradoxes in the relationship between the people and sovereign power are nowhere more evident than in that shrine to modern democracy, the Lincoln Memorial. Ascending the tiers of steps, one enters the darkened portico, on the left wall of which is incised an excerpt from Lincoln's famous Gettysburg Address, ending with "That government of the people, by the people, for the people, shall not perish from the earth." But who are the people? One looks around at a heterogeneous crowd of tourists—American, British, Japanese, Mexican, Chinese, Indian, and so on. Who claims to be the people? Who

1. Carl Schmitt, *Roman Catholicism and Political Form*, trans. G. L. Ulmen (Westport, CT: Greenword, 1996), 25.

legitimates that claim? And there, towering grandly above everyone, Lincoln sits, for all the world like a Roman deity, an Augustus Caesar soliciting worship for the miracle of Pax Romana*—not exactly one of the people, one of the crowd of diminutives swooping, like flocks of birds, in and out of the temple to democratic freedom. It seems that some people are more powerful than other people, for they are people makers. From the steps, one searches across the civic space below, Constitution Gardens. The object of Lincoln's gaze is not the Capitol, which is occluded from this perspective, but the Washington Monument. Lincoln, as the symbol of American democracy, democracy as a republican religion, gazes reflectively at the inauguration of presidential power that occurred with Washington. The state buildings stretching down Constitution Avenue to the invisible Capitol reinforce this sense of an imperium, a democracy upheld by patricians. And the people? One has to descend the steps to that public space made so famous in the civil-rights marches. The people are found here on the plain; they cover the ground from the Lincoln Memorial to the Washington Monument. The people are either the tourists, the venerators with their camcorders, or the remembered dead—the Vietnam dead, the Korean dead, and those four hundred thousand who died in the Second World War. Freedom, one is reminded in a terse paradox, demands a cost. Democracy, it seems, requires sacrificial bloodletting and the piled-up flesh of the people, by the people, for the people. And in a profound expression of these tensions in the relationship between the people and sovereign power—civic space surveyed and surrounded by imperial might—one discovers Friedrich St. Florian's National World War II Memorial. The memorial stands at the center of the park and beneath the Washington Monument, at the confluence of Constitution Avenue and Independence Avenue. It celebrates the American triumph in bringing an end to the Second World War, the American victory that reestablished the new* pax mundi. *And how strikingly close the design of the circle of pillars is to the work of Albert Speers for the Munich Olympics of 1936, the stage set for Hitler's first great international demonstration of power. Only it was opened officially May 29, 2004, by George W. Bush.*

The introduction drew attention to a distinction between micro- and macropolitics and to a trend away from the former toward the latter. This first of three chapters delineating the context within which the call to political discipleship for Christians is announced will examine the implications of this trend with respect to liberal democracy. The history of democracy is a fragile one, as we will see, with some now calling our present condition "postdemocratic." I will argue for the need, in such a condition, to revisit the theological foundations of sovereignty.

"Today the concept and practices of democracy are everywhere in crisis. . . . And the constant global state of war undermines what meagre forms of democracy exist."[2] So say Michael Hardt and Antonio Negri. But democracy is and has always been a slippery term. The *CIA World Factbook*, defining democracy as "a form of government in which the supreme power is retained by the people, but which is usually exercised indirectly through a system of representation and delegated authority periodically renewed," lists several types.[3] Parliamentary democracy (United Kingdom), federal democracy (Australia), federal republic (Austria), parliamentary republic, multiparty democracy, confederation with parliamentary democracy (Canada), constitutional republic (Iceland), and constitutional monarchy (Sweden) are the most prominent.[4] The starting point for the investigation here, however, is not some abstract definition but the fact that the countries constituting the West (the context in which I am most immediately implicated) define their government practices as democratic. The functioning of these democracies differs. Some have proportional representation and others a "first passed the post" electoral system; some have a two-tier system (the House of Commons, the House of Lords) and some do not; some give greater powers than others to local governments (the German Bundestag and the sixteen federal states composing

2. Michael Hardt and Antonio Negri, *Multitude: War and Democracy in the Age of Empire* (New York: Penguin Books, 2005), 231.

3. *CIA World Factbook* (Washington, DC: Central Intelligence Agency), available online at Central Intelligence Agency, www.cia.gov/cia/publications/factbook.

4. Benito Mussolini (and his cowriter, Giovanni Gentile) observed, "If democracy be understood as meaning a regime in which the masses are not driven back to the margin of the State, then the writer of these pages has already defined Fascism as an organised, centralised, authoritarian democracy" ("The Doctrine of Fascism," in *Fascism: Doctrine and Institutions* [Rome: Ardita, 1935], 7–42; originally published as "La dottrina del fascismo," in *Enciclopedia italiana di scienze, lettere, ed arti* [(Milan): Treves–Treccani–Tumminelli, 1932], 14:847–51, available online at World Future Fund, www.worldfuturefund.org/wffmaster/Reading/Germany/mussolini.htm).

the Bundesrat). Each country would view the practices of its government as democratic despite the Greek origins of the word ("rule of the people") and although democracy in these countries is not the exercise of power by the people, whose mandate has frequently been questioned, even feared, by political scientists from Aristotle to Tocqueville on the grounds of "mob rule" or the "tyranny of the majority." The exercise of power by the people in these democracies is indirect—that is, conducted through systems of representation and delegation. This is why democracy in these countries is called "liberal democracy," for "liberal" here signals the withdrawal of state power so that individuals might exercise their maximal freedoms as long as they do not injure or infringe the freedoms of other individuals. So in liberal democracies, government issues through open public discussions between representatives elected by the private balloting of individual subjects. We will see why, because of this association of liberalism and democracy, "liberal democracy" remains a slippery term, a term always under negotiation.

It is appropriate here to make a distinction between democratic polity and democratic culture or ethos, without suggesting one is prior to, and the cause of, the other. The distinction relates directly to that between macropolitics and micropolitics. "Polity" here means, after the *Oxford English Dictionary*, a particular form of political organization, a form of government. Democratic culture or ethos, however, refers to the political values (freedom of the individual, equal opportunities, the right to property, human rights, tolerance, etc.) and practices (freedom of speech, open debates, equality before the law, even sanctioned resistance on critical matters, etc.) that are lived out and fostered by the societies governed by such a polity. It is not a simple case of the polity creating the culture, for democratic polity has evolved with the rise of the modern nation-state and the development of public law from the sixteenth century onward. Certain cultural changes (the rise of the bourgeoisie, who constituted early civil society; the development of natural law and its correlate public reasoning; the turn to the subject; etc.) fostered what Charles Taylor has termed the "modern social imaginary"—ideas about how we should live and how we should organize ourselves.[5] Democratic

5. See Charles Taylor, "The Moral Order: The Transition to Political Modernity," in *Religion and Political Thought*, ed. Michael Hoelzl and Graham Ward (London:

polity and democratic culture exist as a complex interaction and at times can call each other into question. Culture can be said to question polity when the police break up a peaceful protest or when a documentary exposes the suspension of habeas corpus for certain classes of people detained in a democratic country. Policy can be said to question culture when laws ban the right to smoke in public areas or the government demands the distribution of identity cards.

The distinction between democratic polity and democratic culture maps on to the distinction between the public and the private. As the Italian political scientist Norberto Bobbio observes, the origins of the distinction between public and private lie in the difference between public law and private law in Justinian's *Corpus iuris civilis*.[6] It has a checkered history, for until the rise of the state there was no public law as such, only private contracts between particular parties. But Bobbio shows that the distinction between public law and private law is not simply formal but evaluative: there are times when the private is viewed as having primacy over the public and vice versa. Liberalism's demand for a minimal state and an extensive civil society is the modern face of the primacy of the private over the public.[7] Alternatively, "practically speaking, the primacy of the public means the increase of state intervention in the coercive regulation of individuals and sub-state groups."[8] In the terms employed above: there are times when polity seeks to dictate particular social and cultural mores, and there are times when social and cultural forms of behavior challenge the perceived incursions of polity.

Why do these distinctions between polity and culture, public and private, become important for our present analysis? They correlate with macro- and micropolitics and with the trend away from the latter to the former. In order to understand this correlation and its implications for the current political situation, which

Continuum, 2006), 263: "The new normative order was the mutual respect and mutual service of the individuals who make up society. The actual structures were meant to serve these ends, and were judged instrumentally in this light."

6. Norberto Bobbio, *Democracy and Dictatorship: The Nature and Limits of State Power*, trans. Peter Kennealy (Cambridge: Polity, 1989), 1.

7. Ibid., 13.

8. Ibid., 14.

some scholars have begun to call "postdemocratic,"[9] we need to appreciate the fundamental tension that is at the heart of what we call liberal democracy and that continually calls its identity into question. Bobbio has explored this tension, noting that there can be democracies that are not liberal and forms of liberal government that are not democratic. The moral and political virtue paramount in liberalism is liberty, understood negatively as the maximal freedom of the individual from harm or coercion by another, and the moral and political virtue paramount in democracy is equality, understood as the maximal extension of the franchise and equality of opportunity (to education, to ownership of property, to career advancement, etc.). These two ethics rest on two understandings of what it is to be human:

> Libertarianism and egalitarianism are rooted in profoundly divergent conceptions of man and society—convictions which are individualistic, conflictual and pluralistic for the liberal; totalizing, harmonious and monistic for the egalitarian. The chief goal for the liberal is the expansion of the individual personality, even if the wealthier and more talented achieve this development at the expense of that of the poorer and less gifted. The chief goal of the egalitarian is the enhancement of the community as a whole, even if this entails some constriction of the sphere of individual freedom.[10]

The liberal state is older than modern democracy. It flourished on the ground of natural human rights as distinct from the divine and absolutist rights of kings, trumpeting both religious and economic freedom for self-expression and development. It safeguarded these rights and freedoms in legislation (constitutional and juridical), further limiting executive power by fostering a climate of diverse and conflicting opinion. The epithet "laissez-faire" may have described the liberal view that economic progress arose through competition, but it also described the mechanism for progress in liberal culture more generally. "A free market in some opinions

9. See Colin Crouch, *Post-democracy* (Cambridge: Polity, 2004); Richard Rorty, "Post-democracy," *London Review of Books* 26, no. 7 (April 1, 2004): 10–11.

10. Norberto Bobbio, *Liberalism and Democracy*, trans. Martin Ryle and Kate Soper (London: Verso, 1990), 32–33.

became a free market in all opinions."[11] Freedom of conscience finds expression in freedom of opinion, and both enjoy freedom of the press. But competition and conflict are both inegalitarian. The extensiveness of civil society, championed by liberalism, looked upon government as a necessary evil, an artifice constructed on the basis of a common and contractual consent. Liberalism demanded from the state only one thing—one very important thing as we shall see: security.

Democracy, by contrast, views the individual as part of a more important whole, reconciling "individual and society by making society the product of a common agreement between individuals."[12] It fosters cooperation and seeks not only equality before the law (*that* the liberals concede) but also a wider cultural equality that includes the redistribution of wealth. This requires a more extended notion of government, for the state must intervene to ensure the movement toward maximal equality and a culture of interdependence. Freedom of individual choice is curtailed on the bases of public necessity and the common good, a government's executive power now being viewed as positive and socially beneficial. The universal extension of the franchise developed forms of democratic participation in terms of public and accountable electoral systems and government through representation. But democracy challenges liberalism most strongly in its implicit affiliation with socialism and a welfare state.

Historically, the liberal states advocated by figures as diverse as Locke, Rousseau, and Burke developed into the bourgeois (or capitalist) democracies of the nineteenth century and the socialist democracies of the twentieth century. Over time, each type found its need of the other. "The procedures of democracy are necessary to safeguard the fundamental personal rights on which the liberal state is based; and . . . those rights must be safeguarded if democratic procedures are to operate."[13] Nevertheless, a tension remains, and so the identity of democracy is not only pluriform (as the *CIA World Factbook* demonstrates); it is subject to the fluctuations of time and circumstance. When democracy enters into

11. Owen Chadwick, *The Secularization of the European Mind in the Nineteenth Century* (Cambridge: Cambridge University Press, 1975), 21.

12. Bobbio, *Liberalism and Democracy*, 43.

13. Ibid., 38.

a crisis, this tension surfaces most dramatically. Three examples from the twentieth century illustrate this fact.

First Example: Harold Laski and *Democracy in Crisis*

In the spring of 1931, Harold Laski, professor of political science at the London School of Economics and a member of the Labour Party, delivered a series of lectures at Yale titled Democracy in Crisis. The lectures were revised for publication in 1933 with the same title and went into a second printing within three months. Crisis was a word in vogue at the time;[14] it became a quasi-technical term particularly in Weimar Germany in a number of academic fields—for example, economics, politics, sociology, philosophy, and theology. The lexicon of crisis characterized European culture in the interwar years. Crisis was certainly what Laski observed and what he responded to. The 1929 stock market crash had led to a world economic slump that in Britain brought down the MacDonald Labour government (the real hope for social change and democratic development) in 1931. "The year 1933 [when Laski's book was published] marked in many ways the lowest point between the wars in the economic position of Britain, and correspondingly the moment of the greatest social misery—at least for the great mass of the unemployed and their dependants."[15]

The crisis of democracy, for Laski, can be understood from two perspectives. The first is historical: the success of parliamentary democracy (modeled first in Britain) is sporadic and short-lived the world over. Laski observes, "America apart, it is notable that in European countries parliamentary democracy has had nothing like the success which attended it in the home of its origin."[16] He then moves systematically through these European countries (Germany, Italy, Spain, Poland, Hungary, Rumania, Yugoslavia, and

14. See Carl Schmitt, *Political Theology II*, trans. Michael Hoelzl and Graham Ward (Cambridge: Polity, 2008), 39–44.

15. John Oliver, *The Church and Social Order: Social Thought in the Church of England, 1918–39* (London: Mowbray, 1968), 185. See also David Thomson, "The Eclipse of Democracy," in *Europe since Napoleon* (Harmondsworth, UK: Penguin Books, 1957), 702–30; and Eric Hobsbawm, "The Fall of Liberalism," in *The Age of Extremes: 1914–1991* (London: Abacas, 1994), 109–41.

16. Harold Laski, *Democracy in Crisis* (London: Allen & Unwin, 1933), 40.

France), highlighting the instability of parliamentary democracy and the increasing skepticism about its being an appropriate form for democratic societies. After scanning the contemporary political situation in Japan, South America, Australia, and South Africa, he even says to his American audience, "There is in America a wider disillusionment with democracy, a great scepticism about popular institutions, than at any other period in its history."[17]

The second and primary reason for the crisis in democracy (and history's testimony to its instability) is the paradoxical tension at the heart of the argument for representative democracy:

> It assumed the absolute validity of the form of the political state regardless of the economic character of the society it was supposed to represent. It did not see that each economic regime gives birth to a political order which represents the interests of those who dominate the regime, who possess in it the essential instruments of economic power. In a feudal society, broadly speaking, sovereignty belonged to the owners of the lands; custom was registered, legislation was made, in their interest. In a capitalist society, quite similarly, sovereignty belonged to the owners of capital; and the custom was registered, legislation made, in their interest also.[18]

Laski had already examined the nature of democratic sovereignty, and the legitimacy for government gained from this fact, in two earlier works, *The Problem of Sovereignty* (1917) and *The Foundation of Sovereignty* (1921). The second book had an important influence on a political scientist, Carl Schmitt (see below).[19] For Laski, who saw parliamentary democracies still operative in the British dominions and Scandinavia, the paradoxical tension of parliamentary democracy lies in the alliance between capitalism and democracy, that is, in liberal democracy itself. The tension could remain hidden as parliamentary democracy developed, for there was not universal suffrage such that the people could register their opinion, and therefore the sovereignty of the people—and

17. Ibid., 47.

18. Ibid., 50.

19. As far as I can ascertain, there was no direct contact between Schmitt and Laski, but they did have a contact in common, Leo Strauss. Laski recommended Strauss to write a review of Schmitt's *Concept of the Political*. Schmitt eagerly read the review and arranged for it to be published. Schmitt subsequently wrote a supporting reference for Strauss for a Rockefeller Fellowship.

the legitimacy of that sovereignty—was based on a narrow class of those who constituted "the people."[20] Laski explains that such sovereignty is always a fiction: "For the fact surely is that those who possess the engines of power will, for the most part, tend to regard their private good as identical with the general good."[21] Carl Schmitt notes, "Of the more than four hundred million inhabitants of the British Empire more than three hundred million are not British citizens. If English democracy, universal suffrage, or universal equality is spoken of, then these hundreds of millions in English democracy are just as unquestionably ignored as were the slaves in Athenian democracy."[22] Laski would have concurred. In Britain it was the moves made toward universal suffrage—Liberal Party moves based on an abstract notion of human equality—that drew increasing attention to the marked difference between theories of the state based on "the people" and the represented interests in parliament with legislative power. The First World War, the rise of socialism, the organized working-class movements, communism, and the Bolshevik Revolution each facilitated a growing consciousness *of* the people that they *were* the people. In the new political situation after the First World War, Laski (hinting throughout his lectures that there was a revolutionary climate brewing in Western Europe) concludes, "Representative democracy . . . has either to accommodate itself to a world in which the wants of the business man are no longer predominant, whether for good or evil, or it will cease to be either representative or democratic."[23]

20. Carl Schmitt, *The Crisis of Parliamentary Democracy*, trans. Ellen Kennedy (Cambridge, MA: MIT Press, 1985), originally published as *Die geistesgeschichtliche Lage des heutigen Parlamentarismus* [The Situation of Parliamentary Democracy], 2nd ed. (Berlin: Duncker & Humblot, 1926), raised an identical problem regarding the definition of "democracy": "The essence of the democratic principle . . . is the assertion that the law and the will of the people are identical" (26). The people are, then, self-determining. What is presupposed here is what he termed the homogeneity of "the people." "Everything depends on how the will of the people is formed" (27), he adds. In the preface to the second edition, Schmitt argues forcefully to the effect that this "will" is formed through powerful interests and social or economic power groups in parliament. "The masses are won over through a propaganda apparatus whose maximum effect relies upon an appeal to immediate interests and passions" (6).

21. Harold Laski, "Popular Sovereignty," in *The Foundations of Sovereignty, and Other Essays* (New York: Harcourt, Brace, 1921), 228.

22. Schmitt, *Crisis of Parliamentary Democracy*, 10.

23. Laski, *Democracy in Crisis*, 58.

One can see why Laski not only was a member of the Labour Party but was appointed to its National Executive Committee from 1937 to 1949.[24] There is something of Marx's antagonism between the bourgeoisie and the proletariat in Laski's distinction between liberal parliamentarism and democracy.[25] The Labour Party, which, it was hoped, embodied the will of the masses, rose to become the official opposition party in the 1920s after the collapse of the Liberal Party. It held office briefly in 1924 and then from 1929 to 1931. But the collapse of the Liberal Party is indicative of a larger cultural shift, after 1918, away from liberalism more generally. This shift was the catalyst for the crisis in democracy that was revealing itself. Schmitt, more than anyone, examined liberalism beyond the economics of laissez-faire, freedom of contract, and freedom of trade, in terms of what he calls its "consistent, comprehensive metaphysical system."[26] Bobbio's analysis is dependent on Schmitt's. Liberalism was concerned with the free competition of opinions, with the belief that truth arose through debate. Truth was attained through a process that included the power of educated reason, "discussion and openness."[27] Hence, politically, the principles of liberalism will give rise to the institution of parliaments. But in a lecture delivered in 1924 and published in 1926 (the year of the General Strike in Britain), John Maynard Keynes was already referring to the end of laissez-faire economics. In Germany there was an open assault on liberal Protestantism from Barth's second edition of *Romans* (1922) onward and the formation of dialectical theology. A similar assault, albeit from a different theological position, was being waged in Britain by Anglo-Catholics like G. K. Chesterton who, in 1922, published his polemic *The Return of Christendom*.[28] It is in this context that Laski announced the demise of the liberal state and its basis in reasoned public discus-

24. He served as the party's chairman in the election year 1945. Having published *Communism* in 1927, Laski became more vociferous about his Marxism from the 1930s on.

25. Laski owed much also to the work of his colleague at the London School of Economics R. H. Tawney, whose account in *The Acquisitive Society* (New York: Harcourt, Brace & Howe, 1920) characterizes Laski's understanding of capitalism.

26. Schmitt, *Crisis of Parliamentary Democracy*, 35.

27. Ibid., 36.

28. G. K. Chesterton, *The Return of Christendom* (London: Allen & Unwin, 1922).

sion: "Parties have to capture public opinion. But the elements of public opinion do not grow out of knowledge, and they are not the product of reason."[29]

It is the crisis of liberalism (conceived philosophically, culturally, economically, sociologically, and politically) that triggers a crisis of identity with respect to democracy. It announces a crisis of reason, an inflation of skepticism. Laski's comment that public opinion is a product that bears no relation to reason hints at the social construction of knowledge and already half frames the question "Whose rationality?" The cultural production—and therefore politics—of knowledge and the critique of liberalism would become central themes in the work of the newly emerging Frankfurt school. But in the early 1920s, Schmitt, always the more philosophical, in the last chapter of *The Crisis of Parliamentary Democracy*, was already examining "a new evaluation of rational thought, a new belief in instinct and intuition that lays to rest every belief in discussion."[30] What is craved in this skepticism of truth issuing through rational debate is decisiveness, action, even violence.[31] Relying on the work of Georges Sorel on myth (see chap. 4, below), Schmitt argues that Enlightenment reason was a myth no longer sustainable. A new myth is needed—a myth such as Mussolini created of a triumphant Italy. "The theory of myth is the most powerful symptom of the decline of the relative rationalism of parliamentary thought."[32] Although Laski does not follow Schmitt along these theoretical lines, he attempts to create such a myth out of socialism,[33] proclaiming (even preaching), "Socialism, like Christianity, has reached that stage where it cannot be suppressed by persecution, and has become militant in temper because the conditions of victory are within its grasp. It has, it should be insisted, all the characteristics of a great religion."[34]

This first example demonstrates that liberal democracy, always a tense combination of calls for the protection and extension of

29. Laski, *Democracy in Crisis*, 68; see 67–146 for the whole of his analysis of representative institutions.

30. Schmitt, *Crisis of Parliamentary Democracy*, 66.

31. Ibid., 72.

32. Ibid., 76.

33. His attempt has a strong affinity with Georges Sorel, *Reflections on Violence*, trans. Jeremy Jennings (Cambridge: Cambridge University Press, 1999).

34. Laski, *Democracy in Crisis*, 162.

individual freedom (the private, the micropolitical) and for collective social justice or egalitarianism (the public, the macropolitical), is pitched into a crisis when the balance between these calls is tipped one way or the other. The demise of liberalism and the ascendancy of socialism initiate a crisis of identity that forces democracy toward a transfiguration away from liberal democracy to social democracy. This transfiguration has far-reaching implications for the structure of government: (a) the aggrandizement of the state (as it intervenes more to engineer social justice); (b) the increase in bureaucracy (to administer this intervention); (c) the widening of participation by the electorate (which can destabilize the legislative function of parliament by calling for more direct and less "representative" forms of democratic procedure, such as referenda); and (d) more-authoritarian leadership by the party in office. It is significant that the four changes listed above, with the exception perhaps of (c), would be characteristic also of totalitarian regimes—communist or fascist. Schmitt recognized this.

Second Example: The Trilateral Commission

In March 1974 Willy Brandt claimed, "Western Europe has only 20 or 30 years more of democracy left in it; after that it will slide, engineless and rudderless, under the surrounding sea of dictatorship, and whether the dictation comes from a politburo or a junta will not make much difference."[35] A year earlier, a group of private citizens, among them David Rockefeller, Henry Kissinger, and Zbigniew Brzezinski, formed the Trilateral Commission.[36] Originally established for a three-year period, it brought together the countries of the European Union, North America, and Japan "to help think through the common challenges and leadership responsibilities of these democratic industrialized areas in the wider world."[37] The

35. Willy Brandt, *Economist*, March 23, 1974, 12.

36. It thus was technically a nongovernmental organization, but as Noam Chomsky, *Radical Priorities* (Montreal: Black Rose Books, 1981), points out, the president, the vice president, the secretaries of state, defense, and treasury, and the national security advisors of the Carter administration were all members of the Trilateral Commission. Doubts must therefore be raised about the alleged political, even social-scientific, neutrality of the commission's findings.

37. See Trilateral Commission, www.trilateral.org.

formation of the group was a response to a dramatic increase in friction between governments and peoples and a sense that, post–World War II, the United States was no longer in an unchallenged leadership role internationally. These frictions and the response to them have to be placed in the context of the cold war and fears related to socialism. It was viewed as imperative by the commission to cultivate a shared leadership and sense of responsibility, thereby including Western Europe and Japan, in particular, in global planning. The greater sense of national interdependence pointed toward what would become globalization.

The commission undertook to examine key common problems among governments. Hence the first report, *The Crisis of Democracy*, arose out of a question "being posed with increasing urgency by some of the leading statesmen of the West, by columnists and scholars, and—if public opinion polls are to be trusted—even by the publics."[38] The question was whether democracy was in crisis, and the report, made up of three essays (one from each of the three power blocks), concerned itself with the governability of democratic nations. It openly acknowledged that this question was emerging from a mood that was reminiscent of the 1920s.

The essays most relevant to the discussions here are those of Michel Crozier, a French sociologist, on Western Europe, and Samuel P. Huntington, a political scientist at Harvard University and a US government adviser, on the United States.[39] Each essay begins with a description of the problems facing the political situation in the area it treats and an explanation of how the inability to deal adequately with them seemed to point to the collapse of major democratic processes. We will see that, at base, it was a question of a further advance in the liberal-democratic problem evident in the 1920s. For, generally, the findings of the commission concluded that in Europe and North America, it was the extension of the democratic principle, the further erosion of the liberal principle, and the advance of social democracy in the 1960s that were leading to new problems in governability.

38. Michel Crozier, Samuel P. Huntington, and Joji Watanuki, *The Crisis of Democracy: Report on the Governability of Democracies to the Trilateral Commission* (New York: New York University Press, 1975).

39. It is not irrelevant that Huntington was a doctoral student of Leo Strauss, who was in correspondence, as we saw, with both Harold Laski and Carl Schmitt. I owe this observation to my colleague Michael Hoelzl.

The report analyzes several factors affecting the new political destabilization. For Crozier, these include: the new lack of decisionism in a context in which traditional authority is being questioned,[40] resulting in coalition governments;[41] the expansion of a bureaucracy that breeds alienation and a lack of civic responsibility[42] even while there is an accelerated egalitarianism feeding greater expectations of government;[43] the personalization of power, such that key people become public-relations figures;[44] the embryonic cultivation of multiculturalism as a consequence of new waves of immigration into Europe from former colonies;[45] the rise of the media as an autonomous power changing people's perception;[46] the economic factor of high inflation;[47] and, finally, the contradiction between core political beliefs and such principles as freedom and equality.[48] His diagnosis of the problem leads to the conclusion that Europe is politically very vulnerable. According to Crozier's prognosis, since no right-wing reactionary movement can be expected,[49] the future belongs to the Left: "The communist parties have emerged more and more as the parties of order, whose leaders are the only ones able to make people work, and there has always been a very strong tendency to develop state socialism and public bureaucracy interference as the easy solution to manage the impossible."[50]

Huntington's analysis is broadly similar. For him, the key factors in the new destabilization are: a democratic surge strongly advocating justice in terms of equality and producing new active pressure groups[51] and what he terms a "Welfare Shift";[52] the decline of governmental authority based on hierarchy, expertise, and wealth, leading to a fall in public trust and in the credibility of political leaders, particularly the effectiveness of the presidency and leaders

40. Crozier, Huntington, and Watanuki, *Crisis of Democracy*, 25.
41. Ibid., 15.
42. Ibid., 16.
43. Ibid., 25.
44. Ibid., 19.
45. Ibid., 29.
46. Ibid., 35.
47. Ibid., 37.
48. Ibid., 44–48.
49. Ibid., 49.
50. Ibid., 50.
51. Ibid., 59–64.
52. Ibid., 70–74.

in Congress;[53] the decay of the party system, so that issue politics has replaced party politics;[54] the media as a new form of national power;[55] and inflationary tendencies resulting directly from large budgetary deficits caused by the government's welfare program and from union action that forced up wages. Hence while the dollar was being devalued, raising prices, the funding of the welfare program and the wage increases required further money from the taxpayer.[56] Although Huntington does not present a prognosis in terms of the rise of the Left, he does view the further development of social democracy as highly problematic: "Some of the problems of governance in the United States today stem from an excess of democracy."[57] He calls for a return to hierarchical values—the values of the academic and political experts—viewing Japan's position enviably because it still has residual traditional and aristocratic values.[58] There are limits, he suggests, to "the indefinite extension of political democracy."[59]

In the years following the Second World War, democracy increased, so that by the 1970s, 40 percent of public expenditure in Britain, 47 percent in Sweden, and 60 percent in France, West Germany, Italy, and the Netherlands went to providing welfare care.[60] Employment was high, technological advancement was increasing productivity, and higher education became more widely available. Crozier observes that the rise of a critical intelligentsia in France fermented political instability, leading to the Paris riots of May 1968. But that riots triggered acts of student resistance throughout many of the growing economies at that time points to the general rise in education levels and social expectations. A new class was being born as, in France and elsewhere, the number of students tripled between 1960 and 1970. This class represented the

53. Ibid., 76–85. This has to be placed in the context of Nixon's resignation over the Watergate affair in 1974, having taken up office in 1968, and a president and vice president who had come to power for the first time since the Jacksonian revolution without a national election.

54. Crozier, Huntington, and Watanuki, *Crisis of Democracy*, 87.

55. Ibid., 98–99.

56. Ibid., 103.

57. Ibid., 113.

58. Ibid., 114.

59. Ibid., 115.

60. Goran Therborn, "Classes and State, Welfare State Developments, 1881–1981," *Studies in Political Economy: A Socialist Review* 13 (Spring 1984): 7–41.

first wave of a new egalitarianism that led, in the late 1960s, to the rise of micropolitics—movements for civil rights, blacks' rights, women's rights, and gay rights. But the new egalitarianism, while politicizing certain groups, also led to new levels of withdrawal from the public sphere, and from them there has not to date been a recovery. These are the social conditions that Ronald Inglehart's analysis of "postmaterialism" noted in the early 1970s (see chap. 2, below). It was not simply that this new generation was more suspicious of macropolitics, they were also suspicious of the leaders and the parties caught up with it. Technological advancement and higher wages meant the increase in consumer goods, particularly the television and the telephone, which greatly privatized lifestyles. Quality-of-life issues came to the forefront of politics.

> Trade unionists or party members who had once turned up for branch meetings or public political occasions because, among other things, they were also a form of diversion or entertainment, could now think of more attractive ways of spending their time, unless abnormally militant. . . . Prosperity and privatization broke up what poverty and collectivity in the public place had welded together.[61]

The social revolution that followed the Second World War could be maintained while Keynesian economics remained credible and while it was evident to most that they had never had it so good. But the quadrupling of oil prices by OPEC, the oil-producing cartel, in 1973 signaled—some would say initiated—a worldwide economic swing into recession. Prices trebled again at the end of the 1970s after the revolution in Iran. Inflation spiraled out of control, currencies were devalued, unemployment soared, debts increased, an underclass swelled, and social-democratic leaders were in the frontline of those who had to go. That Crozier, writing at this point of great transition, should believe that the Left would win is surprising, even for a Frenchman. The turn to identity politics and the lobbying for specialized issues broke up the support for left-wing resistance. The apocalyptic tones of cold-war rhetoric had turned the communist into a bogeyman, and while the tide of consumerism was rising fast, socialism was already on the retreat—

61. Hobsbawm, *Age of Extremes*, 307.

as the quotation above indicates.[62] Huntington is closer to the mark: although the extremes of communism and fascism were avoided, there was slowly a return to strong right-wing leadership (of which Reagan and Thatcher were representative), and neoliberal economic policy put an end to state-managed corporations.

Liberalism, understood as middle of the road and working through extensive consultation and debate toward rational solutions, became a bad word, but certain characteristics of erstwhile liberalism (particularly asocial and apolitical individualism) remained prominent. Most prominent was the return of laissez-faire capitalism, of free and open economic markets. But this was not the laissez-faire capitalism whose demise Keynes pronounced—that had died around the time Keynes made the announcement. Neoliberal economics bred a capitalism now without conscience. This was not because the economists Friedrich Hayek and Milton Friedman were men without morals. Rather, the social and cultural changes ushered in by the collapse of the traditional values that Huntington drew attention to (the role of authority and the family) and others he did not (the role of the church) nurtured a feral individualism. The values of the old capitalist system arose out of religious convictions—as the examples of Quaker and Nonconformist industrialists confirm and as Max Weber concluded. These values were essentially social: loyalty (to one's employees or employer), trust (that contracts would be honored), the dignity of labor, pride in personal achievement, the sacrifice of immediate pleasure for future security (savings and insurance). The new individualism—fostered by neoliberal economics but generated by an increasing multiculturalism, an attention to personal development (the opening of gyms; self-help manuals), and a youth culture that wanted everything immediately—encouraged a line of ruthless entrepreneurs.[63] They were satirized in characters such as Sherman McCoy in Tom Wolfe's *Bonfire of the Vanities* (1988) and, even more viciously, Patrick Bateman in Bret Easton Ellis's *American Psycho* (1991) (see chap. 6, below). Furthermore, the soulless capitalism that had once more surrendered to Adam Smith's "invisible

62. Inglehart's postmaterialist thesis rests on these newfound levels of prosperity in the West. See chap. 2, below.

63. During the student riots of the late 1960s, a famous graffito on urban Italian walls read *Tutto e subitto*—"Everything and now."

hand"[64] underwent a gargantuan change as, with advanced communications, international trading developed the transnational economics that characterized globalization (see chap. 2, below).

For the moment we will remain focused on the crises undergone by modern democracy and the social, political, cultural, and economic transformations that they have wrought. Democracy, it seems, goes through recurrent identity crises, and political stability depends on which side of its bipolar principles—social/individual, public/private, equality/freedom—can dominate. But perhaps we can go further than simply observing the swings between social and liberal democracy and note a certain vacuum created when the theological foundations for sovereignty no longer hold—a vacuum that both social democracy and liberal democracy skirt.

The French political theorist Claude Lefort points to a profound and ultimately theological issue concerning the history and character of democracy. In the move from the late seventeenth century to the nineteenth century, from the sovereignty of the monarch to the sovereignty of the people, the body of the king (the focus and raison d'être for the first form of sovereignty) is replaced by "the image of an empty space impossible to occupy, such that those who exercise public authority can never claim to appropriate it."[65] On the one hand, the king's body (which was self-fashioned as the terrestrial body of Christ) provided the symbolic grounding for the construal of oneness, of difference contained within homogeneity. The social body, on the other hand, is nebulous and ungraspable, so that the "people will be said to be sovereign, of course, but whose identity will constantly be open to question." Lefort opines that totalitarianism is a response to the questions raised by the paradoxes within democratic polity itself.[66] The egocrat or dictator offers his or her body as a materialization of democracy's own need; he or she embodies the fantasy of democracy's own coherence.

If Lefort is right, then modern democracy is always unstable for three reasons. First, it is a word without substantial content, without grounding. And so it can define itself only negatively—as

64. Mrs. Thatcher indeed named her policy think tank on social and economic matters the Adam Smith Institute. It was founded in 1977 and continues to be influential today.

65. Claude Lefort, *Political Forms of Modern Society: Bureaucracy, Democracy, Totalitarianism* (Cambridge, MA: MIT Press, 1986), 279.

66. Ibid., 305.

in the formula "Democracy is opposed to communism or fascism or militant fundamentalism or theocracy," for the notions of equality, freedom, and the sovereignty of the people are unbounded and fracture along the lines of a thousand qualifications. Absolute equality is the erasure of difference and distinction, the flatline that signals death, the nihilist's void.[67] Absolute freedom is lawless, anarchic, and answerable to no one—the true terrorist—which means that of the triumvirate *liberté*, *egalité*, *fraternité*, only the last remains. But social solidarity, the cornerstone of the sovereignty of the people, sounds an optimistic note (and a universal humanism) to which wars fought in the name of democracy (from Korea to Iraq) give the lie.

Second, while democracy needs to conceive of itself as a political body to which all that compose it—by contracting into the polity of a specific geographical unit such as the nation-state—owe obedience and/or in which they participate, it does not have a body as such. It is only ever an amorphous, ever-changing flux. Democracy is, then, always more an imaginary feat than a substantial reality. It is always in search of a body—a body that continually is absent.[68] This absence is manifest in a lack of sovereign power—a power both sought for and yet denied by democracy. If the sovereign power is located or provided, then we have the egocrat or dictator. But these both assume the power instead of possessing the power intrinsically. When the credibility gap widens too far—as both Hitler and Mussolini had to accept—the offer of the body as a materialization of democracy's own need is rejected. Kingship, by contrast, from its earliest days promulgated ideologies that supported the intrinsic nature of its power by aligning itself with the sacred: the king was divine or the earthly manifestation of the divine.[69] The divine right of kings persisted in the West down to the German kaisers and the Russian czars of the nineteenth century. The body of the king was the physical

67. For an account of the horrors pertaining to absolute freedom, see Terry Eagleton, *Holy Terror* (Oxford: Oxford University Press, 2005), 80–86.

68. For a similar idea in which Lefort is allied with Lacan, see Slavoj Žižek, *The Sublime Object of Ideology* (London: Verso, 1989), 147: "The Lacanian definition of democracy would then be: a socio-political order in which the People do not exist."

69. For a thorough analysis of the history and politics of monarchy, see Ernst H. Kantorowicz, *The King's Two Bodies: A Study in Mediaeval Political Theology* (Princeton, NJ: Princeton University Press, 1957).

expression of the body politic, the corporation into which all who belonged to his or her domain were incorporated. In the hands of an expert apologist for this "mystical fiction,"[70] such as King James VI of Scotland/I of England, the king was not only an icon of the sacred; he embodied the natural order of things—the law of hierarchy to which all creatures were submitted.[71] He functioned sacramentally, as an incarnation of governance. Indeed, when James dined publicly, he sat beneath an ornate baldachin like the eucharistic host. One might say, then, that while pursing equality and freedom, the democrat is always dreaming of the return of the king, the return of the body—and it is this dreaming that makes all totalitarianisms possible. This dreaming goes some way perhaps to explaining why contemporary democracy has imperialistic ambitions.

The remnants of divine kingship, however, were effectively beaten into the muddy fields of Ypres and the Somme or faded with the final screams of the Romanovs. The intrinsic legitimation of sovereign power on the grounds of the sacred and the natural became perhaps the last victim of a triumphal secularism. It lost its credibility, and the "empty space impossible to occupy" was filled by jurists and political scientists and the many books on sovereignty published in the 1920s. The first crisis of democracy then took place—as we have seen. Nevertheless, what remains to be thought here beyond the historical is the theological, for "notwithstanding . . . some similarities with disconnected pagan concepts, the *king's two bodies* is an offshoot of Christian theological thought and consequently stands as a landmark of Christian political theology."[72] The Christian theological thought with which it is most associated is the Pauline understanding of the *corpus Christi* (see section 2 of this book, which develops a doctrine of the church and a metaphysics of embodiment).

A third and final point issues from Lefort's analysis of the paradoxes of democracy: secularization undermines the possibility for democracy because it disregards the theological foundations of sovereignty (section 2 will return to this frequently).

70. Ibid., 3.
71. See Hoelzl and Ward, *Religion and Political Thought*, 89–101.
72. Kantorowicz, *King's Two Bodies*, 506.

Third Example: The Return of the King

Whatever the democratic crisis in the 1970s, "governments of the ideological right, committed to an extreme form of business egoism and *laissez-faire*, came to power in several countries around 1980."[73] The pessimism about democratic governance also continued.[74] It cannot be denied that the 1970s and 1980s also saw the decline of military regimes in several countries around the world (Portugal and Greece, 1974; Spain, 1975; Argentina, 1982; Uruguay, 1983; Brazil, 1984; and later Paraguay and Chile). The crises of political legitimacy were wide-ranging. But what is investigated and argued for here is the crisis and transformation within democracy itself from which a new authoritarianism and decisionist politics emerged. And if the 1980s ended with Margaret Thatcher stepping down from office in 1990 and Ronald Reagan in 1989, their ideological positions were taken up by Tony Blair's New Labour and later by the presidency of George W. Bush.[75] Two books, more often cited than read, captured the political mood: Francis Fukuyama, *The End of History and the Last Man*, and Samuel Huntington, *The Clash of Civilizations*.[76] Their publication coincided with the rise of new critical attention to the work of Carl Schmitt, the advocate for "the state of exception"—which I regard as significant because of Schmitt's owned avowed political conservatism.[77]

73. Hobsbawm, *Age of Extremes*, 248.

74. See the influential study by Jean-François Revel, *How Democracies Perish* (New York: Harper & Row, 1983).

75. In an e-mail correspondence on an earlier draft of this book, series editor, Jamie Smith, reminded me that former President Clinton also had his parallels with Tony Blair—transforming the Democratic Party, as Blair the Labour Party, and not shy when it came to warmongering.

76. Francis Fukuyama, *The End of History and the Last Man* (Harmondsworth, UK: Penguin Books, 1992); Samuel P. Huntington, *The Clash of Civilizations and the Remaking of World Order* (New York: Simon & Schuster, 1996). The article on which *The End of History* is based was published in *The National Interest*, summer 1989, and followed the fall of the Berlin Wall and the collapse of Soviet communism. Indeed, these historical events gave extraordinary credence to the thesis that liberal democracy was the final and most legitimate form of human government.

77. The "state of exception" is a political term indicating a state of national emergency. The term arose from discussions concerning the Weimar Constitution of 1919, which Schmitt helped to draft. Famously, Article 48 of the Constitution gave dictatorial powers to the president of the German Reich: in the event that "public security and order are being significantly disturbed or endangered, the president can utilize the necessary measures to restore public security and order, if necessary with

Fukuyama's thesis argues for the triumph of liberal democracy over other forms of strong government, whether military authoritarianism or communist totalitarianism, but there are inherent tensions in this argument such that imperialism is the shadow side of the "final form." Not least in these tensions is the paradox that liberal democracy was—both before and while he was writing—developing stronger state control contrary to his view that by definition the state is weak in such democracies and does not encroach on the private sphere.[78] This strong-state mentality began with the appeals to nationalism by both Reagan and Thatcher. Although Fukuyama reflects on the rising tide of nationalism following the breakup of the Soviet Union, his universalist thesis is at odds with nationalism, or what I term "the dream of the return of the king." His argument rests on a conviction, persuasively supported and intelligently argued, of an evolutionary process in history toward a worldwide liberalism that is both economic and political.

But Fukuyama is not nearly as simplistic as some of his critics have made him out to be. He is aware of the tensions in his thesis. This is what makes the book so fascinating: the triumphalistic notes blare out of a text that begins with pessimism and ends with the "immense wars of the spirit." Furthermore, the whole of his argument rests on the word "struggle." The struggle is primarily within himself and his own ideas. It surfaces in an affirmation of both Hegel and Nietzsche: the idealism of the former (the end of history and the end of humans brought about

---

the aid of armed forces. For this purpose, he may provisionally suspend, in whole or in part, the basic rights established in Articles 114, 115, 117, 118, 123, 124, 153" (see "Selected Articles of the Weimar Constitution," an Appendix to Carl Schmitt, *Legality and Legitimacy*, trans. Jeffery Seitzer [Durham, NC: Duke University Press, 2004], 105). The controversy that followed concerned whether a president should have executive powers beyond parliament such that he might define and then declare a state of exception. In such a state, an array of individual and public liberties would be suspended for the national good.

For the increasing popularity of Carl Schmitt's work in this period, see "Carl Schmitt Now," special issue, *Telos* 109 (Fall 1996), esp. Ernst-Wolfgang Böckenförde, "Carl Schmitt Revisited," 81–86. Not only were scholarly commentaries on Schmitt and translations of his work into English published; his ideas were also being used to rethink the state of exception as it was being used by democratic governments, and this even before 9/11. See Giorgio Agamben, *Homo Sacer: Sovereign Power and Bare Life*, trans. Daniel Heller-Roazen (Stanford, CA: Stanford University Press, 1998).

78. Fukuyama, *End of History*, 15.

by liberalism, economic and social) and the realism of the latter. "The fact that major inequalities will remain even in the most perfect of liberal societies means that there will be a continuing tension between the twin principles of liberty and equality upon which such societies are based."[79] The central columns of his thesis are erected in part 3 of *The End of History*, and this is also the locus for the greatest tensions, for the logic of his argument depends on human satisfaction. Having defined one key aspect of being human as "the desire of Economic man," he then has to show not only that liberal economics best satisfies this desire but also that liberal democracy is the best "possible solution to the human problem."[80] His second anthropological axiom seeks to define human beings' political satisfaction: the struggle each undergoes for recognition. But here the old tension between freedom, understood as best realized and manifested in modernity economically, and equality, best realized by what Fukuyama calls *isothymos*, or the desire for equal recognition, surfaces most abruptly. And Fukuyama is too much a realist not to raise the issue that the demand for recognition might be so great that self-realization becomes an expression of the will to power, something attained at the expense of others and therefore in essence antidemocratic.[81] The hope, or gamble, is that the desire to be recognized more than others, or what he terms *megalothymos*, necessary for liberal democracy's survival,[82] can be channeled into economic activity—the entrepreneurial and competitive spirit. But the struggle for recognition, even according to Hegel, was the origin of human conflict, whose logic unfolds in imperialistic ambitions.[83] By the transposition of this struggle into the economic sphere, then, what will be created is transnational monopolies and cartels. Furthermore, even Fukuyama has to admit that liberal democracies themselves will have to become imperialistic: "The United States and other democracies have a

79. Ibid., 292.
80. Ibid., 135, 338.
81. Ibid., 172.
82. "Liberal democracy needs *megalothymia* and will never survive on the basis of universal and equal recognition alone" (ibid., 315).
83. Ibid., 182.

long-term interest in preserving the sphere of democracy in the world, and expanding it wherever possible and prudent."[84]

What is significant for my argument is that throughout Fukuyama accepts the secularization thesis and recognizes its dramatic consequences. Despite observing (though not fully appreciating) how Kant and Hegel's thinking with respect to equality and mutual recognition was premised on tenets of the Christian faith and despite noting that passionate believers in liberty and equality such as Franklin and Lincoln "did not hesitate to assert that liberty required belief in God,"[85] his own thesis is rooted in a secularized Christianity and the question "What is man?" In a chapter given over to detailing democracy's discontents, he sees the "need [for] a trans-historical standard against which to measure democratic society."[86] But the standard he proposes is liberal humanism, a universal and optimistic view of human nature. Simultaneously he is increasingly skeptical about the possibility for such a humanism: "Liberal democracies . . . are not self-sufficient: the community life on which they depend must ultimately come from a source different from liberalism itself"[87] (chap. 6, below, takes up this idea when it examines democracy's three fundamentals of freedom, equality, and reciprocal love with respect to the Christian tradition). We have to salute Fukuyama's enormous intellectual effort to convince the West that this is the best of all possible worlds, while remaining, as he himself recognizes in the last section of his book, not only unconvinced that there are no contradictions in liberal democracy that corrode "the legitimacy of the system itself such that the latter collapses under its own weight"[88] but also persuaded that "some new authoritarian alternatives, perhaps never before seen in history, may assert themselves in the future."[89]

Huntington's *Clash of Civilizations* can be read as a counterproposal to Fukuyama's thesis.[90] Both are exercises in futurology.

84. Fukuyama, *End of History*, 280. For an understanding of what such a "long-term interest" means, see Karin von Hippel, *Democracy by Force: US Military Intervention in the Post–Cold War World* (Cambridge: Cambridge University Press, 2000).

85. Ibid., 326.

86. Ibid., 288.

87. Ibid., 326.

88. Ibid., 136.

89. Ibid., 235.

90. Though Samuel P. Huntington, *The Third Wave: Democratization in the Late Twentieth Century* (Norman and London: University of Oklahoma Press, 1991), had appeared before Fukuyama and goes far to support Fukuyama's thesis.

Huntington groups Fukuyama among the neoliberal triumphalists predicting a one-world democracy governed by free trade. He is one of the poor readers of Fukuyama; we have seen Fukuyama is far from being triumphalist. *The Clash of Civilizations* is more about international relations, their past, present, and potential for "fault-line wars"; as such, it is not concerned, as Huntington's work in the 1970s for the Trilateral Commission was, with the character of liberal democracy. But it is valuable for this thesis for two reasons. First, it continues his thesis of a decline in America in the 1970s by vastly broadening its basis and his analysis. The West in toto is in decline—its culture and its ideology. Second, it focuses on what is particularly absent from Fukuyama's Western secularist perspective: the powerful and global resurgence of religion (chap. 3, below, will examine this second aspect when it looks more closely at the new visibility of religion). We need to understand some of the implications of his analysis of the Western decline for the changing nature of democracy.

Huntington provides a thick description of the global context within which the fluctuations in Western democracy were taking place in the 1990s. One point emerges very clearly, that the three other major global civilizations—the Sinic, based around the core state China; the Orthodox, based around the core state Russia; and the Islamic—have strong antidemocratic traditions and a belief in decisionist government. This is the major difference between Yeltsin's and Putin's premierships in Russia. All three civilizations are modernizing but not necessarily westernizing. Although both China and Russia are developing their market economics, all three civilizations reject liberalism. The Sinic and the Islamic civilizations are socialist in orientation. Huntington draws a comparison between Islamic resurgence and Marxism, for they both share a vision of the perfect society, are committed to fundamental social change that includes broad welfare, health, and education provisions, and reject the nation-state.[91] "As Western power declines, the ability of the West to impose Western concepts of human rights, liberalism, and democracy on other civilizations also declines and so does the attractiveness of those values to other civilizations."[92] For Huntington, that the universal values of Western modernity

91. Huntington, *Clash of Civilizations*, 111.
92. Ibid., 92.

go hand in hand with universalism proves to be another form of Western imperialism, but the power base and resources for such imperialism are in decline.[93]

Although, then, democracy seemed to recover from the crisis of the 1970s, it did so by morphing and bringing to power a range of new decisionist leaders who effectively reasserted the liberal principle over the democratic. A king returns. But he does so at a cost, and it is this cost with which we in the West are still living. "In our 1975 volume [*The Crisis of Democracy*] we noted that the challenges to democratic government then observed had produced, at least in the United States, a dramatic decline in public confidence in government. Now, twenty-five years later, while the challenges we enumerated have disappeared, the low confidence in government in America and other Trilateral countries has not only continued but deepened."[94] The cost of the so-called triumph of liberal democracy was public trust. This mistrust was further aggravated by the development of the surveillance society, particularly after 9/11, when issues of national security fostered a politics of fear and spawned various versions of "homeland security." It is a well-known political platitude that if a citizenship feels insecure, then it demands more authoritarian forms of governance. At the opening of the twenty-first century, the word "postdemocracy" is being coined to describe the prevailing political condition.

The Postdemocratic Condition

A Web site established in 2006 to examine postdemocracy states that no one knows yet what it is.[95] In a sense, the use of "post-" from the mid-1970s onward—"postliberal," "postmodern," "postindustrial," "postsecular," and so forth—is adverting to a social and cultural

93. He is not denying that the West still has major advantages as a global player, including massive military capabilities, the ownership and operation of the international banking system, the ownership of all the hard currencies, and the domination of international communications, but he does argue that other civilizations are catching up. Furthermore, the West is retreating economically and demographically, and there "are problems of moral decline, cultural suicide, and political disunity" (ibid., 304).

94. Samuel P. Huntington, preface to *Disaffected Democracies*, ed. Susan J. Pharr and Robert D. Putnam (Princeton, NJ: Princeton University Press, 2000), xxvi.

95. "What Is Post-democracy?" *Postdemocracy*, http://postdemocracy.org/about.

sea change for which we are still trying to find a language. The Web site goes on to say (in a manner reminiscent of Lefort's analyses), "We suspect democracy has become an empty word whose meaning is assumed to be understood but in actuality differs widely among speakers. Hence the need for a postdemocracy theory—a theory that clearly distances the left from neo-con wars of aggression while taking democratic theory in a new, radical direction that supports the rights of local-self-determination against this oppressive, corporate, military world."

It seems, then, that "postdemocracy" is a left-wing response to the return of the king. Early uses of the term related to the election of 2001, which put George W. Bush into the White House despite his loss of the popular vote and the controversy over the electoral vote in the state of Florida.[96] It reemerged with the failure of the American democratic system to oust him in 2005—"more significantly, the failure of voting to offer us a candidate who differed radically from the positions of Bush."[97] So postdemocracy is concerned with the electoral system itself as a tool for democracy, the conservatism implicit in voting, and the decline of party politics more generally.[98]

Most of the recent empirical data concerning electoral participation and levels of public trust, and the analyses of the data, refer to trends in the 1990s. That is, the data available do not cover the more recent shock waves to democracies following 9/11, Madrid, and London; the controversial entry into wars with Afghanistan and Iraq; and the infringements of civic liberties by various democratic governments in the name of national security. But the empirical evidence does overwhelmingly point to substantial changes to civil society generally in the West—with America taking an early lead. Robert Putnam, who has organized researches across eight major countries, has succinctly examined these changes. Most

96. See Ernest Partridge, "On Coping with 'Post Democracy,'" *The Online Gadfly*, http://gadfly.igc.org/politics/postdemo.htm.

97. "Badiou on Voting," *Postdemocracy*, http://postdemocracy.org.

98. See the observations on the electoral system in the French presidential elections of 2002 and the contest between Jacques Chirac, Lionel Jospin, and Jean-Marie Le Pen in Alain Badiou, "Philosophical Considerations of the Very Singular Custom of Voting," trans. Steven Corcoran, and available at http://why-war.com: "Savage belief in the democratic religion . . . grows . . . [while] the vote has become more and more unstable and irrational."

significantly, there is a declining electoral turnout that indicates "a gradual erosion in popular commitment to conventional politics."[99] From the 1950s to the 1990s, the decline was broadly from 80 percent to 70 percent, and it accelerated in the 1990s. Concomitant was a "dramatic decline in party membership"[100] and the public engagement in political parties. Significantly for our examination of postdemocracy, this decline is seen as "a clear indication of how elections have shifted from mass-based participation to vicarious viewing of the campaign on television."[101] (This aestheticization, the media-oriented politics, and their impact on the crisis of representation and on the citizen as spectator will be discussed later.) But the decline is also significant because party membership forms one of three mainline "technologies" (to use Michel Foucault's term)—social institutions involving disciplines that encourage the skills for active citizenship. The other two "technologies" are church and union membership, and these two institutions also saw dramatic declines from the 1970s onward. Furthermore, the empirical evidence points to even greater levels of decline with respect to the younger generation.

Putnam focuses particularly on "social capital," its generation and distribution.[102] Social capital and its wide distribution across all groups of people are absolutely essential for a flourishing democracy. Although some social scientists point to levels of stability in the participation in voluntary associations and informal sociability,[103] these nevertheless constitute soft forms of social capital rather than

99. Robert D. Putnam, "Conclusion," in *Democracies in Flux: The Evolution of Social Capital in Contemporary Society*, ed. Robert D. Putnam (Oxford: Oxford University Press, 2002), 404.

100. Ibid., 406.

101. Russell J. Dalton, Ian McAllister, and Martin P. Wattenberg, "The Consequences of Partisan Dealignment," in *Parties without Partisans: Political Change in Advanced Industrial Democracies*, ed. Russell J. Dalton, Ian McAllister, and Martin P. Wattenberg (Oxford: Oxford University Press, 2000), 58.

102. Social capital is understood broadly as the way family, friends, and networks of associates constitute an important asset politically, culturally, and even economically. "Those communities endowed with a diverse stock of social networks and civic associations are in a stronger position to confront poverty and vulnerability, resolve disputes, and take advantage of new opportunities" (Michael Woolcock and Deepa Narayan, "Social Capital: Implications for Development Theory, Research, and Policy," *World Bank Observer* 15 [2000]: 226).

103. See Peter A. Hall, "Great Britain: The Role of Government and the Distribution of Social Capital," in Putnam, *Democracies in Flux*, 21–58; and Robert Wuthnow,

substantial. The more firmly one is rooted in an institution, the more substantial is the social capital. "The newer forms of social participation are narrower, less bridging, and less focused on collective or public-regarding purpose."[104] In other words, the trend is for social capital to become much more privatized as levels of public and social trust also are on the decline.[105]

Cultural scientists such as Colin Crouch, who has performed the most detailed work to date on the postdemocratic condition, would only concur. There are four key characteristics of this condition as Crouch has examined it. *First*, the will of the people is not obtained but created by various means of persuasion; politics are dominated by their media presentation, particularly by the new telecommunications that provide economic globalism with its life force.[106] In a sense, this is not new—there have always been electoral hustings at which policy is dissolved in a heavy cocktail of promises, propaganda, and rhetoric. Furthermore, as we saw with Laski's and Schmitt's critiques of parliamentarism, certain interests have always been served to the detriment of others. It may be a question of scale. Certainly, after the 2005 campaign in Britain, both the Labour and the Conservative parties were in considerable debt to the tune of twenty and fourteen million pounds respectively, most of which was spent on media campaigning. For a long time in British politics, donations given to particular parties were not regulated, and when a more transparent system was introduced, so was an official system of interest-free or low-interest "loans" to political parties. There is a correlation, investigated recently in Britain, between the people giving these loans and the recommendations (through the prime minister's office) for peerages.

This media domination of politics, to which Habermas draws attention in his account of the decline of the public sphere,[107] must

---

"United States: Bridging the Privileged and the Marginalized?" in Putnam, *Democracies in Flux*, 59–102.

104. Putnam, "Conclusion," 412.

105. See earlier Pharr and Putnam, *Disaffected Democracies*, esp. Russell Hardin, "Public Trust," 31–51.

106. This characteristic is ironic given that freedom of the press was one of the central axioms in the democratic defense against the abuse of power and absolute rule. See Crouch, *Post-democracy*, 20.

107. See Jürgen Habermas, *The Structural Transformation of the Public Sphere: An Inquiry into a Category of Bourgeois Society* (Cambridge, MA: MIT Press, 1989).

also be viewed in relation to media moguls and certain political parties. There is perhaps no coincidence in the fact that the term "postdemocracy" first appeared in Italy when Silvio Berlusconi, one such media mogul, was prime minister.[108] The Australian media mogul Rupert Murdoch was closely associated with Blair's New Labour Party, and the biased coverage by CNN of the war in Iraq led to the banning of that broadcasting channel in South Africa for the duration of the war. Moreover, whereas in the 1970s both Crozier and Huntington viewed the enormous growth of the media as a potential threat to liberal democracy (Huntington even suggesting a need for stricter censorship), clamor for air time on both radio and television by politicians has never been greater. Where credibility is so finely related to image, and persuasive authority to credibility, the media play an ever-increasing role in politics. And so the question arises about the nature and interests of elected representation.[109] "Totally personality-based election campaigning used to be characteristic of dictatorships and of electoral politics in societies with weakly developed systems of parties and debates."[110] To the power of this role must be added a general aestheticization of politics that dates back to at least the work of Leni Riefenstahl and Joseph Goebbels for Hitler.

Walter Benjamin was one of the first to recognize this trend: "The logical result of Fascism is the introduction of aesthetics into politics."[111] What this aestheticization means is the use of the various plastic and media arts—film, architecture, painting, advertising—to generate a particular political myth. This myth has powerful resonance with individuals and societies, and the aesthetic element seeks not only to produce and promulgate this resonance but also to ensure its appreciation. The Nazi mythmaking has been thoroughly investigated,[112] but the questions raised by cultural theorists such as Philippe Lacoue-Labarthe concern the extent to which this aestheti-

108. See also Naomi Klein, *No Logo* (London: Flamingo, 2000).

109. See G. Davies and A. Graham, *Broadcasting, Society, and Policy in the Multimedia Age* (Luton, UK: University of Luton Press, 1997).

110. Crouch, *Post-democracy*, 26.

111. Walter Benjamin, "The Work of Art in the Age of Mechanical Reproduction," in *Illuminations* (London: Pimlico, 1999), 241.

112. See Philippe Lacoue-Labarthe, *Heidegger, Art, and Politics*, trans. Chris Turner (Oxford: Blackwell, 1990); and Philippe Lacoue-Labarthe and Jean-Luc Nancy, *Les mécanismes du fascisme* (Strasbourg: Colloque de Schiltigheim, 1980).

cizing is "decisive in the formation of the modern political sphere."[113] With the increasing emphasis on image and the importance of media in politics, is there not a danger of generating the myth of unlimited capitalist development and the advance of democratic freedom? Are the glamour and internationalism of globalization itself not promoting another myth of bodies freed from the restrictions of time and space, a myth inseparable from Internet surfing and the metaphysics of virtual reality? Are such myths not versions of the romantic sublime so beloved by postmodern theorists?[114] The advance of brand-based politics foregrounds the aesthetic and perhaps also the anesthetic (see chap. 2, below).

The *second* characteristic of a postdemocratic condition is a political sphere that is dominated by economic questions—such that the rise of global capitalism has produced a self-referential political class more concerned with forging links with wealthy business interests than with pursuing political programs.[115] Since the 1980s the boundaries between government and private business interests have been so blurred that public services and welfare policies are increasingly being outsourced and made available for profit-making purposes to private companies. Areas of civic life once held to be the responsibility of governments to protect and secure—health, education, the welfare of its people—are contracted and subsequently even subcontracted. The social has collapsed into the economic. Equality of opportunity, seen as the fundamental democratic right, is severely compromised, for opportunity is subject to a neoliberal economics that demands all sectors be open to the competition of the market. What is significant is that Fukuyama recognized very clearly that for countries given over to full economic growth, "the truly winning combination would appear to be neither liberal democracy nor socialism of either a Leninist or democratic variety, but the combination of liberal economics and authoritarian politics . . . or what we might term a 'market-oriented authoritarianism.'"[116] If anything, democracy is a drag on economic efficiency.[117] The postdemocratic condition, to

113. Lacoue-Labarthe, *Heidegger*, 103.

114. See Eagleton, *Holy Terror*. It is not insignificant that Fukuyama chooses to speak of the fulfillment of his vision as "the Promised Land of liberal democracy."

115. Crouch, *Post-democracy*, 13, 43–46, 78–89.

116. Fukuyama, *End of History*, 123; see also 134–35.

117. Ibid., 205.

the extent it has been fathered by neoliberal capitalist interests, is going to call for strong, authoritarian governments. "The more that there is privatisation and a marketisation model for public-service delivery, particularly at local level, the more a Jacobin model of centralised democracy and a citizenship without intermediate levels of political action has to be imposed."[118] Furthermore, through the outsourcing, governments become increasingly less accountable, and therefore their operations become increasingly less transparent. This new opacity of the state sets it apart from the people so that it is now less responsible and responsive to the electorate. The old system of checks and balances is no longer adequate for calling sovereign power into question.[119]

This diminishment of "intermediate levels of political action" for citizens—coming in Britain at a time when classes in citizenship are compulsorily taught in schools—leads to the *third* characteristic of postdemocracy: not simply the decline in political participation but active forms of depoliticization. I do not wish to suggest that postdemocratic governments actively engage in depoliticizing their citizens, for the depoliticization is much more subtle than that. Carl Schmitt advanced the argument that liberal democracy was itself depoliticizing, for in allowing all sides to have their say, no enemy (and therefore no friend) could be identified.[120] The political, for Schmitt, demanded a clear sense of who were for and who were against the state. Be that as it may, Leo Strauss has pointed out that Schmitt "affirms the political because he sees in the threatened status of the political a threat to the seriousness of human

118. Crouch, *Post-democracy*, 101.

119. In Britain, although Parliament can set up an independent inquiry into an allegation (e.g., under Lord Hutton), the conclusions of the inquiry will raise more questions about the operations of government instead of resolving them. One might also think of the way, in the United States, lawyers raise the question of the legality of Guantanamo Bay, but they effect no changes. Meanwhile, there is George W. Bush's "practice of writing exceptions to legislation as he signs it into law" (Julian Borger, "Leading Lawyers Say Bush Creates Loopholes in Laws He Doesn't Like," *Guardian* [London], July 25, 2006).

120. "[Liberalism's] neutralizations and depoliticizations (of education, the economy, etc.) are, to be sure, of political significance. . . . But the question is whether a specific political idea can be derived from the pure and consequential concept of individualistic liberalism. This is to be denied" (Carl Schmitt, *The Concept of the Political*, trans. George Schwab [Chicago: Chicago University Press, 1996], 69–70).

life."[121] Depoliticization begins with the social atomization that laissez-faire capitalism—committed to the freedoms of the individual and the encouragement of the entrepreneur, the risk taker, the ambitious, and the competitive—necessarily engenders. The intense interest in self-development, continual education, customized spiritualities, and "lifestyles" gives priority to the customer or the client rather than the citizen. Strauss suggests that the case Schmitt is arguing for is that "politics and the state are the only guarantee against the world's becoming a world of entertainment . . . a world of amusement, a world without seriousness."[122] The culture of postdemocracy announces that we have arrived at such a world—a world in which, as the Italian political thinker Antonio Negri puts it, there is "zero degree dialectic."[123] Where there is no dialectic and where the citizen as customer or client is merely requested to be satisfied with the services provided, even the services ostensibly provided by the state through private companies, there is self-determined disenfranchisement in favor of leisure, personal consumption, and entertainment. Fukuyama saw this as one of the dangers of neoliberal democracy.[124] The great historian of the city Lewis Mumford saw this even earlier: if one of the most important functions of city life is its facilitation of dialogue and fellowship, then "for the same reason, the most revealing symbol of the city's failure . . . is the absence of dialogue."[125] It is significant that the many charters of service that set out what each customer can be reasonably expected to receive become the means whereby the possibility of complaint or contestation is neutralized. Satisfaction is primary and it works like a social sedative. Dialectic means discussion and contestation, and as Carl Schmitt noted, politically, "where there is no discussion there is dictatorship."[126] (Hence, a

121. Leo Strauss, "Notes on Carl Schmitt, *The Concept of the Political*," in Heinrich Meier, *Carl Schmitt and Leo Strauss: The Hidden Dialogue* (Chicago: University of Chicago Press, 1995), 112–13. Strauss's essay is insightful.

122. Ibid., 112.

123. Antonio Negri, *Time for Revolution*, trans. Matteo Mandarini (New York: Continuum, 2003), 41.

124. See Fukuyama, "Men without Chests," in *End of History*, 300–312.

125. Lewis Mumford, *The City in History* (Harmondsworth, UK: Penguin Books, 1961), 141. Chapter 5, below, discusses Mumford and the city when it examines the struggle for the city's soul.

126. Carl Schmitt, *Political Theology: Four Chapters on the Concept of Sovereignty*, trans. George Schwab (Cambridge, MA: MIT Press, 1985), 78.

political book such as this must resist these easy satisfactions and therefore cannot be polite.)

Crouch points out that depoliticization and atomism have occurred to such an extent that there is a decline among the social classes that had made possible an active and critical mass politics, so that the concept of civil society is now radically questionable.[127] Indeed, the specificity of the language of "society" seems to be giving way to the amorphousness of the language of "culture"; the social becomes the cultural. As I have pointed out elsewhere, the cultural is a symbolic domain governed by the exchanges of image, metaphor, and myth in a syncretistic transformation.[128] It is the domain of the aesthetic. We might speak, then, not only of an aestheticization of politics but an aestheticization of the social more generally. People do not belong to communities anymore but inhabit various cultures—an observation that is supported by Huntington's attention to civilizations as "culture[s] writ large," which are characteristic of the new post-cold-war situation.[129]

The *fourth* and final characteristic of the postdemocratic condition is a crisis of representation such that powerful minority interests obtain far more attention than their numbers would secure in a ballot and politicians increasingly speak not for their constituency but for their own concerns or at the behest of a party's or professional lobbyist's line.[130] To some extent, this is again a matter of degree, for critiques of parliamentarism have often focused on the problem of how representative is the representative and who or what is being represented by the representative. Where direct democracy is impossible, except on certain rare issues that go to a referendum, mediation is necessary.[131] But the representational problematic is intensified when intermediate levels of political engagement are diminishing and government becomes increasingly opaque. In a speech he delivered to the Council of Europe at its Warsaw meeting in May 2005, President Vaclav Klaus of the Czech Republic likewise understood postdemocracy as the rising power

127. Ibid., 9. See also Michael Hardt, "The Withering of Civil Society," *Social Text* 14, no. 4 (Winter 1995): 27–44.

128. Graham Ward, *Cultural Transformation and Religious Practice* (Cambridge: Cambridge University Press, 2005), 160–61.

129. Huntington, *Clash of Civilizations*, 41.

130. Crouch, *Post-democracy*, 19.

131. Switzerland still maintains its tradition of direct democracy.

of nonelected interests that attain the means to lobby for change.[132] The American political scientist Theda Skocpol best sums up and describes the current situation:

> All in all, the very model of what counts as effective organization in US politics and civic life has changed very sharply. No longer do most leaders and citizens think of building, or working through, nationwide federations that link face-to-face groups into state and national networks. If a new cause arises, entrepreneurs think of opening a national office, raising funds through direct mail, and hiring pollsters and media consultants. Polls are used to measure disaggregated public opinion, even as advocacy groups emit press releases about hot-button issues, hire lobbyists to deal with government—and engage in incessant fund-raising to pay for all of the above. Organizational leaders have little time to discuss things with groups of members. Members are a nonlucrative distraction.[133]

Little wonder, then, that in a manner reminiscent of Laski's observations, the interests of the wealthy and best educated predominate and the people for whom the new democratic condition least works (and likewise the new economic conditions associated with open markets) are the poor and marginalized. The latter lack capital of all kinds, even social. Perhaps the West has made a circle back to the 1920s, where our analysis began. Meanwhile the poor and marginalized "group represents a difficult problem for democrats—they are most susceptible to manipulation owing to the absence of an autonomous political profile and tend to be the most politically passive of groups, whilst being the most rapidly expanding sector in Western societies."[134] Where politicians are disassociated from their constituents, the way is open for corruption.[135]

132. "Debate on Postdemocracy Chaired by President Klaus," Radio Praha, www.radio.cz/en/article/68482.

133. Theda Skocpol, "United States: From Membership to Advocacy," in Putnam, *Democracies in Flux*, 134.

134. Phil Burton-Cartledge, review of *Post-democracy*, by Colin Crouch, *Sociological Review* 53, no. 2 (May 2005): 372.

135. For an endorsement of this view regarding Italy, see Donatella della Porta, "Social Capital, Beliefs in Government, and Political Corruption," in Pharr and Putnam, *Disaffected Democracies*, 202–28.

Conclusion

If some analysis of voter trends is pointing to the rise of political participation in new social movements, like Green parties, peace movements, animal rights groups, alongside an increasing skepticism about the hierarchical nature of political institutions themselves,[136] then today we may be witnessing a titanic struggle between high-handed neoliberals, on the one hand, and disaffected social democrats, on the other. The postmaterialist thesis points to such trends (cf. chap. 2, below, regarding its claims). But even if this postmaterialist thesis was substantially correct, it would not counter Crouch's postdemocracy thesis because its political activities frequently lie outside the traditional governmental institutions of the state.[137] Postmaterialist preferences may be elite-challenging in supporting the eco-warriors, the marginalized, the oppressed, and those without a public voice, but the elites still remain in charge. Nevertheless, there is a problem with the "postdemocratic" thesis, namely, the stability of the modern concept of "democracy" that it employs. For it assumes that democracy in the past was so homogenous, stable, and self-evident we can now talk about its demise. As we have seen throughout this chapter, the paradoxes of liberal democracy have furnished historical swings in one direction and in another. We are not *post*democratic if the history of the West is the history of a struggle to be democratic—in the various ways that term has been understood. Even so, many of the social and cultural features Crouch depicts as postdemocratic are recognizable, so the value of the label, and the conditions it describes, is that it shows how "thin" democracy has now become.

Crouch himself sees no major way of changing what Western governments have set in motion, because there is no "effective alternative to the capitalist firm for process and production innovation and for customer responsiveness where most goods and services are concerned."[138] Phil Burton-Cartledge , one of Crouch's

136. See Russell J. Dalton, "Value Change and Democracy," in Pharr and Putnam, *Disaffected Democracies*, 252–69; Susan Pharr, Robert D. Putnam, and Russell J. Dalton, "A Quarter-Century of Declining Confidence: Trouble in Advanced Democracies?" *Journal of Democracy* 11, no. 2 (2000): 5–25; Iris Marion, "Activist Challenges to Deliberative Democracy," *Rhetoric and Public Affairs* 5, no. 2 (2002): 223–60.

137. See Hans-Dieter Klingemann and Dieter Fuchs, *Citizens and the State* (Oxford: Oxford University Press, 1995).

138. Crouch, *Post-democracy*, 105.

commentators, disagrees, holding that there is always the anticapitalist struggle, the socialist alternative.[139] But socialism, as it was conceived and practiced, failed.

What we need, then, is something more than socialism as it was conceived and practiced, that is, a responsible capitalism based not simply in higher taxation, nationalization, trade boundaries, and welfare provision. The nation in the wake of globalization and the opening up of local markets is much weaker. We need a responsible capitalism founded on a metaphysics that argues against the cruelties of reductive materialism; for metaphysics is concerned with establishing first principles, the conditions on which materialism, in this case, is possible. The way beyond our present deepening postdemocracy is the fostering of a postmaterialist culture that is built not on the shifting sands of ephemeral human desires but on the rock of what is true and good and realistic. In other words, changes to processes, economic or political, have to be preceded by, and grounded on, changes in transcending values and vision. This means the creation of a new anthropology, a new way of seeing ourselves, our purposes and desires, our bodies, hopes, expectations, and teleologies. Green parties and environmentalists, concerned with the rapacious way we are consuming the planet's resources with little or no consideration of future impact, are busy envisaging new nonexploitative cosmologies, new ways of conceiving creation as a gift to be well stewarded and conserved. This is a beginning, and their popularity—they are among the few political interest groups whose participation figures have increased significantly over the years of electoral decline—point to a new ethics of renunciation and reciprocity that ultimately is postmaterialistic.[140] But with Lefort's analyses in mind, this must be built upon in a theological and metaphysical manner.

The call for a new metaphysics is somewhat at odds with postmodernity, and we need to explore this further if we are to avoid being caricatured as "pissing in the wind." For it is no coincidence that postmodernity (like postdemocracy and postmaterialism) arose in the mid-1970s at the same time as the oil crisis and the detachment of the dollar from the gold standard, the rise of neolib-

139. Burton-Cartledge, review of *Post-democracy*, 373.

140. For the rise of postmaterialist politics and the role it might have in revitalizing democracy, see Dalton, "Value Change and Democracy."

eral economics, and the return of the king. They are not unrelated phenomena. Neither are they collapsible into each other—as some left-wing cultural analysts would like to think. For example, the neoliberal universalism of someone such as Fukuyama does not correlate very easily with what Jean-François Lyotard places at the very forefront of his exposition of postmodernism: the death of grand narratives, such as History with a capital *H*.[141] Most of the influential Continental philosophy that provides a metastructure for postmodernity—by, for example, Michel Foucault, Jacques Derrida, Jean Baudrillard, Lyotard, Gilles Deleuze, and Jean-Luc Nancy—comes out of a declining socialist tradition in France during the late 1960s and 1970s. These thinkers were of the generation that had such high hopes for Mitterand—and was so severely disappointed. But there is no doubt that the favored language of postmodernity—"flux," "flows," "libidinal economies," "deferral," "undecidable," "nomadic," "*khora*," "erring," "deterritorialization," "aporia," "body without organs"—and the move toward soft understandings of the subject as agent and of power as diffuse are at best not going to be effective resistors to laissez-faire capitalism and at worst help foster a culture in which such capitalism can have its greatest impact. Furthermore, postmodernism's championing of the kitsch, the surface, the cited, and the performed is hardly going to stem the tsunami of the reified and the commodified. The society of the spectacle and the culture of the spectator and the spectacular legitimate domination by media and the aestheticization of politics. Endless critique in the name of a quasi-transcendental is a critique from an angry dog without teeth. It is not going to answer Negri's point about "zero degree dialectic." A galloping relativism of values and even frank espousals of nihilism are not going to help give content to Lefort's "empty space impossible to occupy" that generates the paradoxes of democracy. Where the passing of judgment becomes ethnocentric, colonial, sexist, racist, and so on, postdemocracy as it is experienced by the majority[142] can all too easily be viewed as postmodern politics. Discussing postmodernization and its

141. Jean-François Lyotard, *The Postmodern Condition: A Report on Knowledge*, trans. Geoffrey Bennington (Manchester, UK: Manchester University Press, 1984).

142. Those taking the decisions and lobbying for and making the policies obviously do not experience it like this.

effects on politics, the American political scientist Ronald Inglehart points to the erosion of a respect for authority and the turn to "maximizing subjective well-being" as the key features.[143] Although Inglehart goes on to relate these features to his own rather thin account of postmaterialist values, they are hardly a sound basis for metaphysics.

So we have to tread warily here, locating perhaps the new metaphysics for which I am calling as a project within postmodernism itself—as the project that remains unfinished within the radical critique of modernity. This is what I will argue, and in doing so, I move beyond postmodernity entirely. But first we have to examine more closely one of the drivers of the postdemocratic condition: contemporary economic theory. For "the encroachment of capital into areas previously deemed essential to the quality of citizenship, and therefore too important to be subject to commercial imperatives," highlights the "role of the World Trade Organisation and the International Monetary Fund in the global dismantling of welfare states."[144]

143. Ronald Inglehart, "Postmodernization, Authority and Democracy," in *Critical Citizens: Global Support for Democratic Government*, ed. Pippa Norris (Oxford: Oxford University Press, 1999), 239.

144. Burton-Cartledge, review of *Post-democracy*, 372.

2

Globalization

When the World Is Not Enough

> There is the assumption that globalization is the continuation of the Christian civilizing project, and that whatever stands in the way is "oriental" despotism, Muslim fundamentalism, etc. To this extent, globalization is counterpoised against the non-West in a mission of redemption and salvation.[1]

Cape Town

Whether you arrive in Cape Town by plane or train, what greets you is the stark contrast between the destitute and the moneyed. From the international airport the road to the city descends through a vast camp of makeshift housing of cardboard, clapboard, and polyethylene; from the central train station the exit wends through a mass of hawkers sitting before their bits of possessions in a passivity that lies beyond despair. And the circling beauty of Table Mountain, Devil's Peak, and Lion's Head burns

1. Eduardo Mendieta in conversation with Jürgen Habermas, in Jürgen Habermas, *Religion and Rationality: Essays on Reason, God, and Modernity* (Cambridge: Polity, 2002), 152.

in the midday heat. This is a restless city of migrants—migrants who have slid toward the tip of the Southern Hemisphere. From here there are only the sea and the melting wastes of Antarctica. The migrants came from Holland, Britain, France, Germany, Indonesia, and Madagascar, vying with the local Bushman and Hottentot tribes and the Bantu from the north. They came with the expansion of global trade from the seventeenth century onward, as explorers and exploiters, slaves and merchants, domestics and financiers, sailors and scientists, adventurers, debtors, and fugitives. They came for the diamonds, for the gold, for the climate and soil that could produce an abundance of grapes and apples. More recently they came as refugees, tourists, and conference delegates—as refugees from nineteenth-century struggles in Botswana, twentieth-century colonial and civil wars in Mozambique, and twenty-first-century political purgings in Zimbabwe; as tourists from Russia, the United States, China, Japan, Europe, and Australia; and as conference delegates from around the world to the International Convention Centre, which dominates the downtown district. They came for the work, the opportunities, the rugby, the beaches, the sunshine, the gemstones, the cricket, the surfing, the wine tasting, the climbing, the real estate, the drugs, the sailing, the rich pickings, and the giant aquarium and Imax at the newly refurbished Waterfront, where the Old Prison is now a hotel. From a terrace bar in the glass pavilions of the Waterfront, charging the prices of a cocktail lounge in Manhattan, you can sip the country's best Pinot Noir looking out to the flat dark smudge in the ocean: Robben Island, where captives like Mandela were housed in the years of apartheid. Boats from the harbor do sunset tours with champagne.

Here in Cape Town the world meets, mixes, and goes its various ways in a multitude of languages and ethnicities. Founded on exchange and barter, the city is a giant emporium, a theme park for trading that stands at the edge of the world.

A distinction between globalism and globalization is made in the argument presented here. "Globalization" refers to a number of activities and processes related to historical developments in trading and capitalism that have been informed by neoliberal economics.[2] We cannot reduce globalization to economics, for it is a far wider phenomenon. Its ideologies of internationalism and the vast contraction of space and time have had an impact culturally, on social and political relations, for example. Nevertheless, globalization is inseparable from specific forms of economic theory, and the political forces (nation-states, liberal democracy) advancing and advocating them are mainly products of Western and North American history. Distinctively, the more abstract term "globalism" refers to a worldview, a universal or global vision, intrinsic to certain ideologies (e.g., Marxism and Christianity), certain practices (e.g., missionizing and peacekeeping), or certain phenomena (e.g., the Internet and satellite television). These worldviews are enshrined in sets of discourse that speak about and disseminate these ideologies, practices, and phenomena and in technologies that mediate this dissemination. The central argument in this chapter is that the historical development known as globalization is the product of a globalism issuing from Christian theology and its ecclesial history. Globalization is thus intimately bound to religion, its triumphal myths of salvation for all, its promises of profoundly fulfilling what a human being yearns for, and its metaphysics. It is therefore no coincidence that the contemporary phase of globalization parallels the return of religion to the public sphere in new, not necessarily institutional, forms. It also follows that awareness of the masked theologies and metaphysics of globalization needs to be drawn out and developed so that postmaterialist values may be asserted and substantiated in the face of radical capitalist expansion.

The Pursuit of a New Postmaterialism

What cannot be underestimated, according to the literature on the crises, disaffections, and fluxes of contemporary democracy,

2. The capitalism characterized by neoliberalism is not the only form of capitalism. Some scholars have argued persuasively that Chinese and Japanese capitalism must be distinguished from Western forms because it is closely associated with family networks; Western capitalism, by contrast, is far more individualistic. This chapter uses "capitalism" in its Western character. With the phenomenal growth of Indian and Chinese production, new world economic leaders are emerging; whether the differences in the nature of capitalism remain is an interesting question. Some economists wish to distinguish Oriental forms of capitalism from capitalism as practiced in the West.

is the move away from central planned economies in favor of the blind and unpredictable forces of the market. The significant years for this shift were the mid-1970s although the road to neoliberal economics was paved in the mid-1940s. In 1974 Hayek won the Nobel Prize for economics; in 1976 the same prize was awarded to Milton Friedman. Hayek's *The Road to Serfdom* and Friedman's *Capitalism and Freedom* were the most influential books in the advocacy of laissez-faire as a means for safeguarding democratic freedom.[3] Indeed, for both of them, democracy is impossible without global free trade. For Hayek, writing in the middle of the Second World War and bringing to bear his profound understanding of Austro-German politics, all alternatives to free trade lead to totalitarianism; the future of Western civilization and its distinctive moral code rested, for him, on the erasure of socialism. For Friedman, monetarism would not lead to the alleviation of poverty but, rather, to another Great Depression.

As we saw in the last chapter with both Fukuyama and Crouch, contemporary liberal democracy or even the postdemocratic condition is intrinsically related to accumulative capitalism. Huntington too is aware of this connection, for he points to the economic factors that prepared the ground for such democratization. Wealth-accumulating nations foster five significant factors that correlate strongly with democratic governance and culture: (a) "feelings of interpersonal trust, life satisfaction, and competence"; (b) higher levels of education; (c) greater resources "for distribution among social groups . . . hence [facilitating] accommodation and compromise"; (d) the opening of national borders to a world economy and "the democratic ideas prevailing in the industrialized world"; and (e) the creation of a confident middle class interested in electoral politics.[4] Some of these factors, according to other analyses, were already on a steep downward curve by 1991—interpersonal trust and the redistribution of resources, for example. But there is a further significant factor about the effects of laissez-faire capitalism to which neither Fukuyama nor Crouch or Huntington allude.

3. Friedrich A. Hayek, *The Road to Serfdom* (London: Routledge, 2001); Milton Friedman, *Capitalism and Freedom* (Chicago: University of Chicago Press, 1962). We will return to Hayek and Friedman later.

4. Samuel P. Huntington, *Third Wave Democratization in the Late Twentieth Century* (Norman and London: University of Oklahoma Press, 1991), 65–67.

Since the early 1970s, the economic and political scientist Ronald Inglehart has been charting, through a series of empirical tests, the effect of this new wealth accumulation on the values that people hold. It is Inglehart who coined the word "postmaterialism." His thesis was simple: as a people moves out of economic instability, where basic survivor values such as food and physical security dominate, their values change—orientated now toward quality-of-life issues such as human rights, personal liberties, community, aesthetic satisfaction, and the environment. It is these values that he designated as postmaterialist.[5] If the thesis holds, then the increasing affluence in the West created through globalization will correlate with an increasing number of postmaterialists and a cultural shift toward postmaterialist values. This is what Inglehart's own measurements, along with his analysis of the three waves of the World Values Survey,[6] indeed suggest: "At the time of our first surveys, in 1970–71, Materialists held an overwhelming numerical preponderance over Postmaterialists, outnumbering them by nearly four to one. By 1990, the balance had shifted dramatically, to a point where Materialists outnumbered Postmaterialists only four to three."[7] Indeed, by 1994, in Europe the indications were "that postmaterialists were coming to be equal in number to materialists," and in the United States, the Netherlands, and Denmark, changes were even more substantial, with the survey results for Denmark showing that "there were more postmaterialists than materialists in that country."[8] Inglehart's work, his index method, and his interpretation of the results have not gone unquestioned, but this does not matter here. What does matter is that "it seems that a fundamental and profound shift in social attitudes is in process across the world"[9] and is set to continue.

5. See Ronald Inglehart, *Modernization and Postmodernization: Cultural, Economic, and Political Change in 43 Societies* (Princeton, NJ: Princeton University Press, 1997), chap. 4. This work, the first that relates postmaterialism to postmodernity, furthers the analysis of available data that Inglehart began in *The Silent Revolution: Changing Values and Political Styles among Western Publics* (Princeton, NJ: Princeton University Press, 1977) and expanded in *Culture Shift in Advanced Industrial Society* (Princeton, NJ: Princeton University Press, 1990).

6. These were conducted in 1981–84, 1990–93, and 1995–97.

7. Inglehart, *Modernization and Postmodernization*, 35.

8. Alex Inkeles, "Surveying Postmaterialism," *Journal of Democracy* 9, no. 2 (1998): 177.

9. Ibid., 178.

Postmaterialism is not necessarily the mark of anticonsumerism or a new asceticism; it is founded on a new capitalism encouraged by globalization. And I have found few figures for the number of people who have actively "downshifted" because of these values—that is, voluntarily decided for a quality of lifestyle in which less is consumed and less is earned.[10] The years of global free trading from the 1980s through to the 1990s and into the twenty-first century *have* enabled many more in the West to enjoy the best things in life. In my parents' generation, the thought of inhabiting the same sphere as those who could regularly eat smoked salmon, sleep in sheets made of Egyptian cotton, own silk shirts by Yves Saint Laurent and wool suits by Christian Dior, walk on floors of Amazonian oak, and wear designer cufflinks of silver and opal was a dream even beyond the slogan coined by British prime minister Harold Macmillan, "You've never had it so good." What were once understood as luxury items have now become widely affordable. Workers from a variety of earning levels can fly from England to Eilat for the weekend or to New York for Christmas presents. Meanwhile an ever-increasing disparity between those who can and those who cannot afford to spend accelerates,[11] and many today are not just satisfied but surfeited. Inglehart's postmaterialism correlates with consumer choice. In a public debate on the relationship of theology, politics, and economics, I asked leading American economists what they thought about the old socialist idea of the redistribution of income as part of a regulated national economy. I was told it was heresy and not even discussable anymore. Economists no longer consider trade boundaries, the nationalization of key industries, increased taxation, and so forth as conditions for optimum wealth generation. What is surprising is that the price for this inflation of consumer desires and expectations is not chalked on the wall alongside the price of langoustine with a lime-and-champagne coolie or a glass of vintage Sauternes. What is surprising is that despite the increase in postmaterialist values, we have all come to accept ignorance—or limitations in what we allow ourselves to know—as perfectly

10. An illustration appears in Richard Eckersley, "The Challenge of Post-materialism," *Australian Financial Review* (March 2005): 24–28, which states that "23 percent of Australians aged 30–59 had 'downshifted' in the past ten years."

11. This pattern may change with what is coming to be known at the "credit crunch."

normal, rational, even unquestionable. Postmaterialism is just not postmaterialist enough.

Now, I believe in the subconscious. There are boundaries to what we see, what we notice, what we deem significant—as anyone who has had to testify to an accident or answer a police inquiry knows too well. Knowledge is partial, and this partiality is governed by many factors. But when I speak of ignorance here, I mean something we intend: we actively desire to be ignorant. One summer I buy a crème cotton suit in Berlin at a large international retailer. I buy with a sense, at that time, of a strong sterling currency. I buy in euros, and even if one euro equaled one pound, this suit is cheap. It is a suit that might have been worn at Humphrey Bogart's club in Casablanca. And it is made in Turkey or Morocco or China. But I delve no further into how it was made, how much it cost to make, how much the person who made it (or part of it) was paid per hour, per day, per month. And, yes, Marx is relevant here, because there is a gentleman's outfitter on a small street in Oxford who sells handmade English leather shoes—and even in a sale for a good pair, you would not receive much change out of three hundred pounds. The difference is probably quality and craftsmanship, to a point, but the major difference is the visibility or invisibility of the labor costs in any production (and the accompanying values associated with the visibility or invisibility of these labor costs).

What I wish to pursue in this study is a deepening of postmaterialist citizenship, which currently is fickle (subject to the rise and fall of economic prosperity) and a matter of consumer choice. I want to provide the values of postmaterialism with a metaphysics and a theology. But for this it is necessary to examine why one forgets about the means and modes of production and why they need to be remembered if my argument is to be established. The shelves of books devoted to globalization increase by the month, but the focus of this chapter is on the correlations between neoliberal economics and democracy, on the one hand, and between neoliberal economics and religion, on the other. It will argue that globalization, like secularization, is a religious ideology—that is, a myth masquerading as natural law, even divine providence.[12] But it is only as it discloses itself as such that we begin to observe and

12. "A law [against free trade] . . . interferes with the wisdom of the Divine Providence, and substitutes the law of wicked men for the law of nature" (Richard Cobden,

are able to analyze the various elements that constitute its potency, to analyze the imaginative strengths that create credencies, enjoin belief, and capture hopes, dreams, and desires. Globalization is a religious creed that is predominantly Christian at its roots and in its ethos. Like Christianity, globalization seeks a major transformation of the world order through historical and material processes. Like Christianity, globalization is not one. The transformations globalization effects issue through complex nodes of interrelated actions and operations that foster a universal vision achieved through high levels of integration.[13] Like Christianity, globalization is concerned with transforming social relations across national borders, establishing new levels of interconnectedness and new transcultural identities, and generating a global consciousness.[14] Globalization, then, like Christianity, is intrinsically imperialist, and we need to uncover how the logics of their imperialisms both differ and are related. By excavating the theological elements in globalization, the postmaterialist values that are being fostered by globalization can become rooted in a theological firmament that can deliver them from the arbitrary whims of the market and the superficial aesthetics of customized lifestyles.

Christian and Capitalist Imperialism

Huntington makes much of an association between the three phenomena we are examining in the first section of this book: the democratic condition, globalization, and the new visibility of religion (and how they are related to postmodernity, on the one hand, and postmaterialism, on the other): "In country after country the choice between democracy and authoritarianism became personified in the conflict between the cardinal and the dictator. Catholicism was second only to economic development as a perva-

---

"Speech Given on Free Trade," September 28, 1843, in *Speeches on Questions of Public Policy* [London: Macmillan, 1870], 68).

13. James H. Mittelman, *The Globalization Syndrome: Transformation and Resistance* (Princeton, NJ: Princeton University Press, 2000), 4, in his own account of how globalization is not a single, unified phenomenon, describes its operations in terms of a "syndrome."

14. On the importance of developing a global consciousness as a spur for globalization, see Roland Robertson, *Globalization: Social Theory and Global Culture* (London: Sage, 1992), 142–45.

sive force making for democratization in the 1970s and 1980s. The logo of the third wave could well be a crucifix superimposed on a dollar sign."[15] It is not nearly as neat as the impression he gives, and in his detailed description of Christianity's expansion into Korea, for example, he observes that four-fifths of the population converted to Protestantism, not Catholicism. But Huntington is one of the few political scientists who point to the role religion plays in international developments both political and economic. Weber saw a traditional link between capitalism and the spirit of Protestantism, and the world's early democracies (the United States and Britain) were predominantly Protestant. But Huntington views the liberalizing Second Vatican Council, liberation theology's mobilization of Catholics, and the globe-trotting missionizing of John Paul II as far-from-insignificant factors in the wave of new democratizing in Latin America, South Korea, and the Philippines. "It seems plausible to hypothesize that the expansion of Christianity encourages democratic development,"[16] he concludes, and Fukuyama's thesis would lead us to add, "and democratic development favors neoliberal economics."

We have already begun to explore the democratic condition; now we turn our attention to the relationship between the production of an international matrix of exchange and the global dreams of Christianity. An investigation into this relationship will enable us to understand how our current globalization lies within a specific Western religious tradition—secularizing, parodying its theology.

The Tale of Two Economies I

At the end of Matthew's Gospel, the risen Jesus makes the following proclamation: "All authority in heaven and on earth has been given to me. Go therefore and make disciples of all nations, baptizing them in the name of the Father and of the Son and of the Holy Spirit" (Matt. 28:18–19). It is one of the foundational texts of Christian missiology. The endings of the two other Synoptic Gospels—Mark and Luke—contain similar, but not as elaborate, statements (although scholars recognize that the last

15. Huntington, *Third Wave*, 85.
16. Ibid., 73.

nine verses of Mark's Gospel are not found in earlier and more reliable manuscripts). What Matthew's statement makes plain is a major theological transposition effected by the coming of the Christ: the transposition from the ethnic specificities of Judaism to the universalism of the Christ through the liturgical practice of baptism in the name of the trinitarian God. In Matthew's day there were more Jewish people living in the Diaspora than in Palestine itself, but nevertheless the picture of the cosmic Christ,[17] possessing all authority in heaven and on earth, and the strong imperative to go into all nations imply that the community of the faithful would be made up of more than those drawn directly from the Jewish genetic pool. Luke's Acts of the Apostles and Paul's Letter to the Romans concur: now the Gentiles were included in the new covenant, the new dispensation of God's grace.[18] The Jewish messiah pointed Judaism toward its global horizons. The writer of Luke's Gospel dramatizes this theological cataclysm and the dissemination it effected: "Repentance and forgiveness of sins will be preached in his name to all nations, beginning with Jerusalem" (Luke 24:47 NIV). Jerusalem, which had gathered together Jewish people from all over the known world for the Passover (when the Christ was crucified), would be the epicenter for a new cosmic polity. The writer of Luke's Gospel, in Acts of the Apostles, narrates how the falling of Christ's Spirit upon the disciples—the anointing that authorized and empowered them to preach the gospel—came during the Feast of Tabernacles, when "Parthians, Medes and Elamites; residents of Mesopotamia, Judea and Cappadocia, Pontius and Asia, Phrygia and Pamphilia, Egypt and the parts of Libya near Cyrene; visitors from Rome (both Jews and converts to Judaism); Cretans and Arabs" were all assembled in Jerusalem once more (Acts 2:9–11 NIV). Peter preached and "three thousand were added to their number that day" (2:41 NIV). The global mission in the name of a universalist salvation had begun. The world was opening up to the tune of a Christian eschatology in which it was believed that all nations had to be evangelized if

17. This theme is emphasized in Paul's Letter to the Colossians and Letter to the Ephesians.

18. There is a religious universalism also in the later parts of the Hebrew Scriptures, associated with a developing messianism; Trito-Isaiah, Ezeziel's vision of the Temple City, and the *Daniel* testify to the advent of a universalization of Judaism ushered in with the messianic age.

the messiah was to return. This is not yet economics because the Roman Empire and the embryonic Christian imperialism are still divided. But this will change.

As the Marxist historian Immanuel Wallerstein observes regarding the establishment of the early world trading system in the late fifteenth and early sixteenth centuries, the pace of globalization is governed by the overcoming of territorial particularity by technological means.[19] The centrality of technological advances in the development of globalization will become more pronounced as we proceed with our examination.

The early church flourished in its own way but became increasingly fragmented through persecution. The degree to which Jerusalem remained its mother church, to be succeeded later by Rome, is still uncertain, as the debates over the rise and fall of early Jewish Christians illustrate. But there is little doubt that a major upturn in the expansion of Christianity came with the conversion of Constantine in 312 CE and the Edict of Milan, issued in 313. The edict, though granting religious freedom throughout the Roman Empire, was the first step in constituting Christianity as the religion of the empire. It explicitly sought and associated divine favor with the imperial commonweal. Constantine wrote, "My design then was, first, to bring the diverse judgements formed by all nations respecting the Deity to a condition, as it were, of settled uniformity; and, second, to restore a healthy tone to the system of the world."[20] His sentiments express here a new political theology that was being composed at the time by Eusebius of Caesarea in his *Ecclesiastical History*: that Constantine was the second Augustus (the man who had created the conditions for worldwide unity and peace in preparation for the coming of the Christ),[21] the vehicle for the providence of the Christian God. Eusebius forged a rhetorical link between the Christian church and the Roman Empire. He wove together, in his propagandizing texts, two distinct economies or movements through

19. Immanuel Wallerstein, *The Modern World-System: Capitalist Agriculture and the Origins of the European World-Economy in the Sixteenth Century* (London: Academic Press, 1974), 15–16.

20. Cited in W. H. C. Frend, *The Rise of Christianity* (London: Darton, Longman & Todd, 1984), 497.

21. See Carl Schmitt, *Political Theology II*, trans. Michael Hoelzl and Graham Ward (Cambridge: Polity, 2008) and his debates with Erik Peterson on Eusebius and Augustine, pp. 60–102.

time—the theological and the political. Christian cosmology was now inseparable from its eschatological teaching on the salvation of the world and its global ambitions. Constantine turned rhetoric into activity by forging the systemic links that lay the foundations for Christendom, by fighting Donatists and Arians, and by opening the first ecumenical council at Nicaea. He thus established the ideological parameters of the *corpus Christianorum*. The imperial administrative and military networks provided Christianity with the technological means for expansion, the means for developing the universalist logic at the heart of its monotheistic credo: "After the victory of the Milvian Bridge [312 CE], Christianity was never again to lack an imperial patron."[22]

With the fragmentation and decline of the empire, Christianity was enabled, even required, to expand and establish (with Latin the *lingua universalis*) the integrating infrastructures on which Western civilization emerged from the Dark Ages into the glories of the various forms of renaissance from the twelfth century onward. The key figure here was the Frankish king Charlemagne, who conquered the lands that now formed the territory of a united Western Europe and was crowned the first Holy Roman emperor by Pope Leo III on December 25, 800. Latin Christendom was established on the basis of this conquest, and our current globalization is a product of that civilization.

The Tale of Two Economies II

When Latin Christendom itself was dissolving—as fledging nation-states grew stronger and the Protestant schism racked the body of the church—Christianity underwent a second major transformation that adapted it for the new forms of expansionism and imperialism that arose in the late fifteenth and early sixteenth centuries with respect to another economy: capitalism. After the forced reentrenchment of Christendom by the advancing Ottoman Turks—in which territories of an earlier expansion by the Crusades were brought under Muslim dominion—Christianity's imperial ambitions were now channeled into two new enterprises, one commercial and the other academic. The first was a new colonization program, and the second was a universalization of Christianity's

22. Frend, *Rise of Christianity*, 482–83.

own identity in terms of "religion." The two enterprises went hand in hand: the several voyages, first of exploration and then of colonization, undertaken as much on theological as on economic and political grounds, paralleled the rise of the generic category of "religion."[23]

"Religion" means what Constantine dreamed of when he sought to "bring diverse judgments formed by all nations respecting the Deity to a condition, as it were, of settled uniformity." In fifteenth-century England, to speak of "religions" was to speak of the various monastic orders. This followed a line of usage found from Augustine to Aquinas in which "religion" was a practice, an order of worship. By the late fifteenth century, however, the word was beginning to be employed by the likes of Nicholas of Cusa and Marsilio Ficino to describe the universal grammar of Christianity as the highest form of religion.[24] Gradually, as new lands and peoples were encountered and the journals, letters, and narratives of these encounters began laying the basis for the new science of ethnography, "religion" became a rhetorical tool for a new universalism inextricably bound to the pursuit of gold. The need, following the warring factions of the Reformation, for a political and theological détente—fundamental to the origins of liberal democracy—gave this meaning of "religion" not just academic respectability (this came much later) but also social and political force.

This universalist idea of "religion" furnished a new anthropology—the universal condition of being human. This was bound to a new ethics, humanism, out of which liberalism and the rights of man were later to arise. The universalism was fused at this time with the concepts of natural law, nature, and an evolving naturalism and gave new persuasive power to the expansionist logic within Christianity itself. The technological possibilities of preaching

23. See Graham Ward, *True Religion* (Oxford: Blackwell, 2003), for an account of Columbus's reasoning with his patrons, Ferdinand and Isabella. The gold he sought was to furnish the pope with the means to conduct a new crusade against the Muslim "infidel" (35–41).

24. Both figures were influenced by the fourteenth-century Catalan philosopher Raymond Llul, who, as far as I can ascertain, was the first to use "religion" to describe Judaism, Christianity, and Islam. See *The Book of the Gentile and the Three Wisemen*, in which Lady Intelligence speaks to a Gentile, a Jew, and a Saracen, encouraging them to converse because "what great good fortune it would be if . . . we could all—every man on earth—be under one religion and belief" (*Doctor Illuminatus: Ramon Llull Reader*, trans. Antony Bonner [Princeton: Princeton University Press, 1994], 90).

the gospel to all nations with new methods of shipbuilding and navigation went hand in hand with the development of a theology that makes conversion to Christ a matter of recognizing the truth about the human situation and the created order. A new egalitarianism, a brotherhood of mankind, is announced in which God's justice is rendered self-evident and natural and the particularities of redemption in Christ are globally available. Natural knowledge revealed broad a priori moral and political truths and, under the influence of the Protestant work ethic, economic truths also.

Wallerstein, in his monumental history of world trade and the development of the capitalist world system, views economics as the dynamic for both modernization and globalization. He gives hardly any place to the theological dynamics that, in fact, governed (even regulated) economic policy throughout the medieval and Renaissance periods.[25] This is a profound oversight, for territorial expansion and the development of the world system was, throughout the fifteenth and sixteenth centuries, a matter of lively theological discussion, particularly among the Jesuits, who were engaged in worldwide missionary activity. When we return the developments of Western Christianity into the picture, we can perhaps understand globalization as issuing from a certain cultural, rather than simply economic, program. Wallerstein raises an interesting question: why did Europe rather than China enter the theater of world trading, exploration, and colonization in the late fifteenth century? Agreeing with and citing the work of William Willetts, he answers, "This has something to do with the *Weltanschauung* of the Chinese. They lacked, it is argued, a sort of colonising mission because, in their arrogance, they were already the whole of the world."[26] I would argue that the colonizing mission felt by a number of European nations—but first and foremost Catholic Spain and Portugal—is endemic to the global logic of Christianity, which forever saw other nations beyond its borders

25. Wallerstein, *Modern World-System*. Keynes had taken some account of medieval economics; see J. M. Keynes, *General Theory of Employment, Interest, and Money* (San Diego: Harcourt Brace, 1964). He based his distinction between savings and investment on his researches, but his interpretation of usury was challenged by B. Dempsey, *Interest and Usury* (Washington, DC: American Council on Public Affairs, 1943). See S. Long, *Divine Economy: Theology and the Market* (London: Routledge, 2000).

26. Wallerstein, *Modern World-System*, 55.

that lacked the gospel. Christian missiology thoroughly informed the Western *Weltanschauung* and was implicated in all the debates and activities concerning embryonic mercantile covetousness and territorial ambitions. It was the dominant ideology out of which the capitalist world system developed. After all, these expeditions and explorations were profoundly speculative; they ran risks that required vision, faith, and hope and drew on imaginations inspired by far more than simple acquisitiveness, opportunity costing, or the *libido dominandi*. As sociologists such as Weber and historians such as R. H. Tawney point out, Western capitalism (and the material exchanges prior to formal monetary systems) is implicated in mind-sets, habits, desires, and household disciplines established by Christian practices of faith. As several prominent economists have also pointed out (e.g., Hayek and Hirsch), the very practice and theory of economics issue from, and proceed on, a moral legacy of truth, fiduciary and redemptive acts, contracts understood as formal covenants, and construals of freedom. It was a legacy first forged in Christendom and later rendered universal when the universalist idea of "religion" turned theological particularity into secular naturalism and moral normativity. The secular age was under way.

Secularization and Dematerialization

Globalization is profoundly related to secularization. As the trading and colonizing fostered new international relations throughout the seventeenth and eighteenth centuries, the ideology that legitimized its ambitions also slowly changed. This is not to say that missionizing stopped. It still continues today and is as virulent in its religious forms of evangelization and conversion as it is in big business with global mission statements, visionary ambitions, and the entrepreneurial pursuit of opportunity. The nature of the ideological change that was slowly emerging throughout modernity can be witnessed in Hume and Kant, both of whom saw globalization as the international extension of "benevolent tendencies" (Hume)[27]

27. See section 2, "On Benevolence," in David Hume, *Enquires concerning the Human Understanding and concerning the Principles of Morals*, ed. L. A. Selby-Bigge (Oxford: Oxford University Press, 1975).

and the mediation of a cosmopolitan peace (Kant).[28] The secular eschatology of early Enlightenment liberal humanism now informed the visions for a world market.[29] By "secular eschatology" I mean that the transcendent role of divine providence yielded to the purely immanent teleology of history and economics but the absolutism and the utopianism remained the same: the theological myth of all being made one in Christ gives way to the secular myth of Kenichi Ohmae's "borderless economy,"[30] in which warring nation-states are transcended and a new international democracy announces itself. "Increasingly, millions of global investors, operating out of their own economic self-interest, are determining interest rates, exchange rates, and the allocation of capital, irrespective of the wishes or political objectives of national political leaders."[31]

Current neoliberal economic policy in the vein of Hayek, Michael Novak, and Joseph Schumpeter is steeped in these secularized liberal ethics, and so the vestiges of the Christian tradition appear frequently in the rhetoric of globalized-market discourse. The debates over whether markets have agency (or corporations have "personalities") or have outcomes that can be seen and therefore prevented and the debates concerning scarcity, risk calculation, and distributional justice all still depend on a moral legacy bequeathed by Christianity.[32] A more recent theological voice has drawn attention (in terms I will develop later) to the cultural currents that bring together the Western Christian tradition and economics.

28. See "Idea for a Universal History with a Cosmopolitan Purpose," in *Kant: Political Writings*, ed. H. E. Reiss, trans. H. B. Nisbet (Cambridge: Cambridge University Press, 1991), 41–53.

29. Some scholars, David Harvey and Anthony Giddens among them, have viewed globalization as a product of modernity. Whereas Harvey relates time-space compression to the logic of capitalism, Giddens relates it to advancing technology. But what each fails to think through is the relationship among the project of modernity, the instruments developed in the realization of that project, and the secularization of a Christian eschatological vision.

30. Quoted in John Gray, *False Dawn: The Delusions of Global Capitalism* (London: Granta Books, 2002), 68.

31. Lowell Bryan and Diana Farrell, *Market Unbound: Unleashing Global Capitalism* (New York: Wiley, 1996), 1.

32. The move off the gold standard in the mid-1970s suggests a major shift in monetary economies from that moral legacy in which promissory notes ought to be redeemable and in which certain deontological duties underpin economic exchange mechanisms.

> The sign designating the dollar, $, was borrowed from the Christian numismatic sign IHS, which stands for *in hoc signo* (by this sign). The Spirit of God represented in the Eucharistic wafer is the currency of exchange, which establishes the identity and differences within the godhead and mediates the opposition between divinity and humanity throughout the history of salvation. . . . Hegel's speculative philosophy actually anticipates the aestheticisation of money, which characterises postindustrial capitalism. In the late twentieth century, something approximating the Hegel Absolute appears in global networks of exchange in which money is virtually immaterial. When read through Hegel's logical analysis of the Spirit, it becomes clear that money is God in more than a trivial sense.[33]

As Mark Taylor knows, Hegel's philosophy was Marx's starting point, and Marx made the same observation in the famous opening section of *Das Kapital*.

Marx will enable us to dissect what is going on here.[34] His analyses of capitalism emphasize two characteristics that are important for the development of the argument offered here. First, the process of producing commodities not only dematerializes the world—"Not an atom of matter enters into the objectivity of commodities as values"[35]—but also establishes the social order as an allegory: "Here the persons exist for one another merely as representatives and hence owners of commodities. As we proceed to develop our investigation, we shall find, in general, that the characters who appear on the economic stage [*die oekonomischen Charaktermasken*] are merely personifications of economic rela-

33. Mark C. Taylor, "Christianity and the Capitalism of the Spirit," in *About Religion: Economies of Faith in Virtual Culture* (Chicago: University of Chicago Press, 1999), 154–58. For further reflections on the relations between coin and eucharistic wafers, religion and the dollar, see Marc Shell, *Art and Money* (Chicago: University of Chicago Press, 1995), 13, 15, 19; and Emilio Gentile, *Politics as Religion*, trans. George Staunton (Princeton, NJ: Princeton University Press, 2006), xi–xiv, on the dollar as a sacred symbol. Taylor and Shell are misguided. IHS is not the medieval acronym for "by this sign," but the acronym for the name of Jesus that St. Ignatius adopted for his monograph for the Society of Jesus, the Jesuits. See the *Catholic Encyclopaedia* at www.newadvent.org/cathen/07649a.htm.

34. Karl Marx, *Capital: Critique of Political Economy*, vol.1, trans. B. Fowkes (Harmondsworth: Penguin, 1990). When the German text is quoted, the page references refer to *Das Kapital* (Berlin: Verlag für literatur und politik, 1933).

35. Marx, *Capital*, 138.

tions; it is as the bearers [*Traeger*] of these economic relations that they come into contact with each other."[36] Marx's allusion here, as the German makes plain, is to the theater of classical Greece and the ornate masks, or *prosōpa* (Latin *personae*), worn by the actors. Our economic social lives, he is suggesting, are forms of fiction, but we are so deluded that we do not realize it. Objects to be bought and sold are "endowed with a will and a soul of their own." Exchange values are "mode[s] of expression" and "form[s] of appearance." Capitalism generates virtual realities as "value . . . transforms every product of labour into a social hieroglyph."[37] The reality of things and their value are screened from us by money and what the market will bear, creating in us a false consciousness. Furthermore, the dominance of economic relations distorts all social relations—making social relations also part of an ongoing piece of theater. The unmasking, literally, of *die oekonomischen Charaktermasken* is necessary in order for there to be a society at all, since society as such under capitalism is what Benedict Anderson terms an "imaginary community"[38]—a necessary fiction akin to the fiction of "democracy," as noted in the last chapter. Marx's project is to rescue the social and establish its materiality, which now is concealed beneath illusion and pantomime. The tool for this job is interpretation, that is, judging "the bearers (*Traeger*) of these economic relations"—providing rules in an attempt to reestablish objects in the nakedness of their use value only.

The problem is that the production of such rules only extends the fictional nature of our economic living, for Marx's books are themselves implicated in the production of commodities and therefore the extension of *die oekonomischen Charaktermasken*. What this means is that the materiality of the social—and the use value of objects that are exchanged and constitute the social—is still being produced for us. We are offered only another false consciousness, so that there is no escaping the matrix generated by capitalism's virtual reality. To establish the materiality of social relations becomes a secularized eschatological task comparable to the establishment of the kingdom of God. The task becomes

36. Marx, *Capital*, 178/*Kapital*, 60.

37. Marx, *Capital*, 1003, 127, 167.

38. Benedict Anderson, *Imagined Communities: Reflections on the Origin and Spread of Nationalism* (London: Verso, 1991).

messianic—nothing less than the overthrowing of all idols (see later in this chapter the discussion of the market's creation of logos, such as Nike and Pepsi, that float free of the material contents of the goods they are labeling).

The second, and related, characteristic of capitalism that Marx unmasks is that all commodities are characterized by their fetishism. The idol and the fetish establish a religious worldview; they are necessarily opposed to the worldview of the icon and the sacrament. Capitalism generates, then, what Marx calls the "mystical" (*geheimnisvolle*), or "mysterious" or "enigmatic" (*raetselhafte*), or "fantastic" (*phantasmagorische*) forms of relation between things, whose only analogy is "the misty realm [*Nebelregion*] of religion [*die religioese Welt*]."[39] Capitalism generates a world of "metaphysical subtleties and theological niceties"[40] in which all things are subjected to the authority of "the universal commodity," money. Money is a transcendental. In the religious world of commodity values, it wears the mask of the antichrist—the beast of the book of Revelation (which Marx cites).[41] The apocalypse of capitalism is being challenged, then, by the eschatology of a new community or a restored community—since Marx believes that once in history this community existed—in which relations no longer exist in "reciprocal isolation and foreignness" (*wechselseitiger Fremdheit*).[42] As such, capitalism is inseparable from gnosticism—except that there is a subtle inversion with respect to the body and the soul. It is capitalist evil that moves through history like Hegel's *absolute Geist* and imprisons the goodness of the material order; the body is captive to the soul in the production (understood in terms of both economic process and theatrical staging) of commodity values. And like Hegel's *Geist* (see chap. 6, below), the magic potency of the money fetish (Marx's language) lies in its power to vanish, "leaving no trace behind."[43] It erases its own presence by becoming "visible and dazzling to our eyes";[44] as an idol, it can only reflect the desire and retroject the values pro-

39. Marx, *Capital*, 165/*Kapital*, 51.
40. Marx, *Capital*, 163.
41. Ibid., 181.
42. Ibid., 184/*Kapital*, 63.
43. Marx, *Capital*, 187.
44. Ibid.

jected onto it.[45] Money has not only the "appearance of value," like other commodities; it is "the form of appearance of the value of commodities."[46] It participates in a Platonic metaphysics in which its abstraction is consummated by its disappearance. The power of capitalism lies in the omnipresence of an absence that circulates in and through desire, is constitutive of desire—an absence that is at once demonized and adored. What the power of capitalism effects is a trade in bad faith, winning allegiance, through seduction, to the incantatory credo of credit.

Marx, then, understands the profound relations between money and religion, capitalism and an eschatological vision, and although he himself does not explore the erotics of fetishism, he perceives that one of the roots of capitalism is desire. Mark Taylor, like Milton Friedman, figures capitalism as freedom, but in Taylor freedom is not freedom of choice but—here he follows Hegel and is in line with Marx—freedom understood as unfettered desire. The glamour of contemporary globalization, the seductive appeal of its internationalism, figures, I suggest, infinite desire, which in Marx's descriptions of gold is expressed the other way around: a desire for an ever-allusive infinite. If this is so, the logic of capitalism, like the logic of Christianity, is not only expansionist but also intrinsically metaphysical: the world is simply not enough. In chapter 5, below, which treats the struggle for the soul of the city, it will become more apparent how Christianity's divine, trinitarian economy differs from capitalism's secular economics, but both are comprehensive systems that allow for nothing outside themselves. Both enjoin participation. Granted, one can opt out of being a Christian, but from within the Christian worldview, even those who opt out are still within the operations of God in the maintenance and redemption of the world. It is conceivable that there are some Robinson Crusoes on islands somewhere who live self-sufficient lives outside the mechanisms of economic exchange. But to the capitalist, such subsistence living is barely living at all. It is a quality of life that needs improving, and not to want such improvement is unnatural. There are small religious, self-governing communities,

45. See Jean-Luc Marion's analyses of the idol in *L'idole et la distance* (Paris: Grasset, 1977); *God without Being: Hors-texte*, trans. Thomas A. Carlson (Chicago: University of Chicago Press, 1991).

46. Marx, *Capital*, 184.

such as the Amish and the Hutterites, who live in splendid isolation in the United States, but they still require the sale of their produce to the outside world in order to survive. They may not have televisions or the Internet, but they remain in communication with local cities, their roads intersect with state highways, and they consume fries and burgers like others in the United States. Capitalism in its expanded global form is a participatory system. I may chose a postmaterialist option and not buy sportswear from Nike because of the charges of sweatshop exploitation, but my index-linked pension, the investments made by my mortgage company and my bank, my credit and debit cards, and online shopping all situate me very firmly in the global economy. Globalization is not simply the effects of free-market economic policy adopted by this country or that, or even the ideology of international operatives driven by multinational corporations, the International Monetary Fund, and the World Bank; it is an environment, an atmosphere. It implicitly possesses and promotes a cosmology. Like a religion, it generates its own mythology, and however much it deals with empirical goods, metrics, positivist facts, and processes that are entirely focused on the concrete, immanent logics of this world, its ethos and ethics are utopian and transcendental, as Marx understood.

In heady, ecstatic language, the mythology it generates speaks of liquid realities, protean selves, the collapse of geographical space into flows, the erasure of national and continental boundaries—and therefore the seasons for fruit and vegetables and the cultural hybridity of drinking Chilean wines, in (now affordable) Italian clothes, from crystal goblets made in China, while sitting on reproduced Shaker furniture from Russian pine and illuminated by scented candles refined from North Sea oil. In this mythic discourse, the traditional attributes of God are made material—omnipresence, omniscience, and omnipotence. The vast homogenizing, synthesizing, and integrating dynamics of globalization perfect the realization of Spinoza's monism: God is the one substance of which all else are modifications. And religious and metaphysical language is continually employed both to argue for and to argue against the deregulation of the commodity market. Noami Klein, in her best-selling book describing the effects of globalization, writes about "Nike's myth machine": "The Manhattan Nike Town on East Fifty-seventh Street is more than a fancy store fitted with the requisite brushed chrome and blond wood, it is a temple, where the swoosh is worshipped as both art and heroic symbol." What Nike is selling is not a product but an experience, "pure ideas about athleticism as transcendence and perseverance," "pure sporting transcendence" that "would be the spiritual transformation of Man over nature."[47] In a world where content disappears and brand names such as Pepsi, Armani, H&M, the British retailer Marks & Spencer, Reebok, and so on float free and ethereally on electronic waves of advertising, we enter a parody of Plato's world of pure forms, where the dominating ideal of the Good is now calculated and calibrated in accordance with "goods." Logos mimic the *Logos*. A culture of simulation is created that is the apotheosis of nominalism—where names bear no intrinsic relation to what is being named. Multinational corporations diversify, and their names endlessly defer any fixed meaning to become polyvalent signifiers. Disney makes movies, sells videos, manufactures toys, has a television channel and radio stations, means Mickey Mouse, fantasy, theme parks, innocence, turreted castles, childhood, holidays, dressing up in costumes, animation, a nongovernmental organization,[48] and so on. While the menial tasks of production are farmed out across the third world, the headquarters "is free to focus on the real business at hand—creating a corporate mythology powerful enough to infuse meaning into these raw objects just by signing its name."[49] In the world of corporate business, goods and services come a very poor second to the creation of "collective hallucinations."[50]

Virtual Immateriality

Capitalism created virtual realities and imaginary communities well before the advent of optic fibers and digital communications. Again, technological advances drive forward and mutate an imperialist logic. The corporate businesses described above are the exposed face of globalization, and modern technology supports enterprises constructed out of light and electronics. Without the

47. Naomi Klein, *No Logo* (London: Flamingo, 2000), 54, 56, 51, 53.

48. See http://corporate.disney.go.com/outreach/index.html, for Disney Worldwide Outreach.

49. Klein, *No Logo*, 22.

50. Ibid.

virtual reality of cyberspace, today's globalization would not be possible. But again beneath the hype of cybernauts who cruise weightlessly and facelessly along highways of information that liquefy time, location, cultural context, and identity lie Christian accounts of heaven, of life beyond bodily imperfections and limitations, of angels and angelic knowledge.[51] The sociologist Manuel Castells has called real virtuality the final turn of secularism.[52] Globalization and the expansion of the virtual are not creating parallel universes—the one imaginary and the other real—they are collapsing the distinction between the imaginary and the real. Hence Castells's term "real virtuality." The world is now re-created again, only more perfectly, as simulacra. This is the realization of the ancient dream of returning to paradise, Arcadia, or the Golden Age. For the ancient Greek philosopher Aristotle and for the English Renaissance poet Sir Philip Sydney, *poiesis*, imaginative recreation, was the only way to redeem the world and return it to its pristine condition.

The beginning of this chapter spoke of forgetting. Inseparable from virtual perfections is a hidden cost: digitalization is the final step in commodification. An object of labor whose use value was once fetishized is now reproduced virtually in pixels and megabytes. This reproduction dematerializes the object even further, and in this dematerialization lie the origins of consumer oblivion. We are deluded into believing that the world we have created in the West and participate in is real. The crème suit bought in Berlin is inseparable from the Hollywood dream of Bogart in Casablanca. The life we are living, even in our postmaterialist options, is a fantasy, and as Neo in *The Matrix* learns, supporting such a fantasy is a world that is sordid, exploitative, and wasted. But the desire that craves such a fantasy, that requires such a forgetfulness, is profoundly theological: we want to live like the pagan gods in Olympian splendor. We want eternal life and heaven, and we want them now.

Globalism, then, as the construction of a world system (of not just economic but cultural interdependence), is one more attempt

51. See Michel Serres, *Angels: A Modern Myth* (Paris: Flammarion, 1995). Serres moves fluidly between traditional accounts of angels and contemporary communication systems.

52. Manuel Castells, *The Rise of the Network Society*, vol. 1, *The Information Age: Economy, Society, and Culture* (Oxford: Blackwell, 1996), 355–406.

by human beings to become divine. It is the continuation of a Prometheanism that goes back to the famous foundation for humanism: the *Oration on the Dignity of Man* by Pico della Mirandolla at the end of the fifteenth century. The text was composed just as world trading was opening up to the new trafficking in gold, silver, tobacco, spices, and gems. And the desire behind the drive, which later became so closely tied to the worldwide promotion of liberal democracy, is infinite freedom—freedom defined as the infinite possibilities for choice, frictionless freedom forgetful of boundaries physical, cultural, or historical. Infinite freedom is a freedom without restrictions, a freedom, then, that ideologically has to transcend the limitations of normal physicality. The "Stargate" entrance to infinite freedom is what sells the Internet—eternity on a desktop, like the galaxy in a tiny bauble hanging from the collar of a cat in the film *Men in Black*. In a manner identical to the branding by multinationals, the Internet shifts us beyond self-serving rational choice—"I like this pair of trainers," "This is a fizzy drink," "This is a car"—toward a lifestyle, even a postmaterialist lifestyle. "It is on-line that the purest brands are built: liberated from the real-world burdens of stores and product manufacture, these brands are free to soar."[53]

But we can take this analysis further. The Internet itself is a vehicle for radical displacement and transportation. (Chapter 5 will examine in more detail this phenomenon, its effects, and the degree to which it differs from Christian eschatology.) I want to explore the implicit metaphysical nature of *this* infinite freedom—given what was noted about political freedom in the last chapter and my concern here about the pursuit of a deeper postmaterialism. For this freedom lies beyond choice, since the experience of choice, since choosing itself, implies limitation. To be able to have all things simultaneously, to possess the fullness of the present as present—only this can fulfill the dreams of infinite choice. Hence one of the key elements in global culture is speed;[54] perfection must be instantaneous. In a conversation with a director for Britain's Channel Four Television Broadcasting, I was told we were looking at the end of television in the near future because customers

53. Klein, *No Logo*, 22.

54. See Paul Virilio's seminal *Speed and Politics: An Essay on Dromology* (Los Angeles: Semiotext[e], 1986).

wanted programs and films they could download instantly. "Of course," he said, "'instantly' doesn't mean that at the moment. But it *will* do."

His remarks open a critical space between the realities and facts of a conceptual object such as freedom and the desire invested in it, for the freedoms of cyberspace, like the freedoms of a market without boundaries and like the freedom pronounced on the monument to those who died in the Korean War in Washington, come at a cost. Free trade was never free, and not simply in the sense that one had to have the financial wherewithal in order to participate in the circulation of proffered goods. Free trade, from nineteenth-century industrial Britain to neoliberal economics, was always nudged and nurtured. The deregulation of the market is continually controlled by at least three levels of organization: the corporate, the national, and supranational bodies such as the World Trade Organization, the International Monetary Fund, and the World Bank. Economic freedom is politically engineered; it is not the natural state of things despite the neo-Darwinian language of certain monetarists. The extent of the real cost (what British Higher Education Institutes have come to know as "full economic cost") of our freedom of choice is hidden. It is because of this concealment that we can forget. The myth of the free and open market dominates despite the counterfactual evidence. The myth circulates seductively; freedom is fetishized, invested with a desire that both knows the truth (there is no free lunch really) and yet continually forgets it.

What remains is the desire itself. But the desire for infinite freedom is the desire for oblivion, or what the postmodern thinker Michel de Certeau once called "white ecstasy." Certeau describes this ultimate *jouissance* in a language culled from various world faiths. In a conversation constructed between two men meeting on a mountain top, Simeon the Monk speaks of the "final bedazzlement," in which there is "an absorption of objects and subjects in the act of seeing. No violence, only the unfolding presence. Neither fold nor hole. Nothing hidden and thus nothing visible. A light without limits, without difference; neuter, in a sense, and continuous."[55]

55. Michel de Certeau, "White Ecstasy," trans. F. C. Bauerschmidt and C. Hanley, in *The Postmodern God*, ed. Graham Ward (Oxford: Blackwell, 1997), 157.

This is the silence of the sublime and the unrepresentable,[56] where transparency meets transcendence.

What cyberspace encourages is the endless reproduction of particularities. Everything is to be reducible to digital coding and pixel imaging. This euphoric transcendence comes from seizing the presence of things in the present and understanding all locations as infinitely transferable. It has other names that fuse together postmodernity, the postdemocratic, and globalization: Heidegger and Derrida's "end of metaphysics"; Fukuyama's "end of history"; Jaron Lanier's "experience of the infinite" (he coined the term "virtual reality");[57] Deleuze and Félix Guattari's "deterritorialization"; Lyotard's "body without organs"; Baudrillard's "hyperreality"; customer satisfaction; the apotheosis of free trade; the call for the complete transparency of institutional operations by government agencies; omniscient surveillance. The desire is for total escape, full immersion. Hence we have the increasing popularity of extreme sports, such as free-fall skiing, white-water rafting, and bungee jumping, and extreme rides at theme parks throughout the world. The logic of total escape culminates in death—death as oblivion. Globalization is the ultimate synthesis of the Freudian psyche: the libidinal economy *becomes* the death drive. Enforced universal democratization is the Freudian stasis, the zero degree dressed in the neoliberal language of freedom. Thomas Friedman, who has written one of the most popular books on globalization, observes that he is frequently asked, "Is God in cyberspace?" His answer is indicative of one of the axioms of globalization: "There is no place in today's world where you encounter the freedom to choose that God gave man more than in cyberspace."[58]

Freedom of choice is harnessed to movement here, albeit in an illusory manner—illusory because to choose is not to move—and where one moves to (whether we can talk of "movement" at all)

56. On the postmodern sublime and the unrepresentable, see Jean-François Lyotard, *Lessons on the Analytic of the Sublime*, trans. Elizabeth Rotterberg (Stanford: Stanford University Press, 1994); and on the relationship between this sublime and the terror of absolute freedom, see Terry Eagleton, *Holy Terror* (Oxford: Oxford University Press, 2005), 48–49, 93.

57. J. Lanier and F. Biocca, "An Insider's View of the Future of Virtual Reality," *Journal of Communication* 42, no. 4 (1992): 156.

58. Thomas Friedman, *The Lexus and the Olive Tree: Understanding Globalization* (New York: Anchor Books, 2000), 469.

when space has collapsed into an indifference with respect to directions and locations is a real question. In Ellis's *American Psycho* (see chap. 6, below), Patrick Bateman's good looks (he is often mistaken for a movie star or a model) and perfectly toned body constitute a three-dimensional display board for an accumulation of brand names: Calvin Klein, Brooks Brothers, Versace, Ralph Lauren. Beneath the display there is nothing, a void. Bateman senses that neither he nor anyone else is anything, confessing, "Where there was nature and earth, life and water, I saw a desert landscape that was unending, resembling some sort of crater, so devoid of reason and light and spirit that the mind could not grasp it. . . . This was how I lived my life, what I constructed my movement around, how I dealt with the tangible."[59] Movement here is not action because there is no agent. So, like creatures released from the pressure of gravity, in cyberspace we float, we surf, we ride, we free-fall, we transcend a variety of human finitudes to become divine. To be global is to be divine. The most globalized figures (Hollywood film stars, sports and royal personalities, entrepreneurs such as George Soros, Bill Gates, and Richard Branson) are stars in the new global galaxies. And these stars inspire cult following; they are saints without shrines who call for veneration and pilgrimage. They promote freestanding, depthless logos with no connection whatsoever to what the Greeks and the New Testament writers termed the *Logos*.

If this is the culture of immateriality fostered by globalization, then it maps closely on to what Michael Hardt and Antonio Negri describe as the production of a new social and working life modeled on networks. The governing characteristic of this new production is post-Fordist "immaterial labor," as distinct from the industrial labor associated with Fordism. They define "immaterial labor" as "labor that creates immaterial products, such as knowledge, information, communication, a relationship, or an emotional response."[60]

> One can conceive immaterial labor in two principle forms. The first form refers to labor that is primarily intellectual or linguistic, such as problem solving, symbolic and analytic tasks, and linguistic

59. Bret Easton Ellis, *American Psycho* (New York: Vintage, 1991), 374–75.

60. Michael Hardt and Antonio Negri, *Multitude: War and Democracy in the Age of Empire* (New York: Penguin Books, 2005), 108.

> expressions. This kind of immaterial labor produces ideas, symbols, codes, texts, linguistic figures, images, and other such products. We call the other form of immaterial labor "affective labor." . . . Affective labor . . . is labor that produces or manipulates affects such as a feeling of ease, well-being, satisfaction, excitement or passion. One can recognize affective labor, for example, in the work of legal assistants, flight attendants, and fast food workers (service with a smile).[61]

Hardt and Negri take pains to emphasize that this new production of immaterial goods does not do away with the older industrial production of material goods. But the immaterial labor is hegemonic in a qualitative sense; it takes place in urban centers in wealthier parts of the world; it is the kind of laboring to which workers in the factories (now established in parts of the globe where education and the quality of life is low) aspire and toward which they migrate. Furthermore, this immaterial laboring is not without considerable effort, but it is effort spent in the production of an immaterial product, such as customer care and the social relations that ease and oil the flows of revenue. The new form of labor, together with the new products it produces, concerns itself with distributional networks. It encourages the denationalization[62] of global capitalism; it perpetuates and utilizes global communications systems; and it evidences postmodern society, "characterized by the dissolution of traditional social bodies."[63] This new form of labor thus fosters the metaphysics of globalization that is traced throughout this section. The Internet is its most profound metaphor, model, expression, and tool; in the face of the Internet, the physical body is just a node in an infinitely extensive matrix. Avatars for this physical body can be found in every cybergame and cybercommunity, so that fantasies of postresurrection life can be lived out now in dimensions disconnected from real time and structured space.

It should, then, come as no surprise that New Age self-help spirituality is in perfect synchronism with the metaphysics and religios-

61. Ibid.

62. This term has been developed by the urban geographer Saskia Sassens, *Losing Control? Sovereignty in an Age of Globalization* (New York: Columbia University Press, 1996).

63. Hardt and Negri, *Multitude*, 190.

ity of globalization—both are hyperindividualist, self-interested, and vision orientated. "The corporate world has always had a profound New Age Streak,"[64] but the longing for self-deification has a thick biblical history under the rubric of "sin." The globalization and New Age spiritualities meet in the pursuit of the pure. The Platonic abstraction of the pure brand finds cultural synergies in the promotion of pure democracy, pure wool, pure freedom, pure water, pure energy, pure soap, digital sound, sugar-free and caffeine-free Coke, high-definition reception, the healing properties of crystals, allergy-free cosmetics, and organic foods. The pursuit of the pure is a close ally to the cult of the instantaneous and the ecstasies of the sublime. It announces a secular asceticism wrapped in the veils of quasi-religious language uncoupled from the exercise of ritual, the practices of faith, and commitment to a tradition and its institutions. Both New Age religious movements and multinational corporations not only believe in the metaphysical nature of persons; they also want to colonize the soul. Scott Bedbury, onetime marketing director of Starbucks, puts it plainly (and in a manner that relates to contemporary fascination with the figure of the vampire in literature, film, and cybergames): we want "to align ourselves with one of the greatest movements towards trying to find a connection with your soul."[65]

The next chapter will explore the new visibility of religion and its association with the new democratic condition and globalization. For now, it is important to return to the thesis of this chapter: the Christian heritage behind this new Western culture. For, though issuing from secularization, the myth of globalization, closely annexed to the myth of infinite freedom, has now become self-consciously religious on several counts, each of which is associated with modern developments in Christian eschatology.

The modern understanding of Christian eschatology emphasized the *modo*, the now, the present, as the time of fulfillment. It emphasized a realized eschatology that was radically detraditionalized. Indeed, with theologians such as Harvey Cox and Johannes B. Metz, it embraced secularism uncritically as a progressive development brought about and fostered by Christianity. Metz describes this existential eschatology as "a mere presential or actual

64. Klein, *No Logo*, 22.
65. Cited in ibid., 138.

eschatology, in which the passion for the future exhausts itself in a mere 'making present' of eternity in the actual moment of personal decision."[66] Detraditionalized religion, a religion without past or future, finds itself expressed in globalization as a cultural, not simply economic, phenomenon in six particular ways.

First, as I have said, it invokes a new vision of infinite freedom—freedom understood economically as the ability to purse one's own desires and control one's own destiny and as liberation from dependencies, political and social, and local needs. Salvation is total emancipation. Second, it fosters belief in an eternal sustainability promising unlimited consumption. It is not just that this kingdom (and its everlasting banquet) can be established and brings history to an end; the kingdom will be governed by a perpetual progressive motion. Third, this motion is determining and inevitable. It is a transcending force, beyond human control, that human beings have to embrace: not so much a providence as a pagan understanding of a fate to be loved. Fourth, this force is dematerializing. Coins and notes are the nominal tokens of a sovereign power that is ultimately ungraspable. There is a metaphysics of money, an appeal to a transcending ontology. The less we see of the actual coins and notes that gave us the illusion of money as a natural substance, the more transactions concern electronic figures transcribed in cyberspace, the more the material is transcended. The eclipse of time and space in this new internationalism and the access to such an eclipse via the Internet assist in this dematerialization. Fifth, globalization offers an all-encompassing worldview in which credit and *credo* are again inseparable. Milton Friedman points out that in a government's monetary control and fiscal policy, there are "mythology and beliefs required to make it effective."[67] What we believe or are led to believe financially is directly related to how substantial the beneficial changes that we register are to our lives. The mythology and beliefs generated around globalization, the effects of which we can see all around us, present us not with a historical process but rather with a universalist vision of the

66. Johannes B. Metz, *The Theology of the World*, trans. William Glen-Doepel (London: Burns & Oates, 1969), 95; see chap. 4, below, on Metz and the critical resistance to this eschatology in his own "eschatological reserve." See also Harvey Cox, *The Secular City: Secularization and Urbanization in Theological Perspective* (New York: Macmillan, 1966).

67. Friedman, *Capitalism and Freedom*, 42.

truth about human beings and the civilizations they nurture and are nurtured by. This new universalism is an outworking of the trajectory we saw earlier with the rise of the generic meaning for "religion" and of the humanism it fostered. Globalization becomes inseparable from globalism. Together they announce a truth about a cosmological community that recognizes what the producers of the 2005 Live 8 set out to proclaim: our radical intradependence. It is a utopian vision of an international community stable and beyond conflict (see chap. 7, below, on the Christian conception of the kingdom of God). Sixth, and last, it is a moral vision that is ultimately Protestant in its orientation; the *amor fati*, though an intense discipline (as Nietzsche recognized), will bring about the rejuvenation of an economy and its people. This is the message still being given the third-world countries by the Group of Eight (G8), which has the power to cancel the vast burden of their debts. It is this "religious" eschatological undertow to globalization that is turning Weber's disenchantment of the world through rationalization into a new reenchantment. It is thereby helping to reverse the processes of secularization founded on an adherence to the material and the rational. "What we are dealing with here is a type of religious fundamentalism."[68] So the promoter of secularism has now become a forceful driver for secularism's implosion. This is important. Globalization evokes a new visibility of religion in the public sphere (see chap. 3, below).

In conclusion, this globalism is a myth formed out of the universalisms of Christianity, and this is why it is significant for theologians. Indeed, from John Gray's analysis in *False Dawn* to Joseph Stiglitz's confessions in *Globalization and Its Discontents* and, most recently, John Rawston Saul's analyses in *The Collapse of Globalism*, globalization as "an end-state toward which all economies are converging[, a] universal state of equal integration in worldwide economic activity,"[69] has been recognized as an illusion. But this is not the point here. As a myth, it governs and generates cultural imaginings; it fashions hopes, beliefs, dreams, and desires. Thus despite the counterfactual evidence of globalization's "achievements"—the accumulating evidence that it does not result

68. John Rawston Saul, *The Collapse of Global Capitalism* (London: Atlantic Books, 2005), 48.

69. Gray, *False Dawn*, 55–56.

in "a universal free market but an anarchy of sovereign states, rival capitalisms, and stateless zones,"[70] or what Saul describes as "a vacuum"[71]—the myth can remain powerful. The imaginative power of such a myth remains socially and culturally determinative. It enables us to forget. Furthermore, the effects of the myth are felt (most notably in terms of advanced social disaffection, depoliticization, and insecurity) even while the market fundamentalists in their designer offices and book-lined studies are changing their minds and spinning other prognostications.

Complex Ironies

When we relate globalization to the crises and transformation of Western liberal democracy, we face several significant ironies, all focusing on the notion of freedom. The first of these ironies issues from my analysis of the return-of-the-king phenomenon in contemporary politics: if the return of strong, top-down decisionist governments distanced from their constituent populations is correct, then neoliberal economics is not so nearly neoliberal as might first appear. Neoliberal and neoconservative shade off one into the other.[72] A great inaugurator of the recent waves of laissez-

70. Ibid., 194.

71. Saul, *Collapse of Global Capitalism*, 6.

72. David Harvey, *The New Imperialism* (Oxford: Oxford University Press, 2003), 17, draws a distinction between Clinton's neoliberalism and the neoconservative or more authoritarian state action of the government of George W. Bush. The case with Britain is much more complex, but the point here is that there is an intrinsic link between neoliberal economics and neoconservative politics, a link made more evident in our own times. Hardt and Negri pick this up but do not follow it through with respect to Huntington's work. His diagnosis of the crisis of democracy, which is detailed in chap. 1, above, is an "antidemocratic gospel that preaches the defense of sovereignty against the threats of all social forces and social movements. . . . [It] did, in fact, serve as a guide in the subsequent years for a neoliberal destruction of the welfare state" (Hardt and Negri, *Multitude*, 33). The link between neoliberalism and neoconservatism is globalization itself. Far from eroding the nation-state, the radical telescoping of temporality and distance instanced by globalization in its current form demand that certain nation-states maintain strong imperial notions of themselves, both at home and abroad. In a network-based cosmopolis, where nodes of power and influence are more important than isolated bodies, certain nation-states fight for the position of being one such node. The corollary is that other nation-states that cannot maintain such a presence at home and abroad become, in effect, new colonies, satellites. And if certain nation-states refuse such subservience, holding to the older notion of the

faire economics, Milton Friedman, proclaims loudly and proudly that a "liberal is fundamentally fearful of concentrated power"; governments have to be limited, state intervention downsized to a minimum. Indeed, democracy itself will be saved by the market: "The groups in our society that have most at stake in the preservation and strengthening of competitive capitalism are those minority groups which can most easily become the object of distrust and enmity of the majority."[73] Why, then, is the enormous economic extension of consumer freedom allied politically with an equally enormous extension of state monitoring that encroaches on erstwhile civil liberties? Why have the freedoms fostered by capitalism developed hand in hand with the proliferation of gated communities and the soaring business of security and surveillance? Certain freedoms are being bought at the expense of other freedoms.

The contradiction can be somewhat weakened by what evidently neither Hayek nor Friedman calculated: the vast and increasing division between those who have and those who have not has meant that those who have need the very latest in theft prevention, from computer-managed window shutters and infrared alarms to closed-circuit television. State control of monetary policy and trading may well pave a road to serfdom, but even from the evidence of Joseph Stiglitz and the United Nations regarding world poverty, competitive capitalism has widened the highway to slavery. The slavery is creating new forms of poverty and insecurity not simply in undeveloped parts of the world such as the Philippines and China but in the enormous rise of part-time, short-term contract and temporary labor across the West. And both those in jobs on short-term contracts and the few who are still permanently employed are finding that work time is blurring with leisure time; laboring is becoming a 24/7/365 activity. Meanwhile, on a map of globalized countries, as Castells has shown, appear whole territories that on older maps would have been labeled "terra incognita," and whole territories are shown on newer maps only because they are sites of commercial pillage.[74] Britain, however, currently boasts that

inviolable sovereignty of each nation-state to pursue its own destiny—North Korea, Iran, and formerly Iraq—then they present themselves, or are presented, as potential threats to world peace, "rogue states" inviting international sanctions.

73. Friedman, *Capitalism and Freedom*, 39, 21.

74. See Mittelman, *Globalization Syndrome*. If globalization is linked to Internet access, Mittleman shows that "the most recent survey of the estimated 112.75 mil-

376,000 of its inhabitants are sterling millionaires, and the prediction is that this will rise to 1.7 million by the year 2020.[75] Perhaps the contradiction between blue-sky freedom and the climate of fear and insecurity is not so startling when placed alongside the protection of property rights, that axiom of liberal democracy. Neither Hayek nor Friedman factored into their calculations what Castells has examined as the explosion of the criminal underworld.[76] They did not foresee the collapse of industrialism in the West and the outsourcing of production to sites around the world where labor is cheaper and less regulated. Friedman ventured that freeing the markets would bring an end to poverty through a universal rise in wages, but by all accounts, globalization has brought no increase in real wages.[77] In fact, it has encouraged the development of an underclass consisting of those who are unskilled, poorly educated, permanently out of work, and ripe pickings for transnational organized crime in drug trafficking, arms dealing, prostitution, and the exploitation of children. The promised trickle-down of jobs and money generated from income tax benefits only certain, already advantaged levels of society. "There is mounting evidence . . . that workplace transience is finally eroding our collective faith, not only in individual corporations but in the very principle of trickle-down economics."[78] Nor were Hayek and Friedman in a position to calibrate social and cultural changes wrought—not necessarily on globalization though certainly on Western democracy—by the war on terrorism.[79]

---

lion Internet users in the world indicates the following distribution by regions: the Middle East, .525 million; Africa, 1 million; South America, 7 million; Asia/Pacific, including Australia and New Zealand, 14 million; Europe, 20 million; and Canada and the United States, 70 million" (226–27). One has to observe here that the two continents with the least Internet access are the two continents, along with parts of Asia, whose populations and/or natural resources are the most exploited by the rest of the world.

75. Press Association, "Millionaire Britons to Rise to 1.7m," *Guardian* [London], Guardian Supplement, August 15, 2006, 10–11.

76. Castells, *Rise of the Network Society*, 101–46.

77. Mittelman, *Globalization Syndrome*, 230.

78. Klein, *No Logo*, 260.

79. There is, however, much research to show how globalization has greatly benefited organized crime, including the sale of arms. See Mittelman, *Globalization Syndrome*, 203–22.

These noncalculations can be marked down as dangerous naiveties on a par with Friedman's belief that "there is no personal rivalry in the competitive market place."[80] But to explore further the irony of an ideology promoting shrinking political governance in the face of tendencies toward more autocratic state rule, we have to recall that the stronger state was developing in and through economic reforms made by political leaders, such as Reagan's attack on antitrust laws and Thatcher's creation of the Adam Smith Institute, and before the threat of terrorism gave unprecedented powers over civil liberties to certain government agencies. We thereby uncover a structural analogy between the aggressive marketing and redistribution of manufacturing and selling by transnationals and the militant democracy of the wealthiest countries, such as that of the G8.

Klein's analysis is suggestive here although she does not proceed along these lines. She charts two indicative processes from the 1970s to the late 1990s. First is the weakening of what, in the introduction, I called micropolitics: the politics of identity that characterized political activity at that time. It was weakened not necessarily by government action but by global economics: "Identity politics weren't fighting the system, or even subverting it. When it came to the vast new industry of corporate branding, they were feeding it. . . . The need for greater diversity—the rallying cry of my university years—is now not only accepted by the culture industries, it is a mantra of global capital. And identity politics, as they were practiced in the nineties, weren't a threat, they were a gold mine."[81] Klein concludes on a note that returns us to the ubiquity of the virtual: "Women's and civil-rights movements by the conflation of causes that came to be called political correctness successfully trained a generation of activists in the politics of the image, not action."[82] The demise of micropolitics on a national level leads dominant nation-states to place as much domestic policy as possible into the hands of the market and to seek the development of their own national status—the nation as a kind of brand itself abroad—in a decisionist foreign policy. This, to some extent, is an old political move; troubles at home require

80. Friedman, *Capitalism and Freedom*, 119.
81. Klein, *No Logo*, 113, 115.
82. Ibid., 124.

diverting attention to activity overseas. Only now the basis for this shift is a profound and complex alignment between neoliberal economics and conservative politics.

The second process Klein charts is the decline in freedom associated with choice as international companies merge or form synergies that increase their monopolization (politically understood as hegemony) over the market. Neoliberalism was all about the expansion of personal choice. But when giants such as Paramount Pictures merge with Blockbuster, or AOL with Netscape, and when Virgin not only sells CDs but also produces them, broadcasts them on its radio stations, and offers them through its mobile-phone communications, options shrink and a strange combination emerges—"a sea of products coupled with losses in real choice."[83] The citizen is customer, catered for by both the state and the commercial world, but it is a customer who, on the one hand, seems to be given a vast freedom to chose and, on the other, is heavily directed toward what to choose. This reflects the way the public sphere, the space where democracy was birthed and fostered, has been hired out to private enterprises. In Manchester, England, on several weeks of the year, the main public space in front of the town hall, created in Victorian Britain for political congress and debate, is rented out to house a Christmas market, a Bavarian beer garden, and a dry ski slope, among other things. The town hall is now in the entertainment business, advertising a list of spectacular events staged throughout the year. It brings people from a wide radius into the city to shop, draining outlying centers of their independent economic wealth. But it also means that the space for protest, for rallies, for citizens engaged in specific public issues is available only when the town hall is not rented out. And CCTV and security people are always on hand to ensure that the environment is safe for the customers.

The political has become the economic, and the economic the political; globalization is the result of the fusion of neoliberal economics with neoconservative politics.[84] In the process, a supposed economic freedom is bought at the price of certain sup-

83. Ibid., 159.

84. The relations between economics and politics have always been close. But as Mittelman observes, "Globalization is emerging as *a political response to the expansion of market power*" (*Globalization Syndrome*, 7).

posed political freedoms as certain Western countries transform themselves into corporations, utilizing the same economic and managerial logics and requiring the same hierarchical forms of organization. The control of a nation correlates to the control of a market; aspirations to global leadership govern both; the decline in civil liberties parallels the effective decline in consumer choice. What is evident is that globalization is not at the vanguard of democratization. Indeed, it cannot be because no one controls the unbounded market and therefore no one is accountable to it, whereas democracy's requirement for checks and balances demands means whereby a public account of governance can be made. Globalization is transforming democracy, undermining what makes democracy flourish—a vigorous civil society.[85] As mentioned in the last chapter, one of the key characteristics of the postdemocratic condition is the increasing government of state policy by economic matters. Does, then, the correlation between aggressive democratic states and aggressive multinational corporations come about because of copycat managerial strategies or because, where power is increasingly understood in terms of economic and military strength, negotiations have to be made between international leaders of commerce and key national governments implicated in empire?

The socialist geographer David Harvey has examined the paradox traced here in terms of a dialectic that operates between a capitalist logic of power and what he terms a "territorial logic of power" on behalf of certain hegemonic nation-states.[86] The logics are not identical, and indeed he suggests that the continuing occupation of Iraq by the United States displays their uncoupling (where territorial gains act as a continual drain on financial resources). But from the 1970s to the war with Iraq, these logics worked hand in hand to develop the United States into a new imperial power. The need for new markets and new spaces for the deployment of capital and its accumulation is closely allied, he argues, to the need to colonize or create client states either by direct means (invasion)

85. See ibid., 228–47, for a more detailed account of the way globalization promotes depoliticization and a political disempowerment. Pithily, in a manner that reminds us of Laski's comments on democracy and capitalism, Mittelman observes, "The beneficiaries of globalization have no inherent interest in promoting democracy" (247).

86. Harvey, *New Imperialism*, 93.

or indirect means (employing loans that effectively render the other country dependent on the loan provider and open to the dispossession of its assets). What both these logics thrive on is crisis and insecurity that at times have been engineered and sustained by the nation-states themselves.[87] One country's financial crisis is another country's financial opportunity (e.g., to bail out or buy products at greatly devalued prices). Having the safety of its people uppermost, a nation must do all in its power to secure itself from potential threats (e.g., employing and advertising its military strengths). The systemic inequalities between winners and losers, maintained through a climate of crisis and insecurity, sharpen the competitive edges between state players. Hardt and Negri, in their own analysis of "Empire," downplay the centralizing role the United States plays in the international flows of capital, and so, for them, the empire created through globalization lacks a dominant state hegemony. Harvey disagrees, maintaining that globalization may weaken and/or compromise certain nation-states, but it does require the exercise of powers by dominant states. For these nation-states—even the United States, where, by 2004, 40 percent of treasuries and 20 percent of Wall Street assets were foreign owned[88]—forge the ways in which international trade is opened and profits accrued for their own deployment. It is states that deregulate, set tax levels, privatize, and promulgate laws of migration. For my argument, it matters little whether Hardt and Negri or Harvey is right about the United States. What is significant about the complex association of neoliberal economics and neoconservative politics, the capitalist logic of power and the territorial logic of power, and the complex ironies their association generates is what they share: a profound and intrinsic desire to expand and to acquire and a continuing need for crises, sources of fear, and insecurities.

As already mentioned, allied to notions such as freedom and the full satisfaction of each and all desires, these expansionist and acquisitive logics bear a religious charge—more specifically, a Christian, eschatological (even apocalyptic) charge.[89] When the logics

87. Harvey points to the Nixon regime's dealings with key Arab oil countries, which led to the dramatic rise in oil prices in the mid-1970s and the exclusive processing of billions of petrodollars through United States banks (ibid., 128).

88. Ibid., 226.

89. With each successive reemergence of fighting, dearth, and devastation, Bible-educated Christians (not necessarily fundamentalists) throughout the world rehearse

are articulated by a Christian country in a dominant hegemonic position, both economically and politically, this charge becomes something closer to a messianic imperative. As George W. Bush has said: "Freedom is the Almighty's gift to every man and woman in this world. And as the greatest power on the face of the Earth, we have an obligation to help the spread of freedom."[90]

Here perhaps we uncover another complex irony that has enormous resonance for the argument of this book with respect to developing a theological metaphysics for postmaterialist values. For although I am seeking to expose the metaphysical vision driving neoliberal accounts of free trade and therefore globalization, there is nothing metaphysical about the mechanics whereby such an economics goes about achieving its desire for maximal profits. Carl Schmitt pointed to this irony: "In modern economy, a completely irrational consumption conforms to a totally rationalized production."[91] The processes of post-Fordism that locate production sites at the margins of the world's markets for mass consumption (and thus continually facilitate the forgetting of where these goods have come from and the processes entailed in their production) reveal that globalization is about materialism, however dematerialized its wrapping. The culture of shopping in malls, gallerias, main streets, and arcades across the world's leading cities has transformed a routine activity into a form of entertainment, fantasy, and diversion. The focus on the customer as consumer, as we saw above, aims to satisfy all wants and present a frictionless excess.[92] Resistance, then, to globalization in the

---

the apocalyptic words of Christ in the Gospel of Mark: "And when you hear of wars and rumors of wars, do not be alarmed; this must take place, but the end is not yet. For nation will rise against nation, and kingdom against kingdom; there will be earthquakes in various places, there will be famines; this is but the beginning of the birth-pangs" (13:7–8).

90. George W. Bush, "President Addresses the Nation in Prime Time Press Conference," April 13, 2004, The White House, www.whitehouse.gov/news/releases/2004/04/20040413-20.html.

91. Carl Schmitt, *Roman Catholicism and Political Form*, trans. G. L. Ulmen (Westport, CT: Greenwood, 1996), 14.

92. For many, it is not capitalism as such that underpins this fantasy of endless consumption but credit—belief in resources beyond one's own, infinitely deferring a payback. The crisis of this fantasy is evident in Britain, where it is estimated that "more than 10,000 people a month are expected to declare themselves insolvent this year as a culture of unsustainable debt grows" (Gabriel Rozenberg, "10,000 People

name of postmaterialism raises considerable difficulties, as those who have engaged in protesting against the environmental damage done by the dislodgement of economics from nature (and civic society) have discovered. "By all the indications, the data indicates an expansion of space for resistance to neo-liberal globalization, but thus far, resistance by nonstate politics has had a limited impact."[93] Postmaterialist values, unwedded to market capitalism, have a hard road to travel—unless they are allied with global religious practices, values, and institutions and rooted in a theological commitment.

A postmaterialism simply locked into economic forces that dematerialize the world is ineffective. It remains entangled with modern notions of freedom—political freedom correlated to economic freedom, a freedom that so easily forgets. But this chapter's explorations have unmasked the theologies and metaphysics invested in globalization and the extent to which globalization is parasitic on a predominantly Christian globalism. A more radical postmaterialism would issue from an engagement with the theology and metaphysics that globalization seeks to mimic; it would recognize the true nature of its desires, discerning the degree of its own fantasies and the depths of its own forgetting. But before we can begin to develop this more radical postmaterialism, one further exploration is necessary. To the analyses of our new democratic condition and the globalization that is not simply its context but in part both its efficient cause and ultimate product, we need to add an examination of the third contemporary phenomenon: the new visibility of religion. This is because there is no pure Christian theology or metaphysics on the shores of which we can be beached. There is no paradisial island (as the television series *Lost* makes plain). Christian theology today is hardwired into the new visibility of religion more generally, and this, as we shall see, makes ecclesial living in global cities a political act.

---

a Month Will Go Insolvent," *Times* [London], January 3, 2007, 4). Hence much of the analysis of this chapter may have to be rewritten in two year's time, following the collapse of banking and credit facilities worldwide.

93. Mittelman, *Globalization Syndrome*, 201.

3

Postsecularity?

The New Visibility of Religion

> The global resurgence of religion may well be a response to the crisis of the liberal state in the West as well as the crisis of the secular and modernizing state in the developing world.[1]

Jerusalem

Let us take a spiraling walk into the heart of the Old City and discover there a symbol of profound significance, past and present. We enter through the Jaffa Gate from the modern development built by Jewish settlers—a gate scarred and pocked by a history of warring. We enter the Christian Quarter but turn right, past the remains of the ancient citadel, the former palace of Herod the Great, up the Armenian Patriarchate Road, and enter the Armenian Quarter. The buildings are of the same gray stone as the wall of the city itself, with doorways opening onto shady courtyards. We follow the road around, past the Zion Gate, and turn left along Ararat and right along Ha-Kinor; the architecture begins to change

1. Scott M. Thomas, *The Global Resurgence of Religion and the Transformation of International Relations* (New York: Palgrave Macmillan, 2005), 40.

as we approach the newly developed Byzantine thoroughfare of the Cardo. We have entered the Jewish Quarter, where some of the most beautiful and expensive apartments in the world, crafted from a honey-colored rock, can be found on all sides. From here we can enter the open space of Hurva Square, where, restored once more to its former glory, is the Hurva Synagogue, the scene of so much factionalism and destruction in 1948 between Arab and Jew. Today it basks in a sunlight shaded around its edges by trees, crossed by tourists who have visited the exclusive shops and now wish to rest at the boulevard cafes or travel on to the Western Wall. We too proceed to the Western Wall, above which rises the Dome of the Temple Mount. Security is pervasive: closed-circuit television cameras trained in all directions from above, soldiers checking identifications, rectangular screening portals, X-ray machines for bags and purses, stacks of plastic riot shields resting against nearby walls.

There are two border crossings here: one as we descend the steps to the Western Wall Piazza and the second as we ascend the wooden steps and walkway to the Temple Mount itself. Armed soldiers stand at the gate to the mount; again identifications are checked and bags are searched, for we are entering the Muslim Quarter, and we finally step into the broad expanse of the mount itself, with its panoramic view of the Old City and the Jewish cemetery on the slopes of Mount Scopus. We cross between the stunning Dome of the Rock and the al-Aqsa Mosque with their exquisite tile work, exiting through the Gate of Damascus, and walk toward the Shaar Ha-Arayot, a narrow road at which we turn left. This takes us to one of the city's famous pilgrimage sites, the Via Dolorosa. The dark, old stone lines each side of the Via, the shops press close, and their keepers, touting for trade, press closer. The air is cooler, there are damp, squalid corners, and cars and bikes pass endlessly up and down because the road leads into the heart of the Arab souk. We reach the souk, with its dense aromas and its sweating shoppers at the Souk Khan El-Zeit—where the Via Dolorosa disappears for a time, only to appear again at a sharp right turn. A second and equally sharp right turn brings us into the Souk El-Dabbagha, where falafel is fried in large open pans and the smell of fresh meat warmed by the sun makes the air sweet and fetid.

We arrive in the middle of the Muslim Quarter, down a way made famous by the Christian Gospels, at the heart of the city: the Church of the Holy Sepulcher. But it is neither Golgotha, to the right of the entrance, nor the tomb of the burial of Christ, to the left, that we are visiting. Moving through the crowds of Christians from every denomination throughout the world, we walk toward a flight of steep stone steps that lead down into the Chapel of St. Helena. The steps are lined by thousands of tiny crosses made by medieval pilgrims, and the way is lit by lanterns. We descend to a marble floor the color of blood, the air thick with the perfumes of ancient incense, the subterranean silence cool and meditative. We enter a room at the center of which hangs a huge magnificent lantern pointing directly down to a mosaic floor. The lantern is surrounded by pillars between which are strings of smaller lanterns of bright colored metal and gemstone glass. Whatever the legends about Golgotha as Mount Moriah, the place on which Abraham intended to sacrifice his son, here is the heart of ancient Jerusalem, for it is not only time that is thickly layered at this site, but also space. The lantern plumblined, for the medieval mind, the center of the cosmos. The earth, the moon, the planets, and the primum mobile, the universe itself, moved around this very point, and all celestial influence was focused here.

Introduction

From our analysis so far, we can conclude that the new changes to the nature of democracy, invoking either crisis or transformation, began in the late 1970s as a response to what had taken place in the early 1970s. Histories of globalization also frequently refer to the 1970s as a turning point. As the last chapter emphasizes, globalism has a long cultural history, and it might well be conceived as a further development of the global logics of Christianity as they were translated into the early capitalism that, after the voyages of discovery and the rape of mineral resources in what became Latin America, developed through the accumulation of gold and silver in Europe. Nevertheless, the dollar's move away from its gold reserves (which dematerialized the monetary standard), the end of the Bretton Woods agreement on fixed rates of currency exchange, the oil price crisis, and the technological advances that made travel and communications so much faster made the 1970s the years when globalization underwent a "step change."[2] "Globalization has helped to create alternative transnational religious subcultures or communities that are revitalizing Islam and Christianity in the global South."[3] Postmaterialism too was an initiative of the 1970s that responded to the neoliberal economics fostering globalization. And according to the American historian and theoretician of contemporary art Charles Jencks, the origins of postmodernity are likewise associated with the mid- to late 1970s.[4] In its philosophical and poststructuralist guise, postmodernism turned to religious discourses as a source of resistance to the rationalities of modernity, as can be witnessed in the Catholic imaginations of Julia Kristeva and Luce Irigaray and the reflections on ritual and sacrifice in Georges Bataille and René Girard, to name but a few.[5] These four political, economic, and cultural trends that emerged in the late 1970s, each of which stimulated a new interest in religion, forced religion out of the private retreats of church, mosque, and temple and into the streets, so that today, as we will later examine, a number of key contemporary thinkers are describing the cultural conditions in the West as "postsecular."[6]

The Social Sciences' View of Religion

Before we explore what is called postsecular and the various forms of this new visibility of religion, it is important to acknowledge that not all sociologists of religion would agree that this development has taken place. Steve Bruce, for example, believes that the

2. See Robert W. Cox, "A Perspective on Globalization," in *Globalization: Critical Reflections*, ed. James Mittelman (Boulder, CO: Lynne Rienner, 1996), 21–30.

3. Thomas, *Global Resurgence of Religion*, 115.

4. Charles Jencks, "Postmodernism vs. Late-Modern," in *Zeitgeist in Babel: The Post-modernist Controversy*, ed. Ingeborg Hoesterey (Bloomington: Indiana University Press, 1991), 4–5.

5. See Graham Ward, ed., *The Postmodern God* (Oxford: Blackwell, 1997).

6. In his well-cited study *The Revenge of God: The Resurgence of Islam, Christianity, and Judaism* (Cambridge: Polity, 1994), Gilles Kepel views the new visibility of religion as beginning in the 1970s with the increasing skepticism that science and technology would save us and that Western modernity was indeed progressing everywhere.

secularization thesis can still be upheld.[7] Three points need to be made here: one regarding the sociological approach to religion more generally, the second regarding secularism itself, and the third regarding the kind of religion that is emerging in this new visibility.

Sociologists and Their Discontents

Sociologists have a vested interest in maintaining the secularization thesis. The foundation of their discipline was the critique of religion at the forefront of the Enlightenment agenda. This critique opened an intellectual space for the investigation of society as such. It was a society conceived in such a way that religion was held to play a certain function, but this function was an expression of a human response to specific social conditions. Religion, for those sociologists, was an effect, and what was needed was to understand the cause of this effect. The public sphere that sociology examined was a flat field of relations without a transcendent horizon. Earlier—and I am advocating no nostalgia for this—religion in the West defined what society was. That is, society was the effect; what was needed was to understand the religious cause of this effect. In the Enlightenment, religion was viewed as one specialized institution among a number of other specialized institutions, and each institution had a function in the formation and maintenance of society. The foundation had changed: society was now the fundament to be examined by new philosophical methods—empiricism, positivism, naturalism, humanism. In the light of this new foundation and its approaches to understanding, the presence of religion was to be explained (away) by the newly minted social sciences.

Other associated disciplines beside sociology experienced similar reversals of their own theological foundations. For example, in the light of humanism, Enlightenment anthropology cannot entertain a theological perspective on being human, nor can psychology. And so, although 82 percent of humankind espouses religious convictions, anthropology and psychology, following in the wake of the Enlightenment sociology, can view such people only

7. See Steve Bruce, *Religion in the Modern World* (Oxford: Oxford University Press, 1996) and *God Is Dead: Secularization in the West* (Oxford: Blackwell, 2002).

as immature, primitive, irrational, neurotic, or insecure. For these social sciences, religion can be understood only negatively in terms of human progress toward some flatline of secularization—some enlightenment utopia in which all human beings are mature, civilized, rational, psychologically stable, and emotionally secure and recognize that their need for religion is a pathological or existential condition. The assumption is that such sociologists, anthropologists, and psychologists themselves are free from such immaturities, irrationalities, and emotional instabilities.

It is no wonder, then, that some sociologists still want to deny a dramatic increase in the visibility of religion, insisting that the West is still on course to its secularized destiny. "Abandoning secularisation as the grand explanatory framework is a real theoretical loss [to sociology]; the frame of reference within which one could attempt to predict not just the future of religion, but the future shape of society itself, is lost. Sociology is bereft of teleological signposts."[8] From another perspective, the cultural analyst Zygmunt Bauman has argued that accepting what is currently taking place in postmodernity means reversing the Weberian notion of "disenchantment." Weber famously described the effects of progressive rationalization in terms of an iron cage that emptied the world of its former magic. Bauman concludes that the new "reenchantment," encouraged by postmodernity, calls for rethinking some of the fundamental categories of sociological analysis itself.[9] Scott M. Thomas makes a similar and related point concerning the methodological atheism of scholars engaged in the study of international relations. Recognizing that "religion has been marginalized in the study of international relations," Thomas attempts to devise new analytical tools to examine the current "struggle over

8. James Sweeney, "Revising Secularization Theory," in *The New Visibility of Religion*, ed. Michael Hoelzl and Graham Ward (London: Continuum, 2008), 15–29. In this important essay, Sweeney explores the possibility of a sociology of religion undertaken with the assumption of religion's essential truthfulness.

9. See Zygmunt Bauman, *Intimations of Postmodernity* (London: Routledge, 1992). See also Charles Lemert, *Postmodernism Is Not What You Think* (Oxford: Blackwell, 1997), 132–64, for an account of the crises in modern sociology and the new sociologies that are emerging. More recently, Gregor McLennan, "Towards Postsecular Sociology?" *Sociology* 41 (2007): 857–70, has engaged the question.

the soul of the world," in which "religious pluralism plays so vital a part of foreign policy."[10]

Even when sociologists recognize a significant change in the role religion is playing in contemporary life, they find reductive explanations for its occurrence. Once more, religion is not a cause; it is an effect of something else. The French sociologist Manuel Castells, in his magisterial three-volume analysis of the new "information age," views the return of religion as a political force (notably in only one uncritical form—"fundamentalism") expressive of resistance among faith communities.[11] This is a challenge to the Durkheimian thesis. The French sociologist Emil Durkheim saw the function that religion played in society as a kind of cement: it enabled society to conceive itself as one homogenized community—a body. And so Castells's view is that any contemporary return to religion is flying in the face of, and responding to, contemporary social atomism. He regards the new visibility of religion as a *response* to certain social conditions. The turn toward religion as a means of consolidating one's identity is, in this view, a response to "social disintegration . . . [as] a chronic feature of the contemporary phase of globalization."[12] The dramatic insecurities and hybrid identities, the liquidation of family life and notions of community, ushered in by postdemocracy and its disinvestment in the welfare state; globalization and its attendant multiculturalism and changes to the patterns of working life; postmodernity with its embrace of the eclectic, the ironic, and the soft senses of ontology and hypersubjectivity—all engender a reaction, and the return of religion is one expression of this reaction.

According to this account, the new visibility of religion is *a resistance* to these dramatic cultural and worldwide transformations. More recently, Pippa Norris and Ronald Inglehart (encountered in chap. 2, above, as the champion of political postmaterialism) argue "that feelings of vulnerability to physical, societal, and personal risks are a key factor driving religiosity and we demonstrate that the process of secularization—a systematic erosion of religious practices, values, and beliefs—has occurred most clearly among

10. Thomas, *Global Resurgence of Religion*, 13, 16.

11. Manuel Castells, *The Information Age: Economy, Society and Culture*, vol. 3, *End of the Millennium* (Oxford: Blackwell, 1998), 335–60.

12. James H. Mittelman, *The Globalization Syndrome: Transformation and Resistance* (Princeton, NJ: Princeton University Press, 2000), 216.

the most prosperous social sectors living in affluent and secure post-industrial societies."[13] As a consequence, then, of "the need for religious reassurance" and "*due to the demographic trends in the poorer societies, the world as a whole has more people with traditional religious views than ever before.*"[14] Once again sociological accounts reinforce the view that the turn to religion is an expression of existential insecurities. The anthropologist Clifford Geerzt was saying this in the 1960s, that religion is a symbolic world order giving expression to deep human anxieties concerning existence as such.

Religion is viewed, then, by certain political scientists, anthropologists, sociologists, psychologists, and cultural historians as *epiphenomenal*, as a response to something rather than a cause of anything.[15]

Besides the moral and intellectual hubris of such negative reductions, it is evident that social scientists never espouse religious faith positively, as something of intrinsic value and import. Worship, prayer, liturgical attendance, reading sacred texts, and practices of devotion are never affirmative human acts. They are always substitutes for a lack of some kind. They are never taken seriously as such. And so what should be sociological descriptions of the relationship between religion and society slide into "normatively prescriptive theories of modern societies."[16]

An act of political discipleship has to challenge such attitudes, has to challenge such reductions, for the social sciences, and sociology in particular; only when the new visibility of religion (emerging in the 1970s) is related to the secularization thesis is religion under-

13. Pippa Norris and Ronald Inglehart, *Sacred and Secular: Religion and Politics Worldwide* (Cambridge: Cambridge University Press, 2004), 4–5. Earlier, the French sociologist Daniele Hervieu-Léger had also argued that new types of religious believing arise from the uncertainties provoked by modernity's deconstruction of tradition. See Daniele Hervieu-Léger, *Religion as a Chain of Memory* (Cambridge: Polity, 2000). There are other sociological accounts that also acknowledge the resurgence of religion, even in its more public, deprivatized forms while viewing religion as fundamentally in decline. See José Casanova, *Public Religions in the Modern World* (Chicago: University of Chicago Press, 1994).

14. Norris and Inglehart, *Sacred and Secular*, 18, 25, italics in the original.

15. "A sociology which is methodologically atheist, confining itself to phenomenological comparative analysis, is inevitably drawn toward an epiphenomenal portrayal of religion" (Sweeney, "Revising Secularization Theory," 21).

16. Casanova, *Public Religions*, 41.

stood as something that needs explaining, or explaining away. But another possibility, which remains unconsidered, is that religion is not an effect, a response to socioeconomic, cultural, and political conditions; rather, it is an independent phenomenon intrinsically involved in the transformation of these political, economic, and cultural conditions. This raises a second point concerning secularism itself.

Secularism and Faith

The historian Owen Chadwick has provided us with a fine narrative of the development of the European secular mind in the nineteenth century. He explains that the secular standpoint emerged through the Christian conscience that would allow either many religions or no religion in a state and repudiated any pressure to religious uniformity.[17] So, since the basis of liberalism is freedom of conscience, the origins of that liberalism were with the religious dissenters. Meanwhile liberalism itself sought the secularization of institutions. Alongside liberalism, the other current of secularism can be found in Marx and the transmutation of theology into anthropology following Ludwig Feuerbach's *The Essence of Christianity* (1841). Although liberalism, Feuerbach, and Marx all held secularization to be an inevitable process, none of them developed a theoretical model for this process. There is no account of secularization in Marx; it is merely a methodological assumption arising out of the Enlightenment critique of religion. It was only in the early twentieth century, with Weber's historical sociology and Durkheim's comparative sociology, that theoretical accounts of the process of secularization emerged. An example is Weber's account of the increasing social differentiation into autonomous rational spheres, which would entail that institutions specialize in certain social activities and that religious institutions are marginal.[18]

The secular intellectual pursuits of the nineteenth-century critics of religion—Feuerbach, Marx, Mill, Nietzsche—did not,

17. Owen Chadwick, *The Secularization of the European Mind in the Nineteenth Century* (Cambridge, Cambridge University Press, 1975), 23.

18. See Max Weber, "Religious Rejections of the World and Their Directions," in *Max Weber: Readings and Commentary on Modernity*, ed. Stpehen Kalberg (Oxford: Blackwell, 2004), 340–44.

however, necessarily have great impact socially. In fact, Chadwick claims that anxieties over the assumed atheism of the working class and anticlericalism more generally had as much, if not a greater, impact. Despite these impacts and because of them, the Victorians built "more and more churches, in the towns of England, Wales and Scotland."[19] (Chadwick has published two rich and important explorations of the flourishing Victorian church.)[20] It is, then, easy to exaggerate the secularization of society and thereby assume that it has a long and detailed history. The view that an increasingly disenchanted and rational world began to overshadow the practice of religion in the eighteenth and nineteenth centuries (Christianity in this instance; Judaism and Islam were even more resistant) has to be balanced by the work of the historians of these periods, many of whom point to the flourishing of the Christian faith in its various denominations and revivals. A similar balanced judgment has to be reached about the description of religion as retreating into the private sphere in the same centuries. Evidence shows that the practices of faith were as public, visible, and politically active as ever despite increasing skepticism from some intellectual quarters. If, therefore, by "secularism" we mean the decline in Christian belief (in this context) or Nietzsche's announcement that God is dead and we have killed him, we are talking about an age that probably began to manifest itself socially and culturally only in the twentieth century after the First World War. Given that the United States has always been viewed as the exception to the secularization thesis and Europe as the model, when did this secularism become so pronounced that the world, for the majority of its inhabitants, became a godforsaken place?

We might distinguish here between two forms of secularism: an operative or procedural secularism, in which certain state institutions maintained a laicized stance in the interests of justice for all, and an ideological secularism, in which religion is viewed as a minority interest, as a locus of superstition and cultic practices fostering group illusions, and so on. Operative secularism can be practiced alongside forms of operative or procedural nonsecular-

19. Chadwick, *Secularization of the European Mind*, 97.

20. Owen Chadwick, *The Victorian Church*, 2 vols. (London: A. & C. Black, 1966, 1970).

ism—in the churches (and church schools), mosques, temples, and synagogues. Daniel Bell distinguishes between the structural operations in a society (what he calls the "techno-economic") and its culture. The structural operations can change through a process of secularization, but cultures rooted strongly in tradition do not change in the same way, for, "in the realm of the imagination, once something extraordinary is produced, it is never lost. Changes in cultures only widen the expressive repertoire of mankind."[21] Bryan Wilson criticizes Bell's "genteel notions"[22] of culture as the civilizing of taste and judgment. Bell himself distinguishes his own understanding of culture from that current among anthropologists. But I find Bell's distinction pedagogically useful, even while accepting that the techno-economic and the cultural have an impact on each other (which Bell also acknowledges).[23] There is no reason his notion of high culture might not be expanded to embrace a more general, Geertzian construal of the cultural. It is in the realm of the cultural that I would wish to situate one of the major forms of the new visibility of religion, as we will see. As the sociologist Eduardo Mendieta puts it, commenting on the turn Habermas has made to investigating religion more systemically, religion has become "the last reservoir of cultural autonomy."[24]

In chapter 4 I will develop the realm of the imaginary and the mythical as terrain ripe for the practice of Christian discipleship. For the moment, I suggest that it is ideological secularism particularly that is being advocated by the secularization thesis and that the hegemony of such "creedal secularism" is only a recent phenomenon.[25] Some scholars have thought that European secu-

21. Daniel Bell, "The Return of the Sacred? The Argument on the Future of Religion," *British Journal of Sociology* 28, no. 4 (1977): 435.

22. Bryan Wilson, "The Return of the Sacred," *Journal for the Scientific Study of Religion* 18, no. 3 (1979): 274.

23. Religion, even at its most privatized, is not insulated from the techno-economic. In its institutional forms, it abides within and affects the structural operations of society. In its less institutional and more customized forms, related to New Age spirituality, it provides rich pickings of alternative lifestyles for sale.

24. Eduardo Mendieta, introduction to Jürgen Habermas, *Religion and Rationality: Essays on Reason, God, and Modernity* (Cambridge: Polity, 2002), 1.

25. Wilson draws attention to the confusion between secularization as a process and "secularism as a creed" ("Return of the Sacred," 270). This is partly a matter of the ambiguities concerning what aspects of religious change secularization covers.

larism of this kind emerged only with the return of disillusioned forces from the battlefields of the First World War. But according to Norris and Inglehart, the downturn in religious practice and the upturn in the hegemony of ideological secularism in Western Europe began in the 1960s. And the data that they provide show that 60 percent or more of the populations of Spain, Italy, Portugal, Belgium, and Austria were active worshipers in the 1970s, and more than 90 percent in Ireland. These figures seem to indicate a greater susceptibility to the secular mind in Protestants in comparison with Catholics, but Bell reports, "In 1970 some polls discovered that 88 percent of people in Britain professed to believe in God and 45 percent thought God is a personal being."[26] Furthermore, "in 1947 eight out of ten people believed in God, with the highest levels of belief expressed in Australia, Canada, the United States, and Brazil."[27] Thus ideological secularism, it could be argued, develops exponentially in countries where the secularization thesis is most adamantly insisted on. The question arises, then, as to whether secularism is a self-fulfilling prophecy made by sociologists of religion. Even in such countries where secularism has been most profoundly examined, it is a recent phenomenon, a blip against a background of centuries of piety, a blip that may well be in the process of being reversed, for "a new religious approach began to take shape in the 1970s based on the search for authentic identity, meaning, and economic development."[28]

Indeed, even as ideological secularism gathered pace in Western Europe in the 1960s and 1970s, as both Catholic and Protestant

More recently Rowan Williams, in his essay "Secularism, Faith, and Freedom" (www.archbishopofcanterbury.org/656), makes the distinction between procedural and programmatic secularism with respect to public debate. Programmatic secularism denies the legitimacy of religious conviction in political argument, whereas a "'procedurally' secular society and legal system . . . is always open to being persuaded by confessional or ideological argument on particular issues, but is not committed to privileging permanently any one confessional group." Most scholars endorse the necessity for an operative or procedural secularism on the grounds of social justice. Many religious practitioners, myself included, would concur. Religious institutions also need the checks and balances of the "outsider" perspective to act critically toward their own ideologies and the social technologies employed to promote them.

26. Bell, "Return of the Sacred?" 423.

27. Norris and Inglehart, *Sacred and Secular*, 89.

28. Thomas, *Global Resurgence of Religion*, 43.

theologies were positively embracing the legitimacy of the secular,[29] and as sociologists were beginning to theorize and systematize accounts of secularization and the imminent demise of religion, the secularization thesis rarely went unchallenged. Writing in 1979, Bryan Wilson, a supporter of what he called a moderate view on secularization, pointed to several contemporary examples, going back to the early 1960s, of scholars who challenged the secularization thesis: Sabino Acquaviva,[30] Thomas Luckmann,[31] and David Martin, who called for the elimination of the concept of secularization;[32] Harvey Cox, who changed his mind;[33] and Daniel Bell. Although Wilson accepted that religious changes had occurred—"Krishna Consciousness, the Divine Light Mission, and the modern Sufi movement . . . various New Thought Cults, Scientology, and . . . some of the Human Potential movements"—he was still undecided whether the so-called return of the sacred is testimony to new empirical information or "a return to the sacred among some sociologists."[34] Nevertheless, by the late 1970s a sociological sea change regarding the visibility of religion was being registered even though the empirical evidence demonstrated that church attendance was dropping and traditional Christian observance was in decline.

Since the 1960s and 1970s, questions concerning the accuracy of the secularization thesis have not gone away because, to quote a one-time defender of the thesis, Peter L. Berger, "the 'facts' are not much disputed: New Religious Movements continue to arise; older move-

29. Vatican II announced a Catholic *aggiornamento*, and official documents such as *Gaudium et spes* recognized the autonomy of the modern world and the role of the church to work within it to transform it. Protestant theologians such as Harvey Cox correctly understood that secularism was the social good that Protestantism always intended; both the Hebrew and the New Testaments preached the need for this secularism. Protestantism had interpreted the Word correctly. See Harvey Cox, *The Secular City: Secularization and Urbanization in Theological Perspective* (New York: Macmillan, 1966).

30. Sabino Acquaviva, *L'eclissi del sacro nella civiltà industriale* (Milan: Communità, 1961).

31. Thomas Luckmann, *Das Problem der Religion in der modernen Gesellschaft* (Freiburg im Breisgau: Rombach, 1963).

32. David Martin, "Towards Eliminating the Concept of Secularization," in *Penguin Survey of the Social Sciences*, ed. Julius Gould (Harmondsworth, UK: Penguin Books, 1965), 169–82.

33. Harvey Cox, *The Seduction of the Spirit* (London: Wildwood House, 1974).

34. Wilson, "Return of the Sacred," 275, 270.

ments like Pentecostalism and Mormonism are expanding; religious fundamentalism thrives throughout the world."[35] Celebrated thinkers such as Jürgen Habermas,[36] Slavoj Žižek,[37] Gianni Vattimo,[38] Jacques

35. Peter L. Berger, ed., *The Desecularization of the World: Resurgent Religion and World Politics* (Grand Rapids: Eerdmans, 1999), 1.

36. Habermas's relationship to religion is a much-debated question. Some scholars, on the basis of remarks made in, e.g., Jürgen Habermas, *Theory of Communicative Action*, vol. 2, *Lifeworld and System* (Boston: Beacon, 1987), and Habermas, *The Philosophical Discourse of Modernity* (Cambridge, MA: MIT Press, 1987), view the methodological atheism of his sociological approach as indicative of a more general dismissal of religion. Others see his work as having important consequences for theology, though committed to a Weberian secularization thesis. But Habermas's recent examinations of religion have also revealed to others, e.g., Eduardo Mendieta (in Habermas, *Religion and Rationality*), how rooted he is within construals of the messianic, transcendent, and metaphysical that are found in the work of leaders of the Frankfurt school. His turn to thinking about religion may have more to do with a Frankfurt school social theorist attuned to the Zeitgeist. He remains committed to a residual Hegelianism that views whatever remains of religion as that which has yet to be sublated by philosophy. See Habermas, *Religion and Rationality*, 147–67. Nevertheless, since 9/11 Habermas has been thoroughly engaged with the new visibility of religion. See esp. Giovanna Borradori, *Philosophy in a Time of Terror: Dialogues with Jürgen Habermas and Jacques Derrida* (Chicago: University of Chicago Press, 2003); and the dialogue between Habermas and Cardinal Ratzinger at the Catholic Academy in Bavaria on January 19, 2004, in Joseph Cardinal Ratzinger and Jürgen Habermas, *The Dialectics of Secularization*, ed. Florian Schuller, trans. Brian McNeil (San Francisco: Ignatius, 2006). See also an analysis of Habermas's postsecularism in Antonella Besussi, "Assoluti terrestri: Post-secolarismo e limiti della filosofia liberale," Dipartimento di Studi Sociali e Politici, Università degli Studi di Milano, www.sociol.unimi.it/papers/2007-06-12_Antonella%20Besussi.pdf; and Virgil Nemoianu, "The Church and the Secular Establishment: A Philosophical Dialogue between Joseph Ratzinger and Jürgen Habermas," *Logos* 9, no. 2 (Spring 2006): 17–42.

37. Žižek has increasingly appealed to the Christian religion, and Saint Paul in particular, as a source to disrupt contemporary liberal democracy. Several works could be mentioned, but his thoughts are briefly captured in Slavoj Žižek, *On Belief* (London: Routledge, 2001).

38. Gianni Vattimo, "After Onto-theology: Philosophy between Science and Religion," in *Religion after Metaphysics*, ed. Mark A. Wrathall (Cambridge: Cambridge University Press, 2003), opens with this statement: "The Twentieth Century seemed to close with the end of the phenomenon that has been called secularization" (29). But Vattimo's "postsecularism," as expressed in this essay and in Gianni Vattimo, *Belief*, trans. Luke Disanto and David Webb (Stanford, CA: Stanford University Press, 1999), is only a deeper secularization. Like Hegel, Vattimo sees the present situation as the fulfillment of a kenotic movement in God that began with the incarnation.

Derrida,[39] and Charles Taylor[40]—leaders in the field of cultural and social theory—have now spoken about a "postsecular" condition. What characterizes this "postsecular" condition is not simply the refusal of religion to go away but, more significantly, the new public visibility of religion. And it is at this point, the point where religion has a public voice, that religion becomes political again.

Resurgence, Not Return

Before the champions of theism start rejoicing triumphantly, it has to be acknowledged that this is not a return of religion. A "return" implies continuity with a past phenomenon: what was once overlaid with ideological secularism has now reemerged; the repressed surfaces in social consciousness. No. This is not a return. And the sociological data is right: attendance at places of worship has declined or, at best, remained relatively stable. What we are witnessing is not a return but a new religiousness that is hybrid, fluid, and commercialized. Some empirical statistics can measure this new phenomenon—for example, the increase in the numbers partaking in pilgrimages. In 1986, 2,491 people received pilgrimage certificates for traveling to Santiago de Compostella. In 2004 this number had risen dramatically to 179,944. Another example is the evidence from the first religious census taken in China, in 2008, which points to three hundred million religious believers in contrast with the one hundred million in the previous official

39. Jacques Derrida, "Faith and Knowledge: The Two Sources of 'Religion' at the Limits of Reason Alone," in *Religion*, ed. Jacques Derrida and Gianni Vattimo (Cambridge: Polity, 1998), 1–78; and Borradori, *Philosophy in a Time of Terror*. For a wider discussion, see Yvonne Sherwood and Kevin Hart, eds., *Derrida and Religion: Other Testaments* (London: Routledge, 2005).

40. Charles Taylor, *Varieties of Religion Today: William James Revisited* (Cambridge, MA: Harvard University Press, 2002), discusses the new visibility of religion in terms of a shift from a "paleo-" to a "neo-" and now a "post-Durkheimian" situation. He does this solely on the basis that, for Durkheim, religion's function in society is integration. It is the cement that joins one individual brick to another and creates the sense of being part of something. In the "paleo-Durkheimian" dispensation, there is a strong sacral correlation between church and society. In the "neo-Durkheimian" dispensation, there is an unraveling of this correlation, so that one belongs to a denominational religion by a choice that is "woven into the sense of identity of certain ethnic, national, class, regional groups" (p. 77). With the term "post-Durkheimian," Taylor describes the new turn toward individual expressivism in which "the 'sacred' either religious or 'laique,' has become uncoupled from any political allegiance" (p. 96).

figures, with a rise in Christian believers from ten to forty million people in the 1990s. A third is the claim of Amazon.com that the highest number of book titles in any single category is associated with religion and spirituality (12,285 titles), with nonfiction in the second position (less than 5,000). The visibility of various religious fundamentalism means that we can access empirical information about growth in numbers. But on the whole, because of the new nature of religious believing, it is not easily captured in statistics; it is too liquid, diffuse, and diverse. As will be demonstrated later in this chapter, the new visibility of religion is most evident as a pervasive cultural presence, the impact of which cannot be easily calculated because it is not institutionalized. Or rather the institutions that produce and promote this new visibility are not the institutions examined by sociologists' surveys, since, in themselves, they are not religious institutions.

The New Visibility of Religion—the Example of the United Kingdom

Having examined some of the questions that arise concerning the secularization theory and sociological method more generally, we now explore the evidence for this resurgence of religion and its distinctive nature.

In the United Kingdom, because of sustained church-state relations that resisted the privatization of the Anglican religion, there has continued to be a tradition of critical intervention by the church in the public sphere; one thinks of the Christian socialism of Archbishop William Temple, for example, in the 1930s and 1940s. Tony Blair, in a speech delivered to a Christian evangelical group, testified that in Britain "the churches are among the most formidable campaigning organizations in history."[41] One might also consider, on the wider European scene, the role played by the Catholic Church and Christian Democratic Parties in the establishment of the European Union. But sometime in the mid- to late 1970s, at the point of what has been described as "the great religious breakdown" and the rise of the permissive society, the

41. Tony Blair, speech to Faithworks, London, March 22, 2005, available online at *Guardian*, www.guardian.co.uk/politics/2005/mar/22/speeches.election2005.

public perception of religion more generally began to change. Two events from recent British history accelerated this development.

The first came in 1974 after the general release of the film *The Exorcist*. Adapted by William Peter Blatty from his book of that title, the film won international acclaim, receiving ten Oscar nominations (two wins) and seven Golden Globes (four wins). It quickly became one of the highest box-office successes, grossing about $250 million in 2005. As the publicity machinery began to operate, it emerged that the book was based on a true story about the possession of a boy in the Georgetown section of Washington, DC (where the book and film are set) in the late 1940s. Then myths about mysterious happenings during the filming began to circulate. Depending on which source is used, four to nine people associated with the production supposedly died, and it was alleged that sets caught fire inexplicably and that one of the lead actors, Linda Blair, had a mental breakdown. After the release of the film in the United States, there were accounts of moviegoers breaking into hysterics, fainting, and even having heart attacks. In some Christian quarters, the book and the film were both viewed as purveyors of satanic possession. In the wake of evangelical groups who were raising their public profile at that time in the United States, evangelical Christians in Britain took to the streets to force local councils and cinema owners to ban the showing of the film. These protests succeeded to a certain extent, with some town councils refusing to give cinemas a license to show the film. Other town councils allowed the film to be shown, and buses were added for adults wishing to see it but living in areas where screenings were prohibited. Across Britain evangelical Christians lined the foyers of such cinemas waving banners, handing out tracts, attempting to persuade people not to enter the building, warning them of the dangers of dallying with the occult, and offering pastoral council to those who had watched the film. Though ultimately unsuccessful (and no such events took place with the release of the two sequels), the demonstrations brought to public attention a growing number of people, across all generations, who, despite a liberal education and the evident scientific leaps made in the twentieth century, believed in Satan as a person and dismissed liberal understandings of Christianity as heresy. Religion (here Christianity) was beginning to challenge the secular space, in which freedom of choice was paramount as long as it lay within the parameters of the law and injured no one else's right to choose.

The second event, which occurred in the late 1980s, is far more significant. It took place on a gloomy Saturday afternoon in the city center of Bradford, England, on January 14, 1989, and centered on the public burning of Salman Rushdie's novel *Satanic Verses*. The burning was ritualized, and the protest was organized. Several prominent citizens of Bradford had been invited, including Labour councilors and members of Parliament. It was not, then, prima facie an act of civil disobedience. Since a wider public attention was sought, the event took place twenty minutes earlier than scheduled because the photographer-journalist from the local newspaper, the *Telegraph and Argus*, had to be elsewhere in Bradford later that afternoon. What is significant is that this local event among Muslims in Yorkshire took on first national and then international significance. On January 17 Rushdie went public on the event, calling for the condemnation, by the Labour Party, of official members who had witnessed the book burning. But the response in Bradford was muted. Only the Labour member of Parliament for Bradford South publicly condemned the event; the rest appear to have been dumbfounded by the publicity the book burning had received.

But the Bradford book burning touched a raw national nerve. The posters proclaiming "Rushdie Must Be Destroyed" introduced a violent and seemingly personal hatred into a public space. The liberal boundary between private and public opinion had been transgressed. There were editorials in the country's newspapers, televised interviews, debates, late-night discussions, and radio call-ins. By the end of January, the book burning had become a symbol of a culture war of which the British had until then been oblivious. In the months that followed, a term new to British public discourse was officially sanctioned: "Islamic fundamentalism." It was a term that gained gravitas when, exactly one month after the event in Bradford, on February 14, the Ayatollah Khomeini issued his fatwa: "I inform the proud Muslim people of the world that the author of the *Satanic Verses* book which is against Islam, the Prophet and the Koran, and all involved in its publication who were aware of its content, are sentenced to death." "Islamic fundamentalism" was a term given more credence in the West with the opening of the Gulf War two years later. A new visibility of religion was entering the secular public sphere, and since that time its presence has continued to grow until today it dominates that sphere.

Three Forms of This Visibility

Fundamentalism

There are, broadly speaking, three forms of this new visibility of religion. The first form has been the most widely discussed and examined: religious fundamentalism. In 1977 Daniel Bell predicted that this would be the "strongest element in a religious revival" among people seeking tradition after the "exhaustion of Modernism."[42] Fundamentalism is not itself a new phenomenon. Among the pious there have always been groups who deemed their piety purer or more authentic—the Jewish Pharisees, the Islamic Wahhabites, and the Christian Donatists are all examples. But it is significant that modern forms of fundamentalism, in many ways, first took root as wars of resistance to other secular fundamentalisms—nationalism, communism, imperialistic democracy, and liberal capitalism, for example. In other words, they became titanic because they were clashing with Titans.

There have been several studies in English of Christian fundamentalism as it grew out of American evangelical movements in the early part of the twentieth century[43] and of the present-day impact of Pentecostalism in China, South Korea, Thailand, and Vietnam, and throughout Latin America.[44] Evangelicalism, with its global Christian Web sites, television ministries, and radio stations, mainly arises, like laissez-faire capitalism, from the Protestant and

42. Bell, "Return of the Sacred?" 444.

43. See Robert Wuthnow, *The Restructuring of American Religion: Society and Faith since World War II* (Princeton, NJ: Princeton University Press, 1988); and Martin Marty and R. Scott Appleby, eds., *Fundamentalism Comprehended* (Chicago: University of Chicago Press, 1991). The "fundamentalists" held to the tenets expounded in A. C. Dixon, Louis Meyer, and R. A. Torrey, eds., *The Fundamentals: A Testimony to the Truth*, 12 vols. (Chicago: Testimony, 1910–1915), three million copies of which were given away free.

44. See David Martin, *Tongues of Fire: The Explosion of Protestantism in Latin America* (Oxford: Blackwell, 1990); Harvey Cox, *Fire from Heaven: The Rise of Pentecostal Spirituality and the Reshaping of Religion in the Twenty-First Century* (New York: Addison-Wesley, 1995); and Philip Jenkins, *The Next Christendom: The Coming of Global Christianity* (Oxford: Oxford University Press, 2002).

Nonconformist traditions, but a shift toward conservative Roman Catholicism was also discernable during the pontificate of John Paul II and with the encouragement given to the work of Opus Dei.[45] Britain has been subject to regular national crusades by globe-trotting evangelists since the 1970s, from Billy Graham to Luis Pilau. And whereas attendance in the Anglican Church has been declining or coming to a steady state,[46] the growth of the house church movement and independent evangelical groups has been vast, paralleling the revival of evangelical and fundamentalist Protestantism in the States.[47] Christian fundamentalism is not without its own violences: "In the United States, abortion clinics are bombed and physicians killed in the name of life and saving the unborn."[48]

Although the word "fundamentalism" is most particularly forged within this Christian heritage, after the Salman Rushdie affair it was also applied to describe certain forms of militant Muslim regimes and even forms of militant Judaism. Tariq Ali reveals that the roots of revivalist Islam and the pursuit of a pure reconstruction of Muslim belief go back to the eighteenth century and Ibn Wahbah, whose daughter became one of Ibn Saud's wives.[49] But only with the backing of the most powerful nation on the planet, the United States, did the Muslim fundamentalists become a force to be dealt with, after a deal, struck in the late 1930s with the reigning Ibn Saud, established the Arabian American Oil Company. After the Second World War, despite Saudi Arabia's "confessional despotism,"[50] the Americans con-

45. On the revitalization of Catholicism on an international scale, see David Martin, *On Secularization: Towards a Revised General Theory* (Aldershot, UK: Ashgate, 2005). For an insightful account of the role played by the Vatican in international diplomacy, especially since the 1990s, see *Economist*, July 21–27, 2007, 61–63.

46. Cathedral attendance has, however, been increasing. This could mean one of several things: people would rather attend city-center churches than their local church; the Cathedral is viewed as a living museum with nostalgic value; people are drawn to the choral and musical traditions such churches continue; attendees can remain anonymous because they blend in with the tourists.

47. Indeed, the difference between a fundamentalist and a conservative evangelical lost clarity in the course of this revival.

48. John D. Caputo, *On Religion* (London: Routledge, 2001), 107.

49. Tariq Ali, *The Clash of Fundamentalisms: Crusades, Jihads, and Modernity* (London: Verso, 2003), 74–75.

50. Ibid., 85.

tinued to support the country not only because of its oil wealth but also because of the rising tide of communism through the Middle East. During the 1920s and 1930s, Arab intellectuals were drawn to Marxism as they were to Hitler and Mussolini.[51] Other Islamic revivals occurred in the 1920s in India and Turkey, and the Muslim Brotherhood was founded in Egypt in 1928. In its fight against communism, the Americans backed a number of these confessional despotisms in Egypt, Indonesia, Pakistan, Iraq, and Afghanistan. "By the Fifties, an Islamist triangulation was in place: Wahhabism, Maududi's JI [the Jamaat-e-Islami in India] and the Muslim Brothers dominated Islamist discourse. These were the groups seen by Washington as an essential ideological bulwark against communism and radical nationalism in the Muslim world. All the armed Sunni-Islamist groups who, at the time of writing, are engaged in a jihad against other Muslims and the Great Satan are the children of this constellation."[52] To these groups can be added the Hezbollah in Lebanon, Hamas in Palestine, the Front Islamique du Salut in Algeria, and the Djemaah Islamiya in Indonesia. The militant face of Islam has had a public and international visibility since the 1950s, with notable landmarks such as the 1965 Fatah guerrilla actions in Israel that led to the Six Day War; the toppling of the United States–supported shah of Iran in 1979 and Khomeini's "revolt against History, against Enlightenment, 'Euromania,' 'Westoxification'—against Progress";[53] the assassination of Egypt's President Sadat in 1981; the Gulf Wars; and 9/11.

Because Protestantism, Catholicism, and Islam are transnational faiths, the extreme espousal of their truth claims can set up tensions of loyalty and subsequently raise suspicions regarding allegiance to the national state. Liberal-democratic states fear the theocratic tendencies in such fundamentalism (see chap. 7, below). We should distinguish between this fundamentalism and the use of "fundamentalism" to describe certain forms of Hindu aggressiveness—such as surfaced with the massacre of almost 1,500 Muslims in February, 2002, in Gujarat—for Hindu fundamentalism is closely related to nationalism (80 percent of the Indian population is Hindu). Pluralism is an important concept in Hinduism,

51. Ibid., 300.
52. Ibid., 177.
53. Ibid., 131.

which is not a missionizing religion and does not view itself as the "true religion." It is difficult, then, to develop an extremist ideology on the basis of religious conviction alone. In response to a revival in Hinduism, however, three conservative groups emerged that were called fundamentalist. The oldest, the Rashtriya Swayam Sewah Sangh, was established in 1924, and from this issued the Bharatiya Janta Party in 1951. In 1964 the Vishwa Hindu Parishad, which explicitly opposed religious conversions in the country, was formed. Because of the overt association of these religious groups with Indian politics, there was never a time when religion was not a public issue in the country. Hinduism has always, then, been a visible religion; nevertheless, the violent attacks on Muslims and Christians has recently earned members of these religious groups the label of extremist.[54]

Fundamentalism has also been extended to describe Jewish extremism. Again, this fundamentalism is linked to Israeli nationalism, although the holding of such extreme religious opinions has to be viewed in the context of the alleged secularism of Israeli politics. Indeed, with the expansion of the Jewish sect that is inspired by the messianic figure of Rabbi Lubovicher, we move beyond the frontiers of Israel itself (he has immense followings in the United States and Britain). But the public face of this fundamentalism is often associated with Israel and the opposition to all withdrawals from territories gained in 1967, which supposedly consolidated the biblical boundaries of the country. Two events in the 1990s that roused international attention to this fundamentalism took place in Israel: the killing of twenty-nine Muslims by Baruch Goldstein in 1994 in the Patriarch's Cave in Hebron and the assassination of Prime Minister Yitzhak Rabin by the extremist Yidal Amir in Tel Aviv in 1995.[55]

I do not wish to enter here into whether there are structural similarities between these forms of fundamentalism or structural similarities between these forms of militarism and other forms of believing that constitute communal, even tribal, identity—the various nationalist parties, for example. Rather, I am sketching out some major differences in the new visibility of religion.

54. See John Zavos, *Hindu Nationalism* (Oxford: Oxford University Press, 2000).

55. See Israel Shahak and Newton Mezvinsky, *Jewish Fundamentalism in Israel* (London: Pluto, 1999).

Deprivatization of Religion

The second form of visibility can be defined in terms of the return of religion to civil society. This has been explored under the label "deprivatization" by José Casanova. Nearly all of his evidence is located in histories of the Catholic Church and Protestant denominations (in Spain, Poland, Brazil, and the United States) and the public faces they assumed only in the 1980s.[56] This does not, however, reduce the groundbreaking nature of either his comparative method or his more generalized conclusions. Still, Casanova's work is unable to take into account future developments over the last twenty years, where deprivatization has escalated in certain countries in the light of terrorism.

As noted, the story of the rise and success of secularism has been told in terms of the development of a public sphere that aimed to be religiously and ideologically neutral in order to operate most effectively, that is, inclusively.[57] Institutions forged as the means of administrating, safeguarding, and producing this public sphere—Parliament, the judiciary, schools and universities, hospitals, the media, and forms of government, local and

56. "What I call the 'deprivatization' of religion is the process whereby religion abandons its assigned place in the private sphere and enters the undifferentiated public sphere of civil society to take part in the ongoing process of contestation, discursive legitimating, and redrawing of the boundaries" (Casanova, *Public Religions*, 65–66). Casanova does not take this deprivatization as itself evidence that the secularization thesis is a myth, although deprivatization does question some forms of the thesis that pronounce the demise of religion and challenges secular ideologues who, without hesitation, dismiss religion from the public domain and marginalize its "private" opinions. Casanova still believes that the trajectory toward the increasing differentiation between institutions in the modern world prevents any religion (in Western Europe) from establishing any hegemony. The most he hopes is that deprivatized religion will foster greater debate in the civic and the political realms (ibid., 234).

57. Social and political scientists tend to render more subtly the distinction between the state and civil society by a tripartite division between the state, political society, and civil society. Ideally, the public sphere is the mediating organ insofar as this is the arena for public contestation in civil society. I have not developed such subtleties in my own thinking, and perhaps I should. My main reason for not doing so is my increasing awareness of the policing of civil society and so a difficulty in locating where such a society is. There is talk in Britain of introducing identity cards and a push by the police to establish a national DNA bank, taking samples from suspects on the street for noncriminal offenses such as speeding and littering. So I would view the public sphere as composed increasingly of state-backed institutions and the media, which generate public opinion. The public sphere still plays a mediating role but, predominantly, this role is not concerned with the public contestation of different opinions.

national—all supposedly espoused this notion of neutrality on the grounds of equality and freedom of conscience.[58] Religious convictions were a matter of private devotion and, if brought into the public sphere, were simply embarrassing. I recall meeting the French social historian Pierre Manent in Paris to discuss the new visibility of religion in contemporary Europe and how it was wrestling with the French commitment to *laïcité*. He described the absolute incredulity of the French when they witnessed Bill Clinton's televised confessions of his affair with Monica Lewinski from the White House. The affairs of French presidents were well known, but no one in France, he said, would confuse the office with the man. As political scientists such as Graham Maddox and Charles Taylor have pointed out, this separation of the private and the public is a very reductive account of the relationship between religion and civil society. In fact, we may reverse the notion that the state banished religion into the private sphere, as Maddox does when discussing the rise of the state in the United States. There, it seems, it was more a matter of religion wishing to withdraw from any interference by the state.[59] Nevertheless, as observed above, most historians of the eighteenth and nineteenth centuries testify to the profound public interaction of church and state. The great disassociation of religion from public life is perhaps a recent phenomenon, but it then becomes represented, and defined as the prevailing condition of modernity, by certain liberals. Foremost among them would be John Rawls.[60] So, when we begin to examine the way in which a new confessionalism is once again entering into the public arena, we have to recall that its absence from the public arena is not old and the idea, held

58. I say "supposedly" because there are evident political emphases in the media and because frequently institutions that are allegedly neutral are charged with discriminations (racial, sexual, religious, ethnic, and class). Such evidence of political bias and institutional discrimination qualifies "neutrality" but not the public sphere as much. As long as (a) the judiciary and published commissioned reports can expose such biases and discriminations; (b) public judgments are passed on them; and (c) monitoring procedures against any future offences are put in place, then forms of contestation continue that keep the public sphere dynamic.

59. Graham Maddox, *Religion and the Rise of Democracy* (London: Routledge, 2002), 166.

60. See John Rawls, *Political Liberalism* (Cambridge, MA: Harvard University Press, 1993), 148–52.

by Rawls and others, that this absence goes back to the late seventeenth century is nonsense.

Two examples of this visibility from recent British history have been presented above, but it is a far wider phenomenon. The trend toward the deprivatization of religion was establishing itself elsewhere in the 1980s—John Paul II's visits to Poland and the development of Solidarity, the role played by the Catholic Church in the Sandinista revolution, the promotion of liberation theologies throughout Latin America, and the war between Iran and Iraq from 1980 to 1988. José Casanova, acknowledging the continuing trend of new religious movements in the 1970s, observes, "What was new and became 'news' in the 1980s was the widespread and simultaneous character of the refusal to be restricted to the private sphere of religious traditions as different as Judaism and Islam, Catholicism and Protestantism, Hinduism and Buddhism, in all 'three worlds of development.'"[61] By the 1990s this new visibility of religion was beginning to have an impact on Europe, which was always viewed as the secular exception and the ideal toward which all other continents were moving. According to the 1999 European Values Study, "in all countries, young people who declare themselves Christian, appear more religious in 1999 than in 1990 and 1981 . . . regardless of whether the indicators are personal religiosity (being a religious person, getting comfort and strength from religion, beliefs, especially in a personal God and life after death) or of institutional religiosity (attachment to ceremonies, appreciation of the spiritual and moral contributions of churches)."[62] The international public in the first decade of the post-cold-war era had also witnessed the resurgence of political theologies in both the breakup of the former Yugoslavia and the Gulf Wars.

Talal Asad succinctly charts the trends by which religion has become more public: it has (a) been engaged in the construction of civil society (as in Poland), (b) promoted public debate about liberal values (in the United States), (c) sought to undermine civil society (as in Egypt), and (d) demoted individual liberties (as in Iran and Afghanistan). He concludes that the secularization thesis fails: "Given the entry of religion into political debates issuing in

61. Casanova, *Public Religions*, 6.

62. Yves Lambert, "A Turning Point in Religious Evolution in Europe," *Journal of Contemporary Religion* 19, no. 1 (2004): 37–38.

effective policies, and the passionate commitments these debates engender, it makes little sense to measure the social significance of religion in terms of such indices as church attendance."[63]

Asad's observations concur with what has become one of the most cited records of deprivatization, Huntington's *Clash of Civilizations* (see chap. 1, above). Much of this book, published in 1996, is composed of potted global histories of nation-states, recent international affairs up to 1995, and statistics of public opinion. There is, then, a datedness about the material, even though some of Huntington's prognoses are startlingly accurate.[64] He does not foresee, for example, the rise of a political Islamic party in Turkey that creates new possibilities for alliances across that region. Nor does he foresee the changes in Russian economic power when its oil and gas profits would begin to emerge. He has also been heavily criticized for the "big game" he plays with unwieldy large concepts such as "civilization," although he is often much more subtle than he has been given credit for. Nevertheless, Huntington does show that the struggle for a new world order has religion at its very heart. Religion is central to the contemporary era of world politics.

According to Huntington, the world can be carved up into nine blocks denoting nine different civilizations: Western, Latin American, African, Islamic, Sinic, Hindu, Orthodox, Buddhist, and Japanese. Four of these are evidently religious blocks, and this is not insignificant, for Huntington views cultural roots as much more fundamental than the economic, political, or social expressions of these roots—and religion is one of the most profound informants of cultural diversity. In what is both a highly controversial and a contestable statement, Huntington asserts, "The underlying problem for the West is not Islamic fundamentalism. It is Islam, a different civilization whose people are con-

63. Talal Asad, "Secularism, Nation-State, Religion," in *Formations of the Secular: Christianity, Islam, Modernity* (Stanford, CA: Stanford University Press, 2003), 182.

64. Take, e.g., his view that India's future lies neither with China nor Russia but with the United States (Samuel P. Huntington, *The Clash of Civilizations and the Remaking of World Order* [New York: Simon & Schuster, 1996], 244), in the light of the recent bilateral nuclear-arms agreement (see *Economist*, August 4–18, 2007, 11–12). It is a pity, however, that the administration of George W. Bush did not heed Huntington's warning that core states should avoid intervening in conflicts with other civilizations, that such interventions would be highly destabilizing for world order (Huntington, *Clash of Civilizations*, 316).

vinced of the superiority of their culture and are obsessed with the inferiority of their power. The problem for Islam is not the CIA or the U.S. Department of Defense. It is the West, a different civilization whose people are convinced of the universality of their culture and believe that their superior, if declining, power imposes on them the obligation to extend that culture throughout the world."[65] This is pre-9/11 rhetoric that is as reductive and brutal as it is honest. But when we understand, as Huntington clearly does, that the West is defined by its Judeo-Christian tradition, we see that the clashes Huntington is registering and predicting are fundamentally religious. This becomes more evident in his chapter devoted to outlining the new global politics, because, of the nine civilizations, the African and the Latin American, he admits, are de facto irrelevant (although in recent trends in Christian expansionism, both move more toward what Huntington calls "bandwagoning" on the West rather than anything else). There are three important swing states: Japan, India (the most important Hindu block), and Russia (which Huntington believes heads up a civilization rooted in Orthodox teaching).[66] He does not treat at this point the Buddhist as a separate traditional culture, and so the three remaining are the Western (defined by its Judeo-Christian heritage), the Sinic (defined by its predominantly Confucian heritage), and the Islamic.[67]

When we view these civilizations as products of specific religious cultures, it is significant that the religions themselves transcend geopolitical borders, that the neat maps of the distinctive landmasses that Huntington provides are woefully inadequate.[68]

65. Huntington, *Clash of Civilizations*, 217–18.

66. His thinking here about Christianity is very vague indeed. Protestant, Catholic, and Jewish traditions all inform Western civilization, but Orthodoxy remains distinctly Slavic.

67. Huntington, *Clash of Civilizations*. "At the broadest level the Confucian ethos pervading many Asian societies stressed the values of authority, hierarchy, the subordination of individual rights and interests, the importance of consensus, the avoidance of confrontation, 'saving face,' and, in general, the supremacy of the state over society and of society over the individual" (225).

68. Ibid., 22–26. This level of generalization seems inconsistent with Huntington's opening pages, where he points out the transnational identities that are forming in the post-cold-war era, and with his comment that "in the contemporary world, cultural identification is dramatically increasing in importance compared to other dimensions of identity" (128).

Although Huntington goes on to discuss the frictions along the fault lines, he pays less attention to how the religious bases of these civilizations establish global networks disassociated with landmasses. The Middle East may be the location of fundamental pilgrimage sites for Islam, but there are strong Islamic cultures in Indonesia and Pakistan, Bosnia and Nigeria. The wealth of Arab countries such as Saudi Arabia, which enables them to support Islamic movements in different parts of the world, does not mean that the Arab world has a monopoly on Islam. Indeed, there are substantial Islamic cultures across Europe, most notably in Britain, France, and Germany. Similarly, Christianity (or Judaism) is a diaspora religion that takes hybrid forms as it adapts itself to local histories and social conditions. A friend of mine collects crucifixes from around the world, and the cultural variance in the representation of Christ on the cross is astonishing. The point here is that Huntington's thesis predicts that the future clash of civilizations will occur at what he terms "fault-line wars" that accord with religious traditions: "Since religion, however, is the principle defining characteristic of civilizations, fault-line wars will almost always occur between people of different religions."[69] But in fact religion may be the hope for the making of a new world order rather than the dry tinder awaiting ignition, for it is nations that go to war, allied with other nations, and these religions transcend nationalities.[70] The old European wars of religion (which were Christian wars between Catholics and Protestants) were territorial wars between fledgling nation-states flexing their autonomous muscle. There will not be wars of religion again like those wars because the major religions are no longer bound to territory and the rule of *cuius regio, eius religio*. Furthermore, what unites the faithful communities of these different religious traditions is a common enemy—the godlessness of cultures driven by secular ideals, capitalist rapaciousness, decadent levels of wast-

69. Ibid., 253.

70. In the closing pages of *Clash of Civilizations*, Huntington alerts us to this possibility very briefly. He points out that the major religions of the world have much in common in terms of shared values. "If humans are ever to develop a universal civilization, it will emerge gradually through the exploration and expansion of these commonalities" (320). I would argue that we need to have as a telos some "universal civilization" (echoes of the Enlightenment dreams of Hume and Kant for universal peace) in order for religious cooperation to become the bearer of new hopes.

age, and a hypocrisy that points to the abuse of human rights abroad and closes its eyes to the inadequate provision for the socially vulnerable at home. Chapter 7 will say more about the hope that the new visibility of religion suggests for a different kind of world order.

It is, then, interesting to observe, when the religious once again enters the public domain and questions "secular neutrality," who is making it visible, why, and what the effects are. The following are two concrete examples. First, at a time when the European Community was discussing whether its Christian legacy needed to be protected in some way, political leaders were affirming the specific religious character of the direction their nations were taking. Although Tony Blair, in a dialogue with Christian evangelicals, stated that faith should be involved in public works but distinct from government as such,[71] he nevertheless resorted to a theological argument for the justification of his decision to send Britain into Iraq: God would be the judge of his private decision to enter what is the public of all actions, war. And both George H. W. Bush and George W. Bush explicitly spoke about the Christian convictions that guided their political decisions. George W. Bush regularly used a messianic rhetoric to describe the role that the United States needs to play in international affairs.[72] The three televised debates between George W. Bush and John Kerry before the presidential election in November 2005 focused on key issues, all of which—whether abortion, the use of stem cells, or the war in Iraq—were inseparable from religious issues. Explicit questions regarding their personal faith were, then, apposite. What is significant, given the outcome, is that Bush drew attention to the strong correlation between his religious practices and sovereign action, his prayer life and his decisions. Kerry, though informing

71. See Blair, speech to Faithworks. Joseph M. Knippenberg of the Ashbrook Center for Public Affairs at Ashland University, Ohio, points to differences between the speeches of George W. Bush and Blair. While both talk about community, Bush is more theological and Blair more sociological. Furthermore, there is a striking absence of biblical references in Blair's speech.

72. As seen earlier (see chap. 1), this is not new. Imperialist nations—nations with a desire to be *the* dominating world power—have frequently employed religious language about a divine destiny to drive home their ambitions for the civilized world, whether those ambitions are for territory or for resources such as oil. The only difference here is the frequency and consistency of George W. Bush's references.

the public of his Catholicism, said exactly the opposite. Repeating a formula first used by John F. Kennedy, he said that he would not be a Catholic president but a president who happened to be Catholic. He rehearsed a liberal line, so that Bush drew the support of important and influential Catholic bishops rather than Kerry. There is a politics of making religion visible in which neoconservative religion, both Protestant and Catholic, is allied to neoliberal economics. It is not, then, only Muslim countries that are declaring their religious allegiances.

The second example is the obverse of the first but just as ideological. In France, *laïcité*—what Jacques Chirac termed "the principle of secularism"—was not coined until 1903, in a law concerned with the abolition of religious education in state schools. The law forbade the placing of religious symbols in public places, including graveyards, and ended financial or political support from the government to religious groups (this meant, in effect, Catholics). This law followed the closure of most Catholic schools in France by Prime Minister Emile Combes. But the law lay dormant until after 9/11, when, in 2003, the French government commissioned the *Stasi Report* concerning the application of *laïcité* in France. This report made the recommendations that have caused so much international trouble since. The revisions to the law turned the international spotlight on the Muslims of France, making the public visibility of wearing the veil even more public. The Muslim population in France, as in Germany, is due to economic policies inviting guest workers to become the new working class of European society. France has the largest such population, and the state, far from being neutral, now moved to legislate for civil society. Two observations need to be made here. First, this was an antidemocratic and antiliberal move, for the liberal-democratic state is supposedly there to safeguard civil society, not to impinge on its liberties, notably the liberties of those with a religious conscience. Second, the appeal to the law of *laïcité* made visible the sectarianism and therefore the ideology of "the principle of secularism" itself. It made manifest that such liberalism is hegemonic. In what might be better termed a clash of ideologies, the cry went up that such secular neutrality was really a form of racism. So there is a question of both the economics and the politics of this deprivatization, even new confessionalism (and those who challenge it).

Religion and Culture

The third form of the visibility of religion is the most pervasive, and yet it is little analyzed by pro- and antisecularization researchers. I have given various names to this visibility: the "commodification of religion" (drawing on analyses by Marx of the processes of reification and fetishism associated with the cultural dominance of capitalism)[73] and "religion as special effect."[74] As a phenomenon it relates both to Huntington's recognition that culture becomes the important domain for attaining a sense of oneself in the post-cold-war world and that religion is one of the roots of culture and to Daniel's Bell's distinction between techno-economic secularism and cultural secularism. As already noted, it was Bell who predicted the religious resurgence in the cultural domain, although he did not see its huge commercial value. There will be "a return to some mythic and mystical modes of thought. The world has become too scientistic and drab. Men want a sense of wonder and mystery." Bell concluded, "The power of myth is beginning to reassert itself."[75] This cultural reassertion is the greatest single source of the desecularization or resacralization of the West. It is related to several trajectories we have already uncovered: a more general reenchantment of the real, a return to the mythic and the supernatural, a hastening dematerialization, the increasing virtuality of the real, and the deepening mystification by many people about the complex scientific workings of quite ordinary things such as computers.

This multifaceted phenomenon that we can call religious because it either treats a religious theme or invokes a religious or quasi-religious experience (of mystery, of the limits of what can be understood, of the hidden and unknown) cannot be divorced from globalization and the teletechnologies that make this possible. In other words, this reenchantment is not simply the reversal of Weber's famous disenchantment thesis. It is the advance of the technological, instrumental reasoning that constructed Weber's iron cage, which is now allowing us to see that the bars are all

73. See Graham Ward, "The Commodification of Religion, or the Consummation of Capitalism," in *Theology and the Political: The New Debate*, ed. Creston Davis, John Milbank, and Slavoj Žižek (Durham, NC: Duke University Press, 2005), 327–39.

74. See Graham Ward, *True Religion* (Oxford: Blackwell, 2003), 114–53.

75. Bell, "Return of the Sacred?" 445, 446.

within our own minds; reality is liquid and malleable. Another way to put it is that culture based on the universalist dreams of unfettered consumer freedoms, bound to the unpredictable but inevitable destinies of vast and virtual flows of currency speculation, will necessarily produce a market in spirituality. The religiosity of the market, treated in the last chapter, reflects on itself in the commercialization of religion, the manufacture of religion as a special effect.

Although the French political scientist Marcel Gauchet could write in 1985 about "the disappearance of enchanters and powerful supernatural beings,"[76] the cultural scene since has been overpopulated with enchanters from Gandalf to Harry Potter and with whole armies of angels and demons, vampires, ghosts, and superheros. Zygmunt Bauman is not the first to write about the "reenchantment" of the postmodern world.[77] Others have written about the reawakening of the gothic imagination,[78] a neoromanticism,[79] and, as we have seen, postsecularity. From Hollywood films representing the afterlife—for example, *Gladiator*, *Titanic*, and *American Beauty*—to the phenomenal success of *The Da Vinci Code* and the names of local bars and shops (in Manchester, England, alone) such as the Font, Gaia, the Eighth Day, and the Parting of the Waves, religion does not live in and of itself anymore. It lives in commercial business, gothic and sci-fi fantasy, health clubs, theme bars, and architectural design and among happy-hour drinkers, tattooists,

76. Marcel Gauchet, *The Disenchantment of the World: A Political History of Religion*, trans. Oscar Burge (Princeton, NJ: Princeton University Press, 1997), 3. Gauchet does, however, admit the continuing metaphysical and ethical implications of the Christian religion for the political ordering of the world (see pp. 86–87), and he follows this up in Marcel Gauchet, *La religion dans la démocratie parcours de la laïcité* (Paris: Gallimard, 1998); and "Fin de la religion?" "Sur la religion," and "Croyances religieuses, croyances politiques," in *La démocratie contre elle-même* (Paris: Gallimard, 2002), 27–66, 67–90, and 91–108, respectively.

77. See Bauman, *Intimations of Postmodernity*, and more recently Gordon Graham, *The Re-Enchantment of the World: Art versus Religion* (Oxford: Oxford University Press, 2007).

78. For a wider discussion of the contemporary Gothic, see Mark Edmundson, *Nightmare on Main Street: Angels, Sadomasochism, and the Culture of the Gothic* (Cambridge, MA: Harvard University Press, 1997); Karen Haltunnen, *Murder Most Foul: The Killer and the American Gothic* (Cambridge, MA: Harvard University Press, 1998); and Fred Bolting, *The Gothic* (London: D.S. Brewer, 2002), 101–17.

79. See Peter Woodcock, *This Enchanted Isle: The Neo-Romantic Vision from William Blake to the New Visionaries* (London: Gothic Image Publications, 2000).

ecologists, and cyberpunks. Religion has become a special effect, inseparably bound to an entertainment value.

We could examine this phenomenon more closely through different forms of entertainment—film, television programs, the plastic arts, architecture, advertising—and any short guide to the postsecular condition would have to do this. A well-known example is the Harry Potter series, in books by J. K. Rowling; films directed by a host of talents, such as Chris Columbus; video games; and assorted retail products. The astounding success of the Hogwarts fantasies will influence a whole generation, and not just in Britain and America but worldwide. Indeed, the impact of the books upon literacy levels across the world is already evident, with four hundred million copies sold by 2007. However much they are profoundly products of a very British imagination, their translations into sixty-four languages (again, by 2007) points to a global hunger not for some sci-fi parallel universe in which utopian desires find their fulfillment but for an alternative way of seeing the world in which we live. The copies sold have made Rowling one of the richest women alive and a serious competitor to the queen for the richest woman in Britain. If the copies were stacked on top of one another, they would be higher than Mount Everest.

The plot for all seven volumes of Harry Potter remained in a bank vault during the time of their writing. Ten million pounds were spent on security when the final, seventh book, *Harry Potter and the Deathly Hallows*, was in warehouses awaiting the day of its publication. That day, July 21, 2007, began at midnight in thousands of bookshops and stores across Britain with Harry Potter parties crowded not just with children but parents, teenagers, and twenty-year-olds caught between the pubs and the clubs, all wanting to put their hands on the first copies. In the United States, the first print run was a staggering twelve million copies, following the sales prediction after volume 6, *Harry Potter and the Half-Blood Prince*, sold nine million copies in the first twenty-four hours. The Harry Potter series calls out for a detailed investigation as a social and cultural phenomenon, for this level of social and cultural success cannot be reduced to an existential angst concerning the breakdown of, and the nostalgic longing for, tradition. Seen more positively, it accords with a desire that subtends the cultural imaginary, a desire that subsequently translates itself into various institutional forms (including a projected theme park in Orlando due to open in 2009). It is a desire that is not limited to children, for there are two editions of each book, one aimed specifically at the adult market. I suggest that part of the naming of this desire can be captured in descriptors such as "postsecularity."

I am not attempting that detailed analysis of the Harry Potter phenomenon here, but religion will play a dominant role in such an examination, for it is right at the heart of a seven-year-long story about transcendent darkness and goodness, transfiguration and betrayal, error, sacrifice, forgiveness, and grace. And the liberal secularists are portrayed throughout mainly as rather stupid, petty-minded, fearful, self-indulgent, and frequently cruel bourgeois Muggles. Although some Muggles do cross the line—for example, Hermione Granger—take up their wands and cauldrons, and step onto platform nine and three quarters at King's Cross station for a journey into the supernatural. There is no doubt in these books where reality lies—with the world of magic, even if this world is divided between the dark arts, which wish to persecute and victimize the Muggle world, and the magical practices of hope and goodness, which do not wish to redeem the Muggle world but certainly want to protect it in some sense.[80] This is not simply a one-way exchange, for Hermione Granger's championship of the marginalized and oppressed (werewolves, giants, and house-elves) acts as a vehicle for modernity's critique of a gothic feudalism still dominant in the world of magic.

Taking the Harry Potter phenomenon and other prominent examples of popular culture (the box office success of the *Lord of the Rings* trilogy, the publishing, staging, and filming of Philip Pullman's *Dark Materials* trilogy) as prime illustrations of the resurgence of the mythological does not necessarily suggest what Habermas called the threat of the "possibility of a relapse into neo-paganism."[81] Admittedly, there are analogues between this remythologization and that found in numerous cybergames, online

80. In what sense is not very clear. The consequences of Harry Potter's ongoing battle with Lord Voldemort for the Muggle world are not developed, although, after the third novel, *Harry Potter and the Prisoner of Azkaban* (in which there is mention of an exchange between the British prime minister and the minister for magic), the two worlds draw closer. The threat of Lord Voldemort to the Muggle world opens the fifth novel, *Harry Potter and the Order of the Phoenix*, in which Harry lies listening to the news on television, waiting for the evil of the Dark Lord to manifest itself publicly.

81. Habermas, *Religion and Rationality*, 159.

cults, New Age spirituality, goddess worship, kabbalah bracelets, and ecoreligiosity. But the Harry Potter phenomenon and others cannot be reduced to neopaganism. Certainly much of the material expresses a gnostic worldview. Nevertheless we have to recognize the Judeo-Christian elements that are also prominent in this cultural imaginary.

Central to the thematic development of the Harry Potter series are notions of transfiguration and resurrection, forgiveness and sacrificial love, messianic deliverance, death and the apocalyptic, the destruction of the soul, feasting and the celebration of fellowship, and the overcoming of death. Pace Rowling herself, who states that the main theme of the novels is death, the attention given to half-bloods (e.g., Harry), Mudbloods (e.g., Hermione), and purebloods and the fascination with the inventiveness of the Muggle world (e.g., Mr. Weasley) make the central motif the mediation between the spiritual and the carnal—a central incarnational value. A protective grace, even providence (often associated with the figure of Professor Dumbledore, the headmaster of Hogwarts, though not entirely), operates on behalf of Harry. So, beneath the frothing brew of charms and potions there lies a strong Christian flavor. Hogwarts is modeled on the British public-school system (indeed, Harry's Muggle antitype, Dudley Dursley, attends such a public school), and although this school, unlike other British public schools, does not have a chapel, a monastic atmosphere emanates from the ancient stones and staircases. The temporal framework of the school year governs each of the books. Halloween is a key feast day within that year, but All Hallows' Eve is also an important liturgical event in the Christian church calendar. Other feast days include the two most important for Christianity—Christmas and Easter—with a Good Friday reference thrown in by having all adventures (bar the last one) start at King's Cross. Furthermore, there is a certain sacramentalism about the world of Harry Potter, with a number of key characters situated at the border between the secular world and the enchanted and with familiar plants and herbs imbued with health-giving analogical properties.

The same Judeo-Christian elements, though not the liturgical year, can be found in the *Lord of the Rings* trilogy. Indeed, it is well known that J. R. R. Tolkien was a committed Roman Catholic. What is different about the Harry Potter septet is that the stories are not set either in the remote and mythic past (as with Tolkien) or in a parallel universe reached through a wardrobe (as with C. S. Lewis). This enchanted world folds into and out of the mundane; it is a countersecular world that at its best is governed by generosity and communal sharing mapped on to this one. Furthermore, secularism, figured as the fear of magic among Muggles such as the Dursleys, is viewed as a pathology—a pathology with which the minister for magic, Cornelius Fudge, colludes in *Harry Potter and the Order of the Phoenix*. In other words, there are not two worlds in the Harry Potter series, only two ways of seeing, experiencing, and living the one reality.

The strong Judeo-Christian elements found in the series parallel other forms of contemporary culture that allude to the same tradition—from Diesel's[82] 2004 advertising campaign set around the notion of sin and the GHD 2007 hair styler advertising campaign focused around logos such as "Thou shalt be saved" and "Thou shalt convert" to the current fascination with angels and television dramas that accept the paranormal as a given.[83] Sociologists, then, need to be more subtle not only about the characterizations and dismissals of current "neopaganism" and gnosticism but about what data are being utilized to uphold the prevalence of secularism. The Christian notion of the *sacramentum mundi* can often bear some relation to what might be termed paganism; witness the herb-gathering Friar Lawrence in Shakespeare's *Romeo and Juliet* and how some of the most revered Christian theologians, including Augustine, have been charged with gnostic tendencies.

What is culturally evident is that although certain philosophers of both the analytical and the Continental traditions speak loudly about the postmetaphysical, contemporary living is shot through with metaphysical themes, desires, and dreams. One might even write of a renaissance of the metaphysical rather than the new visibility of religion—though at the risk of diluting religious faith into philosophical categories. (Chapter 5 will treat some of the ways this metaphysics is written into the fabric of our global cites.)

This cultural face of contemporary religion, which has its origins in Western markets but is disseminated globally, plays two mutu-

82. Diesel is an up-market, high-end fashion retailer.

83. See Graham Ward, "Cities of Angels," chap. 8, in *Cities of God* (London: Routledge, 2000), 205–24.

ally implicated roles. On the one hand, as symbolic capital with a certain charismatic past, it can give places, goods, and even people a mystic charge. Those allured by this charge are not buying religion; they are not consuming the religious or being consumed by it. They are consuming the illusions or simulations of religion. On the other hand, these simulations of religion, religion as symbolic capital, are employed as an aesthetic diversion from the profound uncertainties, insecurities, and indeterminacies of postmodern living. The religious is used rhetorically in the creation of the illusions of transcendence to help simulate euphoria in transporting events. This is in synchronism with the religious eschatology of globalism itself. But it cannot be reduced to it.

The new commodification of religion is not simply an economic matter, for economic matters cannot be disassociated from political and social matters in a capitalist democracy. There are two ways in which this commodification—and the subsequent remythologization of the Western imagination—is political. First, as we have learned from the work of the Frankfurt School, these cultural artifacts are not simply products (mirror reflections); they are producers (they transform the cultural or social imagination). They are "technologies" implicated in social processes that change the nature of our perception, our senses of space and time, our appreciation of the visible and the invisible, our understandings of what the world is and what it is to be human in such a world. Thus they must be treated as political, cultural, and imaginative apparatuses that govern not just our bodies (certain physical shapes are desired and others not) but also our minds. These technologies, which are also the technologies that have nurtured economic globalism, structure our dreaming and desiring. Second, tied to consumerism and related to the dramatic rise in eclectic customized spiritualities, they continue to foster "zero degree dialectic."[84] Where there is no dialectic, where there is the continual suspension of judgment, and where the citizen as customer or client is merely requested to be satisfied with the services provided, there is rampant depoliticization that endangers democracy, there is self-determined disenfranchisement in favor of leisure, a personal lifestyle, and entertainment. Dialectic means

84. Antonio Negri, *Time for Revolution*, trans. Matteo Mandarini (New York: Continuum, 2003), 41. See chap. 1, above.

discussion, and politically, "where there is no discussion there is dictatorship."[85]

Conclusion

The threefold typology is heuristic only,[86] but taken together, these three prominent forms of the new visibility of religion demonstrate the ways in which religion is currently dominating the public sphere at all levels. So, what of all the talk about the postsecular condition, and what is its relationship to the postmodern condition?

During the last three decades, Continental philosophy, critical theory, and cultural studies have grown familiar with the suffix "post-": "poststructuralism," "postmodernity," "postindustrialism," "postmaterialism," and "postsecularity." What does this linguistic phenomenon tell us about our contemporary cultural condition? Adding "post-" to an abstract noun does not render that noun more descriptive. It suggests a cultural and historical shift with respect to structuralism, modernity, industrialism, and secularity. A much thicker account can be given, for example, of the displacements of industrial production from onetime dominant locations in Europe and the United States to much cheaper industrial locations in China and Indonesia and of the development of service and information industries in their place. Still, on the whole, "post-" does not help us characterize accurately the contents of this shift or the other shifts in structuralism, modernity, materialism, and secularity. In other words, the use of

85. Carl Schmitt, *Political Theology: Four Chapters on the Concept of Sovereignty*, trans. George Schwab (Cambridge, MA: MIT Press, 1985), 78.

86. Christian theologians may be somewhat surprised that I have not included here what has come to be called "public theology," which has its most recent origins in liberal, correlational theology and was greatly inspired by the Latin American liberation theologians. The practices of public theology have played a significant role in bringing to the attention of governments the welfare and justice issues of their citizens. It is understood variously as "practical theology" or "social and pastoral theology" and is engaged in a whole range of ethical debates. It is not included here because (a) it has not gained greater visibility since its emergence from Christian socialism and, in fact, may have declined, and (b) it is not strongly theological in its public face, for its concerns are primarily ethical and its practices supplement (which is important) declining governmental welfare services.

"post-" betrays something of a linguistic bankruptcy. It politely disguises a certain embarrassment and ambivalence in the human and social sciences.

Given this linguistic inadequacy, what can we say regarding "postsecularity," since none of the named purveyors of postsecularism (Derrida, Vattimo, Habermas, Taylor, et al.) give detailed descriptions of how they understand this condition or what it signifies? This question is especially pertinent because the notion of "secularity" is, as seen earlier in this chapter, still describing an allusive entity and its historical and cultural provenance is unclear. Is it rationalization, scientism, religious tolerance, religious indifference, methodological atheism, agnosticism, ideological neutrality, or a combination of some or all of these? What cultural condition, then, does the term "postsecularity" describe when the consensus on what constitutes the secular condition is still debatable?[87] Are we talking about "secularization as differentiation of the secular spheres from religious institutions and norms, secularization as the decline of religious beliefs and practices [or] secularization as the marginalization of religion to a privatized sphere"?[88] According to Casanova's argument, and Huntington's thesis would bear him out, the trajectory of secularization in the last two instances does appear to be reversing. "Post-" would, then, in their characterizations of secularization, describe the cultural conditions after secularization, a movement beyond it. But so much depends on the analyses of the relationship of religion, society, and culture between (for the sake of argument) the decade following the Second World War and the late 1980s, and perhaps earlier, as we have seen. So much depends on what is being counted in these analyses, and who is doing the counting. A shift is evident; the labels for the shift need further investigation.

87. McLennan, "Towards Postsecular Sociology?" observes that "['postsecular'] need not automatically signal *anti*-secularism, or what comes *after* or *instead of* secularism. For many the key postsecular move is simply to question and probe the concept of the secular, and to re-interrogate the whole 'faith versus reason' problematic that has so consistently punctuated modern thought" (859). This definition of "postsecularity" as a questioning and probing of the secular, however, is too weak. We are not here treating a skepticism about a sociological notion but new modes of believing itself, new conditions for, and structures of, believing that allow objects of belief once thought obsolete to reappear.

88. Casanova, *Public Religions*, 211.

In the meantime, what relationship might this shift in secularity have to the postmodern condition? As noted, the transformations in democracy, globalization, materialism, the new visibility of religion, and the postmodern condition are all phenomena making their appearance in the 1970s. We cannot, then, isolate one phenomenon from the others and speak simply of causes and effects. Furthermore, as Casanova holds, if certain aspects of the secularization thesis no longer fit the evidence, so that some wish to speak of postsecularity, much secularity still remains that is important operationally to handling what are now very complex multicultural, multifaith societies. Likewise, although the postmodern condition ironizes the project of modernity, the project of modernity is not yet over: rationalization, specialization, and instrumentalization are key economic and political tropes. Modernity still has a complicated and intricate relationship to postmodernity, as secularity has to postsecularity.

Nevertheless, insofar as the postmodern condition was, according to at least Fredric Jameson, Harvey, and the more left-wing cultural interpreters, intrinsically related to "late capitalism" and insofar as it is associated with the eclectic, the surface, the virtual, the fanciful, the spectacular, then the new cultural visibility of religion, religion as special effect, can be related to postmodernity. The critique of Enlightenment reasoning as a universal in the name of differends, difference, aporia, *khora*s, brios, ambiguities, hybridities, instabilities, ruptures, radical exteriorities, and rhizomes could not but have an impact on what was at the foreground of Enlightenment rationalism: a critique of religion and the establishment of a self-authenticating public sphere. As already mentioned, some of the most prominent postmodern thinkers themselves took a religious turn.[89] More recently, important left-wing thinkers such as Terry Eagleton, Alain Badiou, Žižek, and Giorgio Agamben (see chap. 4, below) have explicitly returned to religious discourse as a source for political radicalism and intervention. Postmodernism, then, opened the way for, if it was not actually a response to, multiculturalism, an aspect of globalization. It expressed the apotheosis of laissez-faire (and so continuing one of the themes of modernity)—a hyperindividual-

89. See Graham Ward, *Theology and Contemporary Critical Theory*, 2nd ed. (Basingstoke, UK: Macmillan, 2000).

ist expressivism drawn as much to myth and mysticism as to the kitsch and the eclectic.

But there are elements of the new visibility of religion that do not correlate easily with the postmodern condition, other than as a possible reaction to its worst excesses. Contemporary fundamentalisms, for example, or even the deprivatization of religion, might be viewed as forms of resistance to rampant relativism and the liquidation of specific traditions. Postmodernity's religion is softer, more fluid, evasive, playful, narcissistic—closer to New Age spirituality, Gaia worship, Scientology, religions outside traditional frameworks. Luckmann famously examined this phenomenon as it emerged in the 1960s as "invisible religion."[90] Culturally, such a religion is pervasive but not entirely. Postmodernity's religion was not about discipline, sacrifice, obedience, and the development of virtue.[91] It was more related to the spiritualizing of human subjectivity. It was an intensification of the privatization of religion and so in step with one of the main themes of modernity. But there are aspects of the new visibility of religion that resonate with the return of the king, zero-tolerance policing, the biopolitics that keep public health and the stigmatizing of obesity high on political agendas, and the vociferous demands for public order and responsible citizenship. The Westerners who turn to Buddhism, Hinduism, and Opus Dei; the four million who crowded into the streets of Rome for the funeral of John Paul II; the middle-class South Koreans who pass through five or six megachurch services on a Sunday like the drive throughs of fast-food chains—they want the disciplines and structures of a spiritual trainer in a religious gym. They do not want pop transcendence but the real thing.

This suggests that postmodernity is running out of steam; like capitalism of late, it is experiencing a credit squeeze. Or perhaps it is being forced to be ever more apocalyptic, self-destructive. The developing ethos of fear and surveillance, the ever-increasing signs of climate change, and the massive global effects this will inevitably have on migration patterns and demographics are making the

90. Thomas Luckmann, *Invisible Religion* (New York: Macmillan, 1967).

91. These are key elements in the Harry Potter series. Indeed, Harry's journey through the seven books (and the journeys of his companions Ron and Hermione) might best be understood in terms of a sentimental education in the development of a mixture of Greek and Christian virtues, such as loyalty, courage, perseverance, temperance, patience, benevolence, humility, justice, and fortitude.

postmodern dalliance with relativism and nihilism decadent. The euphoria over the superficial and the kitsch is sobering up—going into rehab—and the more decisionist democracies are demanding new disciplines, new obediences, new belong-or-suffer-the-consequences forms of behavior. Postmodernity's only enemies were monolithic reason and standardization, and even these were not castigated, only resituated, recited in destabilizing, nonstandard contexts, such as Marcel Duchamp's famous toilet in an art museum. But the enemies are being named more frequently now. The challenges that this naming raises for Christian discipleship will take up the rest of this volume.

SECTION 2

THE CHURCH

4

Theological Introduction

What can we learn from the preceding analyses of where we are culturally in the West? Let me make two points. First, the four dominant cultural trends—the postdemocratic, globalization, postmaterialism, and the new visibility of religion—are profoundly related to and implicated in a fifth trend, postmodernity. The new profile for religion affords an opportunity for the practitioners of faith to speak out in what remains of the public sphere, not just for what they believe in but also—and perhaps more important—against the cultural impulses that challenge and compromise the tenets of that faith. For there is no mistake to be made here: these cultural trends define what St. Paul would call the principalities and powers against which Christians must wrestle (Eph. 6:12). The situation also makes demands on believers because in the mists of religion and pseudospirituality that are now arising and passing down Main Street—bookshops selling such titles as *A Quiet Belief in Angels*, advertising hoardings, store chains such as Britain's All Saints, and brands of fragrance such as Eternity, Euphoria, and Truth—discernment is needed in trying to distinguish the authentic from the fake when there is no immediate access to what people are hungering for. In this discernment, it is not the resistance to commodification that will help—for commodification is inevitable while capitalism still remains—but resistance to the reductions of materialism. Postmaterialism is helpful here, but as we saw, it needs

to be securely anchored in something more than market trends and individual lifestyle options.

Second, along with the new opportunities and demands for those practitioners of piety in the public sphere, there will have to be the recognition that it will not be just Christians making such public proclamations. People from other faiths and people from no faith perspective at all will stand up for what they believe.[1] But difference must be heard, must be articulated, because the vitality of the public sphere depends on this. And the vitality of the public sphere challenges one of the major social trends we have observed: depoliticization. We need, then, more contestation and something much deeper than liberal tolerance—for example, a theologically grounded respect for the human person. Such a theological grounding would deepen postmaterialist inclinations. I recall a visit to the monastery in Sergiev Posad, Russia. Standing in a room thick with incense and the smell of lit candles, I participated in a mass that was being sung. A deep bass voice was intoning the Orthodox liturgy. Swinging a bejeweled thurible, a deacon draped in a gilded vestment approached the laity. Three times he swung the thurible, enveloping us in a perfumed cloud. And then he offered one low, slow bow to the people before him. A friend whispered, "He bows to the image of God in you." We bowed in reply. It did not matter what my past or my present circumstances were, what sins of commission or omission I might have committed. All that mattered was that being human was profoundly sacred not just in and for itself but because it figured forth the divine. "To detract from the creature's perfection is to detract from the perfection of divine power."[2] Let us not, then, be afraid of public contestation; rather, let us seek ways in which it is rooted not in liberalistic humanism but in the profound respect for the image of God in all of us that the Orthodox liturgy enacts. (Chapter 5 will provide for this anthropology a theological framework in terms of the relationship between eschatology and ecclesiology, and chapter

1. In response to the resurgence of religion, academic atheists have recently staged a well-publicized campaign, winning critical acclaim. See Richard Dawkins, *The God Delusion* (London: Transworld, 2006); Daniel C. Dennett, *Breaking the Spell: Religion as a Natural Phenomenon* (London: Viking, 2006); and Christopher Hitchens, *God Is Not Great: How Religion Poisons Everything* (New York: Atlantic Books, 2007).

2. Thomas Aquinas, *The Summa Contra Gentiles*, trans. English Dominican Fathers (London: Burns, Oakes & Washbourne, 1928).

6 will develop this anthropology in more detail.) Key to the interventionist politics I am announcing in this book is something I wish to call eschatological humanism, which provides the body (in its many material forms) with a metaphysics.

If more contestation is needed and if there is a necessary wrestling with principalities and powers, then, following Schmitt, the reassertion of the political begins with a naming of the enemy. The analyses presented in the first section on "The World" allow us to begin this naming process. The enemy is hydra-headed. First is depoliticization as we move toward a world of entertainment, amusement, and a superficial aesthetics (see chap. 7, below). Then there is dematerialization as we move toward increasingly pervasive virtual realities that facilitate a certain cultural amnesia toward production costs. This is closely related to the rampant commodification of all goods and values, including goods and values specifically associated with traditional faiths. These three trends are associated with a dogmatic secularism, which, even though its progressive thesis is being challenged and a new remythologization of the real is taking place, still insists on the godlessness of the world, the arbitrariness of creation, and the Promethean ability of human beings to order, discipline, and control.[3] Finally, there is the perpetuation of the myth of the infinite freedom of hyperindividuals, liquid subjectivities that erode social and shared responsibilities in favor of a centrifugal atomism. These many heads belong to one body, a body whose name may elude us but whose lineaments can be traced in the interrelatedness of these trends.

At the same time, there are elements that can build toward practices of hope. First is the liberation of religion from private conviction, which—although it may be open to political manipulation—has facilitated, for example, effective diplomatic mediation. The increasing role of the Vatican in world diplomacy and the work of the Council of Christians and Jews and the Muslim Council of Great Britain can be taken as signs of this trend. Second is the appeal to a new postmaterialism in politics (see chaps. 2 and 6). Third is the return to the importance of myth. This is crucial because the institutions we construct and the values they espouse

3. In his magisterial history *A Secular Age* (London: Belknap Press of Harvard University Press, 2007), Charles Taylor describes this as "exclusive humanism" or "self-sufficing humanism" (see 19–21, 26–28, 636–42).

and promulgate are closely related to the cultural imaginary.[4] Our ideas are informed by a molten core of imagined possibilities that the cultures we inhabit furnish. This imaginary opens a space for what is possible. From these possibilities new institutions arise; for example, the creative and imaginative energies of the Harry Potter series develop new industries and productions (see chap. 3, above). Religious practices in a secular age are concerned with changing the cultural imaginary—that is, rereading and rewriting what appears to be the case in ways that are both critical and constructive. In a time of remythologization, new beliefs become believable as the conditions for believing, the structures of believing, change.

In the first decade of the twentieth century, Sorel developed a highly influential account of the imaginative power of myth. He expanded the view of myth to include images and narratives of heroes, ideals to die for, revolutions, missions for utopian kingdoms of eternal peace, homogeneities (national or ethnic), gnostic battles between good and evil, apocalyptic struggles between civilizations, and—perhaps most terrifying and fascinating of all—war, conquest, and expansion or the obverse, holocaust and infinite, inconceivable suffering.[5] The politics of cultural transformation is inseparable from both the critical deconstruction of certain prevailing myths and alternative mythmaking. Sorel sought to understand what needs made the belief in such myths believable. For Sorel, "Myth arises from peoples' need for faith and vivid objects of the imagination in order to commit themselves to great collectives causes potentially involving personal sacrifice."[6] For him, myth was a historical force whose power lay partly in the nature of human weakness. It is able to move the masses deeply if it is believed. "As long as there are no myths accepted by the masses, one may go on talking of revolts indefinitely without ever

4. In my analysis of the cultural imaginary in Graham Ward, *Cultural Transformation and Religious Practice* (Cambridge: Cambridge University Press, 2005), 159–66, I drew on the work of twentieth-century thinkers from Paul Ricoeur to Cornelius Castoriadis.

5. Georges Sorel, *Reflections on Violence*, trans. Jeremy Jennings (Cambridge: Cambridge University Press, 1999), 20–21. He quotes John Henry Newman appreciatively: "What imagination does for us is to find a means of stimulating these motive powers; and it does so by providing a supply of objects strong enough to stimulate them" (28).

6. Christopher Flood, "Myth and Ideology," in *Thinking through Myths: Philosophical Perspectives*, ed. Kevin Schilbrack (London: Routledge, 2002), 186–87.

provoking any revolutionary movement."[7] Myth, then, frames action, inspiring it and giving it a meaning that is not simply arbitrary or pragmatic. We saw this with the myth of globalization in chapter 2. The power of a myth cannot be separated from practices (even violent practices) because it commits the believer to such practices. It commits one to "combat that will destroy the existing state of things."[8] Although a utopian element pertains to myths, they have a life of their own and survive while belief in them remains. And so a "myth cannot be refuted since it is, at bottom, identical to the convictions of a group, being the expression of these convictions in the language of movement."[9] Myth's power to become an imaginative catalyst to act distinguishes it from the intellectual, bourgeois constructions of utopia. Parliamentarism and political liberalism, for Sorel, were "the best examples of a utopia that could be given."[10] Furthermore, myths are aesthetic, for the power of their ideology lies in the "idolatry of words,"[11] in the appeal they make through images to the imagination—to an imagined glory, an imagined heroism or martyrdom. Sorel used "myth" and "legend" as synonyms.

As already noted, the increasing aestheticization of politics and the marketing strategies of multinationals are both concerned with the generation of myths and the production of desirable, vivid objects (see section 1). The success of such myths is measured by people's commitment to them—an existential and financial cost. But it is a cost they are prepared to pay because they need to believe in something. And as also noted, the myths generated by democracy, postdemocracy, and globalization can frequently be traced back to their roots in Christianity. The politics of Christian discipleship is about first unmasking the theological and metaphysical sources of current mythologies and revealing the distortions and perversions of their current secularized forms. Then we need to reread and rewrite the Christian tradition back into contemporary culture. This is already happening in the third form of the new visibility of religion, which employs religious symbols, idioms, and mythemes in films, books, television programs, and advertising.

7. Sorel, *Reflections on Violence*, 28.
8. Ibid., 29.
9. Ibid.
10. Ibid.
11. Ibid., 48.

But this needs to be supplemented by a more informed theological commentary because these symbols, idioms, and mythemes are being disseminated mainly to a public who have grown up through the secularization that occurred after the Second World War. To a large extent, they are unschooled theologically and therefore unable to read, and therefore be critical of, the religious material they are receiving. Hence the need for a reschooling, a rereading and rewriting of the Christian tradition in this instance. This is not done simply by professional theologians (see chap. 5, below). I will argue that this critical and yet constructive activity concerns all the micropractices of Christian living and every public attestation of the truth in Christ. We read and write not only with our eyes, minds, and laptops but with every gesture and muscular inflexion of our bodies. We perform the Christian gospel in every social and cultural engagement, and in these performances we deepen a hopeful trend toward postmaterialism and extend the public role that religion can play in the elaboration of new political, social, and cultural futures.

These performances are the concern of section 2. The following three chapters tackle the many-headed hydra. In particular, they critically challenge aspects of the enemy with theological resources: hyperindividualism (chap. 5), commodification and dematerialization (chap. 6), and depoliticization (chap. 7). These performances are intended as acts of political discipleship. But we need the theological framework within which such performances are intelligible. We need to understand the foundation of any political theology.

A true political theology can commence only with eschatology, for eschatology examines the God of history, the God in history. We can theologize political themes (as the various liberation theologies have). We can use theology to legitimate certain political ideologies (as Eusebius of Caesarea did with respect to the imperial governance of Constantine the Great). We can employ theological categories to critique political ideologies, and even remind secular politics of the theological heritage of such concepts. But none of this activity announces a political theology, for a political theology begins with the sovereignty of the one God and the operations of that sovereignty in and across time. A Christian action is political not because it takes place within the polis and is implicated in the struggle for the city's soul (see chap. 5) but because the God who acts in history is political, for this God exercises authority, power, and judgment in order to establish a kingdom.[12] It is essential to understand the work of providence and the eschatology that trawls the fathomless depths of the mind, will, and purpose of God for creation.[13]

The chapters that follow explore Christian action and ecclesial eschatology as it confronts the city's own aspirations for the future. Beginning our political theology, as we must, with eschatology enables us to make a highly relevant interjection into contemporary culture. In the previous chapters, one characteristic of our times comes to the fore—whether it surfaces in the imperialist forms of democracy, the secularization thesis, the metaphysics of globalization, or the kingdom visions of fundamentalists. This single, common characteristic is the investment that is being made in defining or controlling the future. It is significant, then, in a responsible call to political discipleship in the face of so many competing secular and nonsecular eschatologies, that I orientate my argument around this particular theological doctrine. I take my cue from Johannes Baptist Metz.

The Eschatological Remainder

The eschatology proposed here is defined in terms of "the remainder." To understand both the nature and the political importance of the eschatological remainder for Christian discipleship, we need to see how this formula differs from, and yet piggybacks on, two phrases adopted from two very different thinkers: the "eschatological reserve" or "eschatological proviso," coined by Metz, and the "remnant/remains," examined more recently by Agamben in his study of messianic time, the time that remains. Each phrase is part of an articulation of a relationship between theology and

12. I am indebted here to Oliver O'Donovan, *The Desire of the Nations: Rediscovering the Roots of Political Theology* (Cambridge: Cambridge University Press, 1996), who reminds theologians that political theology begins with "Yhwh reigns." "The political act is a divinely authorized act. . . . The 'political hermeneutic' is discovered and explored in a particular context of discipleship" (20–21).

13. The economy of God's grace in creation can be understood as providence when one looks back and as eschatology when one looks forward. What relates them both is the fulfillment of time by the will of God.

politics; Metz's phrase is at the heart of what he terms "political theology."

Metz recognized in the late 1960s that both "in the West and the East every impressive *Weltanschauung* and humanistic ideology of today is oriented toward the future."[14] The pursuit of the new, the hungry desire driving modernity, meant a forgetting of what was and a perennial dissatisfaction, after a brief enthusiasm, with the novelties of the present. Human beings as they have emerged through the Enlightenment are continually looking ahead. Metz saw an association here between a sociohistorical epoch that fused futurology and anthropology and a profound theological association between eschatology and anthropology. Secularity brought this association into focus, insofar as Christianity always accepted the secular as *saeculum*, as the ordinary time in which the world worked, and modern secularization, which directed human beings toward their future condition, was an outworking of this more traditional understanding of the secular.

In the wake of Vatican II, Metz's theology sought to rewrite secularism in a way that Christianizes the anthropocentric focus of what he called "pure secularity"[15]—a humanism without God. It can do this because Christianity is not opposed to secularism; in fact for Metz, the acceptance of secularity is made all the more possible by Christianity because it is the incarnation of God as a human being that hands "over the world to human freedom." Christian eschatology, then, receives its fulfillment in God's absolute acceptance of the world, an acceptance that respects the autonomy of that world.[16] Metz certainly does not uncritically accept secularism with its autonomous "hominization" and its Promethean belief in human beings' ability to redeem themselves. Secularity's attention to the future, he observes, is toward that which is without destiny and without providence, and he is all too aware that the hominization of secular life does not entail its humanization. Nevertheless, in taking secularism seriously and rooting it in the incarnation itself, the tension (and crisis) between Christian faith and living in a secular society can be negotiated. It is

14. Johannes B. Metz, *The Theology of the World*, trans. William Glen-Doepel (London: Burns & Oates, 1969), 85.

15. Ibid., 43.

16. Ibid., 63.

in this negotiation that Metz's understanding of the association of eschatology and anthropology, theology and politics emerges.

In many ways, I am doing something similar to Metz: relating theology to the world, reading what I see around me as not necessarily working against divine providence but rather as given to us in that providence. Furthermore, I make making these theological moves on the basis of the incarnation. This means that although human beings may distort, devise elaborate parodies, and use for their own ends the histories and the cultures that are given to them, nevertheless "the Incarnation is not a 'principle' that is *applied* subsequently *within* history (to particular phenomena), but the inner *principle* of history itself."[17] This is the basis of my own political theology. So why do I not simply accept Metz's "eschatological reserve" or "eschatological proviso"?

One of the aims of my work here is to refigure Metz's ideas because of the way he draws a distinction between Christian eschatology and other ideologies of the future. "What distinguishes the Christian and the secular ideologies from one another is not that Christians know *more*, but that they know *less* about the sought-after future of humanity and that they face up to this poverty of knowledge."[18] Because of this, the church "must institutionalise that eschatological reserve by establishing itself as an instance of critical liberty in the face of social development in order to reject the tendency of the latter to present itself as absolute."[19] The "eschatological reserve," then, insists on a critical rupture between the present and the future on the basis of a profound agnosticism, a negative theology. "Christian eschatology is . . . but a *theologia negativa* of the future."[20] The word "reserve" adverts to an ecclesiological skepticism of the futures being projected and to a critical engagement with them. Whatever conditions prevail in the world, the eschatological judgment will reveal how these accord with, or differ from, the justice, love, peace, and solidarity of the kingdom. The eschatological reserve is, for Metz, fundamental to a theology of crisis, a dialectical theology of encounter. It is a theology that has to accept the legitimacy of violence because

17. Ibid., 23.
18. Ibid., 97.
19. Ibid., 111.
20. Ibid., 97.

the crisis is a violent interruption. It is a theology that emphasizes grace over nature.

The "eschatological remainder" that I am seeking to define and that colors all that the next three chapters propose differs from the "eschatological reserve" at several points. First, it emphasizes a certain continuity between the kingdom that is already among us and the kingdom that is to come. The contours of the kingdom that is already among us do not readily present themselves, and they are not—following Augustine (and Metz)—identical with the institution of the church or, rather, the different ecclesial institutionalizations that call themselves churches or Christian denominations across the world. (The next chapter will show the extent that this is so when it describes the operation of the church as distinct from the institution of the church.) Yet, by faith, we believe that Christ is among us now as well as coming again, and the body of Christ also. By "a certain continuity," I mean that we are already living within the future messianic return. Eschatological remainder alerts to a messianism operative now—a messianism that Agamben explores. Such continuity views eschatology not as what is lacking in all the secular ideologies of the future but what is excessive and superabundant to them.

If the language of continuity sounds vague, the theology behind it is more robust, as the second difference between "eschatological remainder" and "eschatological reserve" makes plain. For "eschatological remainder" also emphasizes the supernatural mystery of Christ-with-us in that his body is both present and incomplete. It is on this basis that we can speak of an operative messianism. The presence of Christ with us now is discerned in the Eucharist, within every act of faith, among the congregation of the faithful, and analogically in every identification of justice, peace, love, joy, and community. The operations of Christ's presence is found in every identified manifestation and every recognition of the gifts of the Spirit. It is that which remains, that which abides, when human sinfulness and human limitation are taken into account, and it humbles all our ecclesial praxes. It is the profound, secret operation of that which can never separate us from the love of God. It is an index of the mysterious—that is, the sacramental excess that invests the everyday realities of things. Metz's theology lacks that understanding of the analogical relation between what was, what is, and what is to come. Hence he has to fall back on dialectics, a dialectics that accepts as given the dedivinization and disenchantment of the secular world, an empty dialectics if the vigorous secular ideologies of the future can be countered only by a Christian agnosticism. Indeed, Metz positively embraces this disenchantment as Christian: "Hence Christianity, as it understood more and more from its own origins, had to appear not as a growing divinization, but precisely as an increasing de-divinization and, in this case, profanization of the world, dispelling magic and myth."[21] Thus the eschatological reserve is not only toothless but capitulates too much to the prosaic dictates of secularity's hominization. Not less metaphysics but more and better metaphysics is needed, and needed most particularly in a time of reenchantment and postsecularity (see chap. 3).[22]

Third, the *theologia negativa* of the eschatological reserve suggests an apocalyptic judgment that heralds the coming of the kingdom. I wish to correct this suggestion with a *theologia positiva* that would draw a distinction between the apocalyptic and the eschaton and emphasize that although the kingdom is not yet and therefore remains incomplete, nevertheless it persists, perdures. This is the point where a pneumatology, or theological treatment of the Spirit, is necessary. The messianism of a "politics which are to come" is already being practiced beyond all earthly powers, dominions, and sovereignties. Acts of charity persist. There remains an operation of God that shapes ends beyond ourselves and the circulating processes of living in the world. Metz conflates providence with history, but because the Spirit of Christ moves in and across time, providence is not the same as history. The providential operations of God in creating and sustaining the world in its being empowers spiritually our practices of hope, love, and faith. And this emboldens Christians to speak out prophetically. The prophetic church is not at odds with the church that awaits its final redemption. Metz's "ideologies of the future" are not, as he believes, diametrically opposed to the prophetic mission. They will inform it, to some extent, by providing a language in a specific cultural situation where the prophetic voice cannot

21. Ibid., 34.

22. Since Metz's ideas were formulated in the late 1960s, it might well be suggested that I am simply rewriting his eschatology in the social and cultural context of the early twenty-first century. If I understand Metz correctly, this is a task he would see as necessary. The world he faced then and the world we face now are not the same.

announce itself. Our imaginings of the kingdom that has come and the kingdom that is to come, though drawing on the biblical heritage and ecclesial tradition, will also be drawn into the circulation of more-secular concepts and construals. Neither the church nor the Christian lives out a purely countercultural position. In fact, as Metz observes, the secular ideologies of the future (be they Marxist, socialist, totalitarian, democratic, or neoliberal) are profoundly indebted to the biblical heritage and ecclesial tradition. These secular and parodying eschatologies are shot through with messianic resonances. The Nonconformist socialism of David Lloyd George, the Anglo-Catholic socialism of Archbishop William Temple—both foundational figures in the establishment of the British welfare state—cannot entirely be divorced from the secular socialism propounded by Marx, Engels, the Chartists, the reformers, the trade unionists, the cooperative movement, and the Fabians or from the metaphysics of left- and right-wing Hegelianism. The work of Lloyd George and Archbishop Temple is associated with movements they inherited. They are not identical to these cultural trends because their thinking was deeply rooted distinctively in Christian eschatological thinking. What remains in secular eschatologies, though imperfectly understood, though woven from metaphors and myths drawn from Ezekiel's city of Babylon with its hanging gardens, bears still some relation to the kingdom that comes down from above as a bride adorned for her bridegroom.

It is thus that the eschatological is distinct but not entirely divorced from the apocalyptic, the coming in judgment so vividly represented in Christ's speech to the disciples in the Gospel of Mark and in the Revelation of St. John. The return of Christ will, no doubt, surprise us all—perhaps most especially the church. It may very well erase in a moment the appropriateness of all our categories for, all our descriptions and imaginings of, the kingdom. What we now see in a mirror darkly may then seem very remote in the face-to-face. Nevertheless, the notion of the eschatological remainder announces a commitment to the belief in a certain continuity. To employ Hegelian language, however distant from our imaginings, the coming of the kingdom will also be accompanied by a "recognition" (*Anerkennung*). Pace Metz, when we stare into the darkened mirror, we nevertheless perceive, and continually we strain to perceive more clearly.

What is so significant about this eschatological remainder for political discipleship is that it not only informs it but also empowers Christian agency, which is simultaneously both individual and collective. We need to understand something about this distinctive agency (see chap. 5), but first we will consider the work of the second thinker informing this notion of the eschatological remainder, Giorgio Agamben.

Agamben's contribution to the development of eschatology here is twofold: first, what he has to say about messianism and, second, how he relates this messianism to the contemporary political situation (although in his work up to 2008 he is more suggestive than systematic).[23] Agamben describes the political situation as a "postdemocratic counterfeit" of "democracy as a 'community of dispute'" (see chap. 1, above).[24] Agamben, it seems, would concur with Negri's depiction of the postdemocratic condition as one in which there is "zero degree dialectic" (see chap. 1, above). His contribution to the notion of the eschatological remainder comes from his nuanced, highly insightful, and theologically sophisticated commentary on Paul's Letter to the Romans. Agamben's wide-ranging interdisciplinary scholarship enables him to make imaginative connections outside the range of purely biblical criticism. We will be encountering Paul's texts throughout the second section of this study.

Throughout his commentary, Agamben is concerned with transformation, and he examines the power to transform in terms of the "messianic concept of the remnant,"[25] the time that remains. Some of Agamben's suggestions concerning "remnant" and "remains" are useful in the discussion here of "remainder," especially his notion of the richness, the excess, of that which remains undisclosed, although there will be differences. Agamben's commentary explores Paul's text in association with the messianic thinking in Marx's understanding of the work of the proletariat and, most particularly, with Walter Benjamin's con-

23. Agamben's suggestiveness, even allusiveness, may have much to do with how he perceives the ungraspable nature of the "messianic now"—how this messianism cannot appear concretely but only in the interstices of two related but noncoinciding temporalities.

24. Giorgio Agamben, *The Time That Remains: A Commentary on the Letter to the Romans*, trans. Patricia Dailey (Stanford, CA: Stanford University Press, 2005), 58.

25. Ibid.

ception of historical materialism. Indeed, the links that Agamben makes across the history separating first-century Paul from twentieth-century Benjamin constitute something of a genealogy of certain key philosophical and juridical concepts, such as *Aufhebung*, vocation, and the "state of exception." This genealogy outlines the secularization of these concepts. Agamben's attention to the time that remains leads him to thinking through the New Testament's distinction between *chronos* as chronological time and *kairos*.[26] He reads *kairos* not as another form of time but the specific seizure of chronological time, ordinary time, secular time, the "time of the now."[27] On this basis of messianic time as the time in which *chronos* is seized, Agamben concludes that the "messianic world is not another world, but the secular world itself, with a slight adjustment, a meagre difference."[28] The messianic operates (indeed, he calls it "operative time") immanently, opening up a "now" that is full of possibilities because it is outside the law but not the law's annulment—rather, the law is fulfilled in the "now." Agamben understands the "now-time" as one of pure presence (he translates *parousia* not as a second coming but as "presence"), a pure event "pressing within chronological time, working and transforming it from within."[29] It is the disjointedness and yet inextricable nature of these times that installs a dialectic.

There is an inner debate here between Agamben and Derrida, for Derrida's notion of *différance* describes the continual deconstruction of "presence." For Derrida, there is an infinite deferral of a presence that language is both attempting to represent and continually betrays. There is no present as such for Derrida, and Agamben concludes that deconstruction suspends the messianic.[30] For Agamben, the messianic means fulfillment, and it is this fulfillment that has the power to transform because it reveals an excess, a remnant. Remarkable, for Agamben, is the way the seizure of the "now," because it aims at the fulfillment of time, recapitulates the

26. Ibid., 62–69.

27. Ibid., 2, where Agamben is translating Paul.

28. Ibid., 69.

29. Ibid., 68.

30. Ibid., 103. For Derrida's understanding of "the messianic without messianism," see Jacques Derrida, *Specters of Marx: The State of the Debt, the Work of Mourning, and the New International*, trans. Peggy Kamuf (London: Routledge, 1994), 49–75.

past as each instant is related to the messiah. It is in this way that the past is redeemed because past events receive in this new relation their true meaning. Pauline "faith" is the character of living in the zone of indistinction that messianic time announces. It is both a condition of existence (and therefore passive) and an operation that performs the messianic within the secular, the law-bound, and the chronological.

All this is extraordinarily illuminating in terms of characterizing the work the remainder does and in not divorcing that work from the historical and material situation in which the remainder operates. But the remnant and the remains in Agamben are highly abstract, metaphysical notions. They are secret, mysterious (he even at one point writes of "transcendence") aspects of temporality. All too briefly he alludes to Israel as a figure for the remnant but then quickly universalizes it in a way that renders the remnant again in abstract terms: "*At a decisive moment, the elected people, every people, will necessarily situate itself as a remnant, as not-all.*"[31] Earlier he refers to one of the conditions of messianic living as living "not as"—living, that is, both within and beyond the legal and political conditions governing any chronological temporality. But all too quickly the materiality of the remnant or remains evaporates because Agamben never relates Paul's letter to the church and the Christian disciples whom Paul is addressing.

Furthermore, Agamben's concentration on the messianic time as the time of the "now" that recapitulates the past leads him to distinguish between messianism and eschatology. Paul, he insists, is an apostle, not a prophet. His thinking is not orientated, then, toward the future in the way that eschatology necessarily is because it is conceived as a thinking through of the "end times" (the eschaton). Messianic time must not therefore be confused with eschatological time (which Agamben conflates with the apocalyptic). "The widespread view of messianic time as orientated solely toward the future is fallacious."[32] The fulfillment is in the "now" and not in a third aeon situated between this world and the next. Hence the parousia has nothing to do with a return of Christ. But

31. Agamben, *Time That Remains*, 55. The italics are original. The "not-all" refers to the divisions that the law imposes between Jew and non-Jew. The messianic questions all ethnic identifications, all political separations and distinctions—indeed, all politics of identity.

32. Ibid., 77.

this view of eschatology is narrow and not as "widespread" as Agamben believes. The Christ event is also left behind too quickly. Like the remnant, he briefly alludes to it and then sweeps it up in a generalization about the messianic for Paul. He never deals with the scandal of the incarnation on the ground that Paul's messianic thinking proceeds only on the basis of the resurrection of Jesus, the messiah. "To believe in Jesus Messiah does not mean believing something about him."[33] Messianic time has nothing to do with the material history of Jesus—his words, his work, or his death on the cross.

The second contribution that Agamben's notion of what remains makes to this thesis is a political one. The Pauline concept of the remnant "allows for a new perspective that dislodges our antiquated notions of a people and a democracy, however impossible it might be to completely denounce them."[34] To understand this political intervention that Agamben's commentary on Romans makes possible, we have to view the commentary in the light of a political examination that Agamben began in an earlier work, *Homo Sacer: Sovereignty and Bare Life*. There, on the basis of Schmitt's notion of the sovereign as the one who can declare the state of exception, he develops a critique of contemporary democracy that returns us to some of the ideas presented in chapter 1, above. In the state of exception, the sovereign suspends certain legal aspects of the constitution; it makes manifest the nature of modern sovereignty itself—that the sovereign is both within and beyond the juridical.[35]

The paradigmatic declaration of the state of exception to which Agamben continually refers is Hitler's Decree for the Protection of the People and State, of February 28, 1933. Following Schmitt, Agamben holds that the state of exception both allows for the possibility and value of the law to be manifest and, at the same time, opens a space where the law is "utterly unfathomable" because one is now unsure what the legal norm is anymore.[36] For Agam-

33. Ibid., 136.

34. Ibid., 57.

35. See Carl Schmitt, appendix in *Die Diktatur: Von den Anfängen des modernen Souveränitätsgedankens bis zum proletarischen Klassenkampf* (Berlin: Dunker & Humblot, 1994), where he writes about the state of exception in article 49 of the Weimar Constitution. This was a democratic, not a totalitarian, sovereignty.

36. Ibid., 105.

ben, fascism's declaration of the state of exception manifested itself in a particular spatiality—that of the Jewish extermination camps—and revealed "bare life," that is, life without rights, outside the protection of the law, life reduced to *bios*. He believes that this instantiation of the state of exception is what all modern notions of sovereignty are based on, whether the sovereignty is fascist, totalitarian, or democratic. It is this notion of sovereignty that facilitates the creation of liberal democracy, making possible the establishment of places of detainment such as Guantanimo Bay, where the law is suspended and can be suspended because sovereignty is beyond the law. The state of exception renders the political action of the majority invalid; only the one who declares this state of emergency can act politically, because sovereign power is now in their hands. The questions, then, remain: If all modern polities are founded upon the same principle of sovereignty, how, in this "postdemocratic counterfeit" that dominates the West, are political alternatives possible? How can left-wing thinking, historical materialism, imagine other possibilities? How can there be resistance?

Agamben is not the only contemporary left-wing thinker to locate resources for political resistance in Christianity, and Paul in particular. Badiou[37] and Žižek[38] have both seen the "radical" potential of employing Pauline thinking, along with Eagleton[39] (who maintains a Catholic reticence toward Paul but nevertheless points to Christianity as the site of neglected possibilities). The important word for Agamben is "radical," with its Latin understanding, "at the roots of," "original," for his answer is to draw attention to an alternative form of the state of the exception—that announced by Paul's elaboration of messianic time. "The remnant is an exception. . . . Paul radicalizes the condition of the state of exception,"[40] for Paul too renders the law inoperative,

37. See Alain Badiou, *Saint Paul: The Foundation of Universalism*, trans. Ray Brassier (Stanford, CA: Stanford University Press, 2003).

38. See Slavoj Žižek, *The Fragile Absolute; or, Why Is the Christian Legacy Worth Fighting For?* (London: Verso, 2000), esp. chaps. 11 and 15; and Žižek, *The Puppet and the Dwarf: The Perverse Core of Christianity* (Cambridge, MA: MIT Press, 2003), esp. chap. 4.

39. See Terry Eagleton, *Sweet Violence: The Idea of the Tragic* (Oxford: Blackwell, 2003).

40. Agamben, *Time That Remains*, 106.

suspending the law with his insistence on faith as the fulfillment of the law and prior to it. The state of messianic exception exposes an original condition of anarchy and antinomianism that can be compared with Hobbes's theory of the origins of the state. But it is a "mystery of lawlessness" that points to a more original fulfillment, a justice that comes through the unconditional entrustment of oneself to God. Paul illustrates this more radical fulfillment by comparing Abraham's act of faith, which brings about a true justice, and Moses's act of establishing the law of commandment. Agamben concludes, in a way that returns us to our contemporary "postdemocratic counterfeit," that "the unveiling of this mystery entails bringing to light the inoperativity of the law and the substantial illegitimacy of each and every power in messianic time. . . . Profane power . . . is the semblance that covers up the substantial lawlessness [*anomia*] of messianic time."[41] We can understand from this why the "postdemocratic" is a "counterfeit." All profane politics is a "counterfeit," a "semblance." This notion rehearses Schmitt's thesis about the theological origins of major concepts of the modern state.

At this point we encounter a problem—the problem of secularization. It is entirely unclear how this Pauline messianic politics can be utilized as a form of left-wing resistance to the "juridicizing of all human relations in their entirety"[42] and open a space for the critique of modern notions of sovereignty when such messianic politics is divorced from the object of Paul's faith and the work of the church. Yet it reveals another social and political imaginary, a distinctively messianic one, but it divorces this politics from the specificities of Christianity. Paul's faith is in Jesus the Messiah as the historical incarnation of God and in the kingdom inaugurated not only by his resurrection but by his "having been born of the seed of David" (see Rom. 1:3). Agamben is both eloquent and stunningly astute about faith as a "principle of actuality and operativity" and about the sovereignty of grace, which "does not provide the foundation for exchange and social obligations; grace makes for their interruption. The messianic gesture does not found, it fulfils."[43] But faith does not precede grace; grace already makes

41. Ibid., 111.
42. Ibid., 135.
43. Ibid., 90, 124.

faith possible. Messianic time, as the examples of Abraham and the Hebrew prophets show, is rooted in divine providence. And divine providence relates the first things (protology if you like) with the end things (eschatology). Outside an acceptance of this divine order and its operations in the world, then, the possibilities for political critique and resistance opened up by the state of messianic exception cannot be utilized. Agamben mentions the church only derogatively. He does not relate Paul's thinking to the wider theological framework that Paul's letters elaborate: the ecclesiology announced in his understanding of the body of Christ; his Christology, which identifies the messiah with God the Father; and his pneumatology, which makes possible, in and through the messiah's resurrection, the *plērōma*, or fulfillment, that Agamben recognizes is essential to this new suspension of the law. Agamben holds that any messianism drawing attention away from the fulfillment of the "now" toward a future fulfillment is committed to endless deferment. But this is exactly where Christian eschatology differs from the Derridean messianic with messianism without the messiah; Christian eschatology places faith not only in what the messiah has done but also in what the messiah will do in bringing all things into God. Agamben makes much of Pauline faith and love, but there is no analysis of the third in the Pauline trilogue of virtues—hope. And hope is futural in its attentions; it is the hope of salvation in Christ.

The Pauline practices of faith are also practices of hope—a commitment to what has yet to come to pass. The messianic contraction of time is this living that recapitulates the past and draws down the future into the present. Too much concentration on the "now," on presence as the present, cannot offer a politics of resistance in a culture of new capitalism that worships and commodifies the present.[44] Agamben, like Metz, endorses a very modern eschatology that focuses on present realization—the eschatology that is the foundation, even if secularized, for the myth of globalization (see chap. 2, above). For Paul, faith, love, and hope are labors in grace in and across time; they are labors precisely because, as Agamben recognizes, *kairos* is not divorced from *chronos* in that both are created. *Kairos* is the time of grace and *chronos* the time for grace.

44. See Graham Ward, *Cities of God* (London: Routledge, 2000), 152–81, which constructs a genealogy of presence and present from Aquinas to Žižek.

The laboring issues from the continuous acts of discernment in and through prayer that are inseparable from our participation in the Triune God.

My emphasis on the eschatological remainder borrows from and modifies Agamben's messianic remnant and the time that remains ecclesiologically, christologically, and pneumatologically. The church as the substantive remnant exists only in its performance of a specific temporality, "*the time that time has to come to an end* . . . the only real time, the only time we have."[45] But—and here I owe much to Agamben—it announces a new and better politics, a new and better sovereignty that, in our present condition, can help to facilitate "democracy as a 'community of dispute.'"

As I insisted at the beginning of this book, the recovery of contestation is fundamental. Contestation and dispute are synonyms. Here the contestation is between Christianity and the secular powers we have already named. So let the contestation begin.

45. Ibid., 67–68, italics in the original.

5

The City and the Struggle for Its Soul

> People come together in the city to live; they remain there in order to live the good life.[1]

What is it for the Christian to act? We need to answer this question because to act is fundamental to being political, and fundamental also to discipleship as following, obeying, worshiping, and so forth. This presentation on the politics of discipleship must explain what it is for a Christian to act. All the enemies named in the first three chapters are forces that act within the world not only on people but through them. The enemies are never anonymous. But the Christian acts within a present and a future opened up by Christ. He or she acts within the context of the church, as the church acts within the context of the city and the eschatological hope for what is and is to come. The character of eschatology *is* hope, and the anchor point for this hope is the resurrection of Christ. There would be no eschatological remainder without the

1. Aristotle, cited in Lewis Mumford, *The City in History* (Harmondsworth, UK: Penguin Books, 1961), 134.

resurrection. It is the Spirit of the risen Christ who announces both the kingdom come and the kingdom that is yet to come. The church participates in the resurrection by establishing and performing the kingdom come and yet to come. When the kingdom is fully come, then the church and its sacraments of grace are no longer necessary, for then the relationship to Christ is immediate (see chap. 7, below). But before that time arrives, within the time that remains, there is political discipleship. So now we need to examine more closely Christian agency itself and then its role in the struggle for the soul of the city in which it operates.

The Christian Act

Given the eschatological remainder, what is a Christian act as distinct from any other act? In the opening passages of the *Nicomachean Ethics*, Aristotle deliberates on an investigation into the ethics and ends of any action (*praxis*). He determines that the science that most adequately addresses "what people shall do and what things they shall refrain from doing," the realization of the Good that is not secured for one person only but for the wider community, is political science. He concludes that "our investigation [into the ethics and ends of any action] is in a sense the study of Politics."[2] We might note here that "the Good" is *to kalon*—which is also "the Beautiful." Praxes therefore have to be examined ethically, aesthetically, and politically. For Aristotle, they also have to be examined theologically, although he does not undertake such an examination. But he recognizes that the securing of the Good is also a divine achievement (*theioteron*).

In his *Politics*, in a discussion concerning the actions that maintain a democracy, Aristotle advises, "It is a good thing to prevent wealthy citizens, even if they are willing, from undertaking expensive and useless public services [*leitourgia*], such as the giving of choruses, torch-races, and the like."[3] The Greek *leitourgia*, from which "liturgy" is derived, was a technical political term for a service rendered to the city or state. It was a service that might be laid down by the law; it was conducted with honor if not solemnity. It

2. Aristotle, *Nicomachean Ethics* 1.2, trans. Terence Irwin (Indianapolis: Hackett, 1985).

3. Aristotle, *Politics* 5.8 (1309a).

is a work, or a labor (*ergon*), with respect to a people or community (*leitos*). And so, elsewhere in *Politics*, *leitourgia* can be used nontechnically to refer to any act of service.[4] It seems, however, as far I am aware, that nowhere does Aristotle explicitly say that *praxis* stands to *leitourgia* as genus to species, that all specific acts of service concretize the universal form of action.

This close relationship between the politics, ethics, and aesthetics of liturgical practice (*leitourgia*) becomes prominent when we examine the specificity of a Christian act. It is Paul who brings together the two uses of *leitourgia* in a verse at the end of his great chapter on *kenōsis* in Philippians. After outlining the nature of Christ the servant in the *carmen Christi* (Phil. 2:5–11) and the nature of faithful, sacrificial obedience (Phil. 2:12–18), he refers to two of his close friends, Timothy (Phil. 2:19–24) and Epaphroditus (2:25–30). Of Epaphroditus he writes, "he nearly died for the work of Christ, risking his life to complete [*anaplērōsē*] your service to me [*tēs pros me leitourgias*]" (2:30). According to some commentators, Paul is employing *leitourgia* as a euphemism to avoid explicit mention of the exact nature of the service—a gift of money. This may be so, but there is more here. Service on behalf of the ecclesial community is a political act in the sense maintained by Aristotle, that political action concerned the building up and maintenance of the community. Service is also a political act because it announces what one is committed to and where one's allegiances lie. Service is also theological, for *anaplērōsē* is related to Paul's extensive use of the noun *plērōma* regarding the operations of the Spirit in the world (the filling up, the plenitude, the bringing to completion), and the verb *plēroō*.[5] In Philippians 2:17 (RSV), with reference to cultic sacrifice, Paul says that he is "to be poured as a libation upon the sacrificial offering of your faith [*epi tē thysia kai leitourgia tēs pisteōs hymōn*]."

4. Aristotle, *Politics* 3.5 (1278a).

5. See Graham Ward, *Christ and Culture* (Oxford: Blackwell, 2005), 77–80, 183–218, for an exposition of *plēroō* and its relationship to *kenoō* in Pauline teaching. Cultic use of the word *leitourgia* is later than Aristotle. Such use is thought to have developed in Hellenistic Egypt, and the word becomes prominent in the Septuagint to translate Hebrew cultic terms. See H. Strathmann, "λειτουργέω, κτλ," in *Theological Dictionary of the New Testament*, ed. G. Kittel and G. Friedrich, trans. Geoffery W. Bromiley (Grand Rapids: Eerdmans, 1967), 5:221–22, on *leitourgeō* and *leitourgia*.

The Christian act has to be understood in terms not just of the church but also of the church's participation in Christ, the church as the body of Christ. That is, the Christian act is integral to the church's participation in the operations of the Triune God within realms created in and through Christ as God's Word. Discipleship is thus not simply following the example of Christ; it is formation within Christ, so that we become Christlike. And the context of this formation is the church in all its concrete locatedness and eschatological significance.

There are six key elements in such a theological activity, constituting the politics and poetics of Christian action: an agent (the one doing the action); the nature of the action done by that agent; the evaluation of the action done by the agent; the object with respect to which the action is taking place; the effect (both on the agent and on the object of the action); and, finally, the inner intellectual and/or affective workings that lead to an action (variously considered as intention, desire, hope, and judgment with respect to both the act and/or the object of the action, these workings can be called "disposition" or even, after Davidson, "pro-attitudes").[6]

Agency

We proceed with an examination of the first element, the agent, from a Christian theological perspective—that is, on the basis of the framework of Christian participation in the eschatological operations of God in the world through the church. Participation implicates any agent in a relational ontology. This is summed up in Christ's words to his disciples: "he dwells in me, and I in him" (John 6:56 KJV). This statement can be taken as axiomatic for an account of a Christian act. In this act, therefore, we are not dealing with an autonomous subject who, in full knowledge of the facts of a situation, acts consciously in and for himself or herself. In the conception of a Christian praxis, there is no room for such a modern notion of self-sufficiency.[7] This already implicates us in a different construal of freedom than that operating in the notion of

6. See Donald Davidson, *Essays on Actions and Events* (Oxford: Oxford University Press, 1980), 4.

7. See Charles Taylor, "The Rise of the Disciplinary Society," chap. 2 in *A Secular Age* (London: Belknap Press of Harvard University Press, 2007), 90–145, for a historical account of the formation of such atomized (and secularized) selfhood.

the liberal secular subject. In fact, what characterizes this Christian agent is a surrender, a sacrifice, in which he or she is bound by what Augustine calls a *vinculum caritatis*. This does not mean that Christians have no sense of their singularity, their uniqueness—no self-identity. The Christian agent is not a cipher. It is frequently assumed that theologians, such as myself, who find resources for creative theological thinking in poststructuralist authors work uncritically with these resources. This is certainly not always the case. Some poststructuralist authors espouse a very weak sense of the subject, and some of them seem to leave little or no room for agency because the self is reduced to a nodal point in an extensive and extending grid of forces—for example, Deleuze, Foucault, and Derrida. In speaking, then, of a relational ontology in a Christian act in which the subject is always participating in that which transcends himself or herself—indeed, not only transcends but grounds any sense of there being a he or a she—I do not wish to implode notions of selfhood but to refigure them.

Most significantly, in a Christian act identity is not dissolved into the anonymity of an economy of knowledge/power (Foucault), an economy of semiotic, libidinal, and social flows (Deleuze), or an economy of *différance* (Derrida), all of which operate solely on a plane of immanence, although we might learn something of the nature of economy itself from each of these three thinkers.[8] The Christian acts in Christ, and the Christic operation, though working within the world (immanently), also works beyond it, externally to it (transcendently); in other words, such an act announces the eschatological remainder.

Furthermore, the Christian act is not anonymous. We have to tread cautiously here, bearing in mind that with respect to God, as the apophatic theologians have taught us, we can only stare into unsayable glory. Aquinas likewise emphasizes that our knowledge is not of God in himself but of the effects of God's operations in the world. But there is a world of difference between the anonymity of differentiating power found in Foucault, semiosis as found in Deleuze, Derridean *différance*, and "ineffability." Derrida confuses

8. Admittedly, Derrida does deal with what he calls a "quasi-transcendental," and this has exercised the minds of numerous scholars who argue about the extent to which Derrida is constructing a transcendental argument in a Kantian fashion. With Derrida we have at best an *effect* of transcendence that language cannot erase. The effect is—and, for Derrida, can only be—examined immanently.

the effect of *différance* that renders all things ultimately unsayable and ineffability in his essay "How to Avoid Speaking: Denegations," where he gives an interpretation of Pseudo-Dionysius's mystical writings. Reading them as discourses rather than sources for prayer and meditation, Derrida writes:

> We could recognize in the negativity without negativity of these utterances—concerning a transcendence which is nothing other than (and wholly other than) what it transcends—a principle of multiplication of voices and discourses, of disappropriation and reappropriation of utterances. . . . A predicate always conceals another predicate, or rather the nakedness of an absence of predicate—as the (sometimes indispensable) veil of a garment can at once dissimulate and reveal the very fact that it dissimulates and renders attractive at the same time. Hence the voice of an utterance can conceal another, when it then appears to quote without quoting it, presenting itself as another form, namely, as a quotation of the other.[9]

But one cannot worship the passage of endless deferral that is installed by *différance*, nor can one receive grace from it. More significantly, although the divine is incomprehensible, the Christ is not without identifying markers. For God in Christ is Jesus of Nazareth. The Christian act, then, can be identified by Christ-likeness; it will in some sense be an *imitatio Christi*. I say "in some sense" not to introduce a vagueness but a complexity. What we are dealing with in the Gospels are testimonies to the life, work, and person of Jesus of Nazareth, depictions and descriptions that are also interpretations that hand themselves over to us, who interpret them. Nevertheless, what characterizes a Christian action points back to something of that historical person, the gendered Palestinian Jew who was God incarnate. For those who "follow after" will act in accordance with what the American philosophical theologian Robert Scharlemann calls an "acolouthetic reason";[10] the disciples' actions can be parsed only according to the grammar of a life hidden in Christ.

9. See Graham Ward, ed., *The Postmodern God* (Oxford: Oxford University Press, 1997), 167–90; and Kevin Hart's excellent introduction to Derrida's text (171).

10. Robert Scharlemann, *The Reason of Following: Christology and the Ecstatic* (Chicago: University of Chicago Press, 1991), 124.

The chiastic structure of the relationship described in the statement "he dwells in me, and I in him" in John's Gospel (KJV) is related to the notions of both self-identity and freedom through servitude. There is a paradox at the heart of the word "subject," for, on the one hand, it reflects subordination (*sub-jectum*) but, on the other, it invokes sovereignty, the one in control. This paradox is circumscribed in the Johannine formula. There is an "abiding" *in* Christ, but there is also an abiding *of* Christ. There is an abiding *in* me, but also an abiding *of* me. This coabiding is complex and richly suggestive of the messianic remainder. It is the chiastic heart of an *ekklēsia*. Why chiastic? Observe the curious manner of the reciprocal relation with respect to the eucharistic body, the liturgy of incorporation and incarnation itself. By the act of receiving the Eucharist, I place myself *in* Christ—rather than simply placing Christ within me. I consume but I do not absorb Christ without being absorbed into Christ. Only in this complex coabiding are there life, nourishment, and nurture because of, through, or by means of this feeding; there is both participation of human life in God's life and participation of God's life in human life. Something comes into its own in this relationality. The incarnation is fully realized only by the participation of God in human life and the participation of human life in God.

Two points follow from this. First, Jesus is the Christ only in relation—both to God and to other human beings; the act of redemption is a relational act. Christology concerns not the identity of this one subject but an operation effected in and through this complex coabiding in a specific location. This will be important for the ecclesiology that follows. Second, although there is a profound difference between the human and the divine, there must exist within the nature and self-understanding of the Trinity a quality that has affinity with what it is to be human. To create human beings, there must abide in God an image and likeness of what it is to be human. A Christology emerges from these two points that emphasizes movement, a redemptive operation. The Gospel of John continues, "I live because of [*dia*] the Father, so he who eats [*trōgōn*] me will live because of [*di'*] me" (John 6:57 RSV). *Dia* is a word implying transit—movement effected not only within but also by means of the ensouled body.

Let us consider further two characteristics of this spiritual embodiment. First, I embody Christ's body and this body embodies mine. In other words, the bodies here are emphatically carnal and carnally relating, but their colocation, like Agamben's "remains" that exist in the interstices between two times (*chronos* and *kairos*), is unthinkable. We continually return to that chiasmus "he dwells in me, and I in him" (KJV). The coming together of the two bodies does not create a third body whose location can be separated off. It is exactly the opposite: the coming together of the two bodies effects a reciprocal dislocation of both bodies. There is an "abiding," but it takes place in this complex space whose boundaries fold back upon themselves. One body relates to the other, but each is relocated with respect to a coabiding. In this realm, tied as it always must be to the specificities of place, the mutual indwelling that characterizes what Paul calls *koinōnia* announces the presence of an *ekklēsia* always living beyond itself because it is always interpenetrated by that which refigures its boundaries. The *ekklēsia* is thus much less the institution and much more the history of a body that continually overreaches itself—a notion that might be rethought in terms of "tradition." It is the history of its corelation, its indwelling and being indwelt. The church, then, has a history, a tradition, a temporality. It is not that location is eclipsed. A location remains, the body—or collected bodies—of believers that is material and particular. This location is the church, but the church does not stand in splendid isolation as some cathedrals appear to do in the squares and piazzas of Western Europe. If in the eschaton, according to both the vision of Ezekiel and the vision of John the Divine, the temple is located in "a structure like a city" (Ezek. 40:2), then we have to recognize that ecclesial living is also simultaneously civic participation. In this civic participation, members of any particular church are also at the same time members of other civic associations.[11] In this way, Christian action ripples through city living.

The bodies of Christian believers, individual and collected, constitute and contest social and political meaning, institutional and behavioral norms, with respect to their dwelling in Christ and Christ in them. Because of the eschatological remainder, this coabiding is not reducible to the particular and material location or the social and political meanings embedded in them.

11. Graham Ward, *Cultural Transformation and Religious Practice* (Cambridge: Cambridge University Press, 2005), 72–85.

The *ekklēsia* is a location of liminality, a corelation that lives always on the edge of both itself and what is other. We might see this liminality in action through a peripatetic teacher such as Paul, moving from one ecclesial community to another, from one *koinōnia* to another, not simply relating these nodal points but involving them with issues beyond their own frontiers, persuading them to participate in community life in other terrestrial centers. This is the effect, for example, of his plea for money for famine relief. The churches of Macedonia are related to Corinth, and both to Jerusalem, and greetings are exchanged and hospitality offered.[12]

This interrelationality within which the subject comes to an understanding of himself or herself cannot be separated from the practices in which this interrelationality takes place. For example, with respect to Christ being in me and I being in Christ, practices such as prayer, confession, praise, and participation in ecclesial liturgies constitute the economies within which this interrelationality is unfolded. But these practices are not limited to church attendance. In fact, these practices are executed most frequently outside the institutional framework of the church, spilling over and affecting all other social practices: the managing of a school, the nursing of the sick, the administering of the law, cooking for the hungry, and pulling pints for the thirsty. I say "interrelationality" here rather than "intersubjectivity" for two reasons. First, relations are far larger than the subjects engaged in evaluating them can measure; relations by nature exceed subjects. Death, divorce, and departure all testify to the profundity of relations; subjects invariably underestimate the existential impact of these events. Second, intersubjectivity assumes already the independence and atomization of subjects; it accepts as given the modern, secularized individual. Returning to these interrelational practices, it seems that each practice embodies a process of subjectification. That is, the subject undergoes a certain formation or production of himself or herself in and through the practice. Theologically, this is conceived of as vocation—being formed in

12. See Rowan Williams, "Does It Makes Sense to Speak of a Pre-Nicene Orthodoxy?" in *The Making of Orthodoxy*, ed. Rowan Williams (Cambridge: Cambridge University Press, 1989), 1–23; and *On Christian Theology* (Oxford: Blackwell, 2001), 11–15, on the role played in the early church by the epistolary form.

Christ. And this formation has a teleology. We will return to this in the next two chapters when we examine Paul's understanding of the body of Christ as a network of associated functions, commitment to which forms subjects. In the words of the writer of the book of Revelation (who picks up a reference to a suggestion in the book of Deuteronomy), "To him who conquers I will give . . . a white stone, with a new name written on the stone which no one knows except him who receives it" (Rev. 2:17 RSV)—and presumably the one who wrote it (the Son of God). In several biographical sketches of Christian saints, von Balthasar takes up this idea in terms of a lifetime living out a certain statement about the nature of God—a divine name if you will, carved out of the lives of each of those who serve God.[13] Again this supports what we are treating here: the Christian as agent is not a figure consumed by the divine but a person actually personalized and particularized by being divinized, not a subject without a sense of self or a subject in full conscious possession of self but a subject on the way to a final recognition of who he or she is in Christ. The acts that these subjects engage in, participate in, cooperate within (these descriptions are synonymous) form the particularity of the agents they are.

Governing agency, then, are the principles of interrelationality and subjectification. The Christian embodied agent always lives beyond himself or herself in and toward other bodies (the eucharistic body, the ecclesial body, social bodies of various kinds, the civic body, and the body of Christ).

The Action

The second element of an action is the nature of the action done by the agent. It would follow from our investigation of selfhood and participation that the orientation and interpretation of any action would be christological. We might indeed attempt to catalog various types of action—teaching, commanding, obeying, entertaining, and so forth. But because all Christian action participates in the economy of love, all action becomes liturgical. That

13. See Hans Urs von Balthasar, *Elizabeth of Dijon: An Interpretation of Her Spiritual Mission*, trans. A. V. Littledale (New York: Pantheon, 1956); and Balthasar, *Thérèse of Lisieux: The Story of a Mission*, trans. D. Nicholl (New York: Sheed & Ward, 1953).

is, the final determination of an act in Christ is doxological—an act of worship that is political because it proclaims an ultimate allegiance.[14] This appears an easy set of inferences to make, but to be clearer about what is philosophically entailed here, we must go further. To ask about the nature of an action seems to drive us toward the isolation of an act and how that act is named, as if the single act is the most basic element in action, but this is far from certain. As a number of language philosophies of the twentieth century have shown, the word is not the most basic element of meaning. Meaning emerges at the level of the sentence, and even then, as Wittgenstein taught us, the meaning of the sentence cannot be divorced from the context within which that sentence is situated. Similarly, the nature of a single act—giving someone sleeping in a doorway a handful of loose change, for example—cannot be determined in isolation from the relationship of the agent to giving charity as a whole, the social and economic circumstances circumscribing both agent and action, and the social and/or religious mores that encourage or discourage such an action. The act of giving away loose change may be an act of compassion, an act of condescension, an act of obedience (having been told to do it), a way to alleviate guilt, a way to make a political statement about the failure of the welfare state, and so forth. In other words, the nature of the action can be determined only at the level of practices with respect to a certain social, cultural, and historical context. To take an example: Judas's kiss can be understood only in terms of the Gospel narratives as a whole. I say "as a whole" and immediately we are aware that no narrative is a self-contained whole; it is forever generating new readings when situated in new contexts. But at least when we read Judas's kiss in the context of the narrative we have, we can name it as an act of betrayal. The point here is that an act cannot be read outside the larger practices of which it is a part.

If the nature of an act cannot be determined without an appreciation of the practices that situate the act, where does this situating end, so that the nature of the act can be named? The act

14. "The [Christian] community is a political community by virtue of being a worshipping community" (Oliver O'Donovan, *The Desire of the Nations: Rediscovering the Roots of Political Theology* [Cambridge: Cambridge University Press, 1996], 47), for worship is an act that performs an allegiance.

of giving away a handful of loose change was *an act of charity* toward someone poor and homeless. Judas's kiss was an *act of betrayal*. These are the names given to these acts. To equate this naming or judging of an act with an inquiry into the sixth of our key elements (the inner intellectual and/or affective workings that lead to an action)—to equate this judging with an inquiry into intention, motivation, desire, willing, and wishing—is premature because it resolves the problematic of naming the nature of the act at the level of the subject. At the level of the subject, if we take into consideration various textual clues and postulated reconstructions of Judas's discipleship, his kiss was an act of exposure: the exposure of a messianic impostor. But as we have seen above, the subject comes to an understanding of self not only interrelationally—that is, in and through encounters with the other-than-self—but also through the practices in which the subject participates, the practices of subjectification. In other words, the act takes its nature and naming from the practice of which it is a part. The practice operates as a hermeneutical framework that governs the interpretation of acts.

What does this mean in terms of Christian activity? It situates even the smallest and most local of actions—the giving of loose change—within an economy of divine action governed by both a soteriology and an eschatological remainder. Such a framework takes us far beyond conscious willing and intending. This is why Gregory of Nyssa and Augustine consider desire the primary animator of the ensouled flesh. Our desire for God participates in God's desire for us—not only for us but also for the redemption of creation. There are in the Christian act, then, not only a telos but also a utopic moment. The act is both now and proleptic. It reaches toward a future fulfillment. The act is thus always an operation not just of love (toward God) but of faith and hope. "Hope bespeaks the possibility of what escapes the realm of the possible; at the limit, it is relation recaptured where relation is lost."[15] It is apparent from this examination of the act that although each agent will have some knowledge of what the act engaged in is, this knowledge quickly sheers off into mystery. We simply cannot name the nature of our acts, as we cannot adumbrate the consequences

15. Maurice Blanchot, *The Infinite Conversation*, trans. S. Hanson (Minneapolis: University of Minnesota Press, 1993), 41.

of any action, for its nature and its name concern what role the act plays in the divine economy.

The Evaluation of the Action

The third key element of an action is the evaluation of the action done by the agent, for to name the act would be to give it its meaning, and to give it its meaning we would have to be able to evaluate it in terms of its final end. The naming is already an act of judgment. But this is not to say that Christians are like somnambulists or puppets. When they act, they will no doubt name that act (I am giving away some loose change) and evaluate it with reference to themselves (because I cannot bear the shame this other person's poverty evokes in me). But the import of the action done in Christ goes far beyond this naming and evaluation, for the action participates in economies that suspend the local in the universal.

It is important not to fall into a nominalist heresy at this point. The naming and judging undertaken by the agent with respect to the Christian act are not arbitrary. It is not that this naming and judging bear no relation to how it is named and judged with respect to God. Saint Augustine observes, "Ignorance is unavoidable—and yet the exigencies of human society make judgment also unavoidable,"[16] since all contingent judgments await an eschatological judgment. Nevertheless, if there is a participation in the operations of God, then the contingencies of the necessary acts of naming and judging will find their consummation, not their overthrow, in the eschatological judgment.[17] Participation implies analogical relations: our naming and judging participate analogically in God's naming and judging as the act labors in a hope for its consummation. Not that we are unable to make mistakes, to name wrongly (deceiving both ourselves and others), to misjudge. But analogical thinking (or imagining) is, as Gregory of Nyssa explains in his *Life of Moses*, inseparable from anagogical living. That is, the naming and judging are part of a practice of ascent, part of the technologies (in the Greek sense of *teuchō*,

16. Augustine, *De civitate Dei* 19.6.
17. Thus I speak about an eschatological remainder, not an eschatological reserve.

"make, construct") of discipleship. We name and judge far better the more we are subject to God.

The Object of the Action

The fourth key element of an action is the object with respect to which the action is taking place. It is the manner in which a Christian act is irreducible to its execution in the present that renders it irreducible to conscious motivations and irreducible with respect to its naming and evaluation. The same irreducibility pertains to the object of the action. The objects of an action can be separated from the objectives of an action only heuristically. The object of Judas's attention was Jesus's cheek—grammatically. In the act of giving away a handful of change, the first object of the action is the change itself. This object is then handed over to the second intransitive object of the action: the person to whom the change is given. But the object of the action has been chosen in accordance with a specific objective: Judas's choice of the cheek demonstrates to all parties his intimacy with Jesus. The object of the change is chosen in the circumstance because giving the street person one's handkerchief or a used bus ticket would not effect the purpose one wishes for the action. So an object cannot be isolated from the practice governing its choice as an object. I do this rather than that. To forestall again the emergence of the autonomous subject, we can rewrite this from another direction: I do this act that has been prepared for me, rather than that act that has not been prepared (the chiasmus again). The present object/objective, then, is an intimation of a future and final object/objective. What is this object/objective? We return to the processes of subjectification, for I suggest that the future and final object/objective is the submission of all things to Christ. The act, then, becomes an offering; it inhabits the logic of sacrifice—a positive logic, not a negative one. From such a perspective, the object/objective is to facilitate all things becoming what Paul terms "a living sacrifice" (Rom. 12:1). The particular object of any act is thus situated within the schema of redemption, like a composer who submits notes, tones, intervals, and rhythms to the sovereignty of the musical score. In being so situated, each object finds the place of its contribution to the divine order, an order that cannot be known before its accomplishment. The object is, then, situated in the eschatological remainder.

We can become more specific here, for this order is characterized traditionally by those transferable transcendentals, the so-called names of God: justice, beauty, goodness, and truth. The object/objective of the Christian act is to articulate what is just, good, beautiful, and true in, with, and beyond whatever is the grammatical object on which the agent works. In such a laboring, the agent is priestly, the act liturgical, and the object sacramental because each participates in the unfolding of God's grace. The agent is not superior to the object, is not sovereign over it in the way some modern philosophies have exalted subject over object, the human over the givenness of the natural realm, and made it possible to conceive the human task as the taming and exploitation of the natural order. Here the relationship between the agent and the object is symmetrical—the person to whom one gives is not inferior. It is the one I attend to, for both I and he or she are given to each other in this opportunity to offer, to sacrifice.[18] Augustine famously distinguished use from enjoyment and gave enjoyment a higher theological purpose: to enjoy a thing is to participate in the worship of God. God must be enjoyed; he cannot be used. So what I am saying here is that through the act by which I enjoy something, I do not simply use the object, and what I enjoy is the goodness, beauty, justice, and truth of God. Such enjoyment also partakes of the eschatological remainder; it is a joy I do not necessarily experience but that nevertheless I hold by faith. God is being served, and so the Christian's action is always a form of prayer; it is liturgical.

The Effect of the Act

Only when an action is understood in this way can we approach the fifth of the key elements of an action—the effect of the act (both on the agent and on the object of the action). What takes place through the act of offering—of both oneself and the object upon which one is acting—is a transfiguration. But before we explore this transfiguration, let us see what has happened to

18. This is entirely distinctive from a Derridean ethics of the undecidable, in which I give to this cat while bearing the burden of the arbitrariness of this cat with respect to the million other cats that might also need my assistance. See Graham Ward, "Questioning God," in *Questioning God*, ed. John Caputo, Mark Dooley, and Michael Scanlon (Bloomington: Indiana University Press, 2002), 274–90.

a philosophical category often examined with respect to defining an action: effect. The language of "effect" invokes the language of causality. Aristotle distinguishes between material, efficient, final, and formal causation when discussing the economics of motion in the cosmos.[19] The reduction of the construal of action to the autonomous subject, the emphasis on the will as animator of action, and the emphasis on action as occurring only in the world we can see around us gives priority to efficient causation. In modernity, efficient causation dominates; it is the basis for instrumental reasoning. The I authors all action, and that which is executed is an effect of the will-to-cause. There is no final, teleological causation. Several difficulties arise with this model of causation when it is applied to Christian action. First, to unhinge efficient cause from final cause leads to pragmatism if not arbitrariness. Second, the action and animation entailed in a Christian act operates on a divine as well as a human level. The human action participates in a divine soteriological providence. As argued above, this does not erase the I: the I cooperates, or rather the authoring of the I is authorized. Some philosophical theologians have, then, distinguished between primary and secondary causation with respect to divine and human action. This, however, has a tendency to reify the divine and human positions, so that an absolute dichotomy rules them. To some extent, there is a *diastēma*, a distinguishing distance, between the uncreated and what is created; it is a *diastēma* that human sinfulness aggrandizes with respect to the human perspective, and we are plunged into an ever deeper befuddlement the more we recognize the absence of the divine. But the logic of the incarnation and the logic of living and acting as a Christian *en Christō* infer that the *diastēma* allows always for the transits of grace and adoration; the *diastēma* facilitates, does not impede, salvation. If, then, we shift the discourse describing these transits from one of causation to one concerning relations—that is, if we see these transits of grace and adoration in terms of a living relationship—then we are treating, in a more Augustinian manner, the way the desire of those who love each other cooperates to bring about a desired end: all things being one with Christ. It is, then, the final, eschatological cause (if we wish to continue using this language) that informs Christian action at all levels, and the I

19. Aristotle, *Physics* 2.

acts because it desires what God also desires; it is obedient to that desire. The employment of primary and secondary causation as a means of explaining divine and human action can also tend toward a conception of God in terms of some theistic *potentia absoluta*. In the model suggested here (this account of the Christian act), however, God does not force but fulfills human agency.

The shift in discourse can be justified on the grounds that analysis of the relationship between cause, action, and agency is undertaken on the basis of "accounts" given of agents determining something and acting. This is the third problem with respect to the language of causation. We never treat "cause" as such; we treat descriptions of cause, and the descriptions forge links so that the language of cause and effect appears "natural." Lack of attention to this representational or discursive operation leads to the confusions and debates concerning reason and causal explanation. Granted, rationalization is a subset of causal explanation because explanation requires grammatical articulation and grammatical articulation requires an act of reasoning that associates subject, object, and action. Both "cause" and "reason" are intrinsic to saying/writing; they cannot be attended to outside it. But this observation does not reduce all things to the level of language; it merely draws attention to the inevitable linguistic construction of events.

The fourth problem with describing action in terms of the will-to-cause is the sheer fallibility of human willing, attested by the examples of both Paul and Goethe's Mephistopheles. See Paul's wrestling in Romans: "I do not understand my own actions. For I do [*prassō*] not do what I want, but I do [*poiō*] the very thing I hate. . . . I can will what is right, but I cannot do it. For I do [*poiō*] not the good I want, but the evil I do [*prassō*] not want to do I do" (Rom. 7:15–19 RSV). And see the double inversion of this when Mephistopheles first introduces himself to Faust: "The evil that I would do always turns to good."[20] These examples do not deny the will and its involvement in bringing about specific effects within the world. But they emphasize both the limitations of that will—an act of love can bring about tragedy, as all tragic dramatists are aware—and also

20. Johann Wolfgang von Goethe, *Faust: Der Tragödie erster Teil* (Munich: C. H. Beck, 1972), scene 3. Translated by A. S. Kline as "Part of that Power that would/ Always wish Evil, and always works the Good." See www.tonykline.co.uk/PITBR/German/FaustIScenesItoIII.htm.

the limitations of one's own consciousness. We are not transparent to ourselves. As Augustine points out in his *Confessions*, we pose to ourselves one of the greatest questions with which we wrestle.

On this basis, no single agent can calculate the effects of his or her action. The profound interdependence of all things with respect to the providence of God implies that my act of giving away a handful of change can have consequences beyond my own immediate willing in executing this act. It can have consequences for my own spiritual development or its hindering, for other people who witness this act and are affected by my spiritual development or its hindering, and for the person who receives this attention. In the context of what Aquinas calls the effects of God's operations in the world, any object, because it is situated in the eschatological remainder, can become a means of grace. It can be transfigured, and thereby its sacramental nature becomes apparent. Von Balthasar, speaking of the Jewish understanding of wisdom, captures this transfiguration when he describes "the realm of creation [becoming] transparent, allowing us to discern the presence of the divine Spirit within it."[21] Each created object that we hold up to God bears the watermark of the Logos, through whom all things came to be. The effect of a Christian act is never reducible to a set of physical or visible properties. Every effect of a Christian act is related analogously to the raising of a piece of bread at the Last Supper and its identification as "This is my body."

Dispositions and Affections

The sixth element in our poetics of actions is the inner intellectual and/or affective workings that lead to an action. A point that is important for understanding both the fifth and the sixth key elements needs clarification: I am not saying that because we are not totally in control of ourselves, of our actions, or of the consequences of these actions, the act itself is therefore irrational. Stuart Hampshire once remarked that the connection between reason and action is "mysterious."[22] On Augustinian lines, I would agree (he would not, however, accept such lines). But to be mysterious—

21. Hans Urs von Balthasar, *Theo-drama*, vol. 4, *The Action*, trans. Graham Harrison (San Francisco: Ignatius, 1994), 220.

22. Stuart Hampshire, *Thought and Action* (London: Chatto & Windus, 1959), 167.

theologically understood—is not to be irrational or without reason, for Christ as Logos is both word and reason. In a Christian act, our own reasoning operates within this Christic reasoning. Put another way, as in Aquinas, faith perfects human reason. I can, then, give a rational account of my action, but the significance of my action cannot be limited by the account I give of it. The limitations are twofold: first, other accounts from friends, strangers, enemies, or colleagues also are able to rationalize my action, framing it perhaps in a different way. Second, my limited reasoning participates in a higher logic according to which the axiom "I in you and you in me" qualifies notions of personal sovereignty. Both these two limitations emphasize that there is no transparency with respect to intention, but this does not mean that the act is done without deliberation or that a rational account cannot be given for it. For the agent, these alternative frames of interpretation—that given by other people and that given by the Christian faith tradition in its unfolding meditations on the operations of the divine—are hierarchized. The latter is primary or of greater import than the former.

When we come to our sixth key element of action—disposition or pro-attitudes—we need to bear this in mind. Traditional Christian accounts of action, owing something to Stoicism, have emphasized that the role of the passions can distort rational judgments, that there must be a striving for *apatheia*. This has frequently led to a tension between affective states and reasoning—sometimes to a dualism. There appears to be a tension, from the perspective of the twenty-first century, between the fundamental operation of a desire in the theology of Gregory of Nyssa and the goal of *apatheia*. "Desire as much as you can," he advocates. "I boldly add these words: 'Be passionate about it' . . . passionate love [*erōs*] for the divine beauty."[23] But a rational account can be given for affective states in a Christian act even while it is recognized that we have no access to our affective states outside such accounts. There is a long tradition that conceives sensations of the world, acts of intellection, and the stirring of desire as all entailing "movements of the soul."[24] The Greek word

23. Gregory of Nyssa, *Commentary on the Song of Songs*, trans. Casimir McCambley (Brookline, MA: Hellenic College Press, 1987), 47.

24. John of Damascus, *De fide orthodoxa* 2, in *Schriften des Johannes von Damaskos*, ed. Bonifatius Kotter, 2 vols. (Berlin: Walter de Gruyter, 1973), 2:248. Aquinas quotes John when he speaks about the passions and the soul: "Every passion of the

is *kinemapsyches*. It is found in the work of John Damascene, and it is indebted to Aristotle.[25] More recently, neurobiologists such as Antonio Damasio have also drawn attention to the fact that acts of judgment cannot be divorced from feelings and emotional states.[26] Without entering into the difficulties and debates concerning *De anima* 5 and the prime mover, it can be said that in a doctrine of participation, the movement of the soul is situated within the motion of divine action itself. Anagogy is the movement of the soul. Paradoxically, it is related to the verb *anagō* (to lead up, to ascend, to exalt), but what it effects is an entry into a deeper knowledge—in exaltation to God the soul knows its own situation in a radically different manner. Thus we can see, once more, that the authority of the Christian agent is circumscribed since the agent's disposition or pro-attitudes are undergoing a discipline, a formation *en Christō*.

What, Then, Is a Christian Act?

There remains that most abstract of questions: what, then, is a Christian act? In the *Nicomachean Ethics* 6, Aristotle makes a famous distinction between *praxis* (doing, acting) and *poiēsis* (making, creating): "The genus of action is different from that of production, for while production has an end other than itself,

soul is a movement of the sensitive appetite, in consequence of an apprehension of the senses. . . . Properly speaking, passion is a movement of the appetitive power; and more properly still, it is a movement of an appetitive power that has a bodily organ, such movement being accompanied by a bodily transmutation. And, again, most properly those movements are called passions, which imply some deterioration. Now it is evident that fear, since it regards evil, belongs to the appetitive power, which of itself regards good and evil. Moreover, it belongs to the sensitive appetite: for it is accompanied by a certain transmutation—i.e., contraction—as Damascene says" (*Summa Theologica*, question 48).

25. Aristotle distinguished between motion (*kinēsis*) and actuality (*energeia*). They were not dualistic concepts but constituted two poles of a spectrum. *Energeia* was the perfection or realization of all that was potential. *Kinēsis* was the movement that moved all things toward their formal (in the Aristotelian sense of "form") completion. The form is the "*logos* of the essence" (Aristotle, *Physics* 2.3 [194b27]). See L. A. Kosman, "Aristotle's Definition of Motion," *Phronesis* 14 (1969): 40–62.

26. See Antonio Damasio, *Descartes' Error: Emotion, Reason, and the Human Brain* (London: Picador, 1995); and Damasio, *Looking for Spinoza: Joy, Sorrow, and the Human Brain* (London: Heinemann, 2003).

action cannot."[27] In *De anima* the movement of the soul, *kinema-psyches*, is understood as *praxis*.[28] *Poiēsis* comes from elsewhere. It has a practical aspect to it, since it is related to *technē*, but it cannot be reduced to this aspect, for, as Agamben (reading Aristotle through Heidegger, which raises a number of other questions) has recently put it, *poiēsis* "does not bring itself into presence in the work, as acting (*praxis*) brings itself into presence in the act (*practon*)."[29] *Poiēsis* bears a transcendent charge, an ontological weight of bringing something into being, of genesis. The poetic action brings into existence something new, and in that action it also brings about a knowledge of something new. After Aristotle, then, we might characterize Christian acting as a *praxis* that participates in a divine *poiēsis* that has soteriological and eschatological import. It is a *technē*, a crafting, a production of redemption.[30] As already noted, this acting is liturgical, but—returning again to Aristotle—it is also political, ethical, and aesthetic.

The Church

The church, then, as a body of Christians, is constantly active; it is a network of actors reaching into many different parts of city and rural life. It is not only this collection of hymn-singing people, listening to the exposition of the Word and receiving that Word in the sacrament, but also a multidimensional, multigendered activity, living continually beyond its means, transcending by grace all its physical, cultural, and historical limitations, being in relation, productive of relation, being in communion, productive of communion across both space and time. The church is this body of action, this body in action that is both temporal and eternal, material and spiritual. There is no body without this activity, for it is the body of Christ only in and through this continuous operation. This great

27. Aristotle, *Nicomachean Ethics* 6, trans. Irwin, 1140b.

28. Aristotle, *De anima*, trans. D. W. Hamlyn (Oxford: Clarendon, 1993), 433a.

29. Giorgio Agamben, *The Man without Content*, trans. Georgia Albert (Stanford, CA: Stanford University Press, 1999), 75.

30. The Pauline passage from Romans quoted above uses the verbal forms for *poiēsis* and *praxis*. Creative doing—the doing of what is good—Paul also relates to *poiēsis*.

extensive Catholic body is not in the world or entirely of the world, but it is engaged in creating the world anew, reassembling the social.[31] A case could be made that the study of the church should not be called ecclesiology because this word suggests that there is an objective entity out there. When we think about ecclesiology in this way, we reiterate the child's mistake of thinking that the cathedral, the basilica, the minster is the church. The object of studying the church is, rather, ecclesiality, in the same way the study of society is always the study of sociality. Indeed, ecclesiality is only another form of sociality. Neither the church nor society is there as such, as some uniform and foundational stuff. The church is only what this body of Christians do. Even the church as an institution is not there as such, as an object to be observed. The institution is "made to appear" through a series of social acts by various institutional agents: architects, stonemasons, carpenters, glassmakers, weavers of cloth, bankers, and bishops. No one encounters the church as an institution. We encounter this space, this use of land, this person or that, this artifact or that, this order of service or that—all caught up in a circulation of social activity, a circulation that is perpetually in motion and therefore perpetually subject to change. The church—like the social, as the social—is achieved in the interactions of various agents (including objects such as a Communion wafer, a prayer book, and a parish newsletter).

This renders any notion of the church complex in several senses. First, its boundaries are porous not simply because it is irreducible to institutional frameworks but because there is only one panopticon position from which a judgment can be made concerning who is inside or outside this church, who is or is not acting in and as Christ in any particular situation. And this panopticon position belongs to God alone. Second, the church is characterized by being excessive with respect to both place and the evaluation of any act that

31. The phrases "reassembling the social" and "network of actors" are borrowed from Bruno Latour, *Reassembling the Social: An Introduction to Actor-Network Theory* (Oxford: Oxford University Press, 2005). Latour is a Christian thinker, although the theory he outlines touches on the religious only tangentially. "Network is a concept, not a thing out there. It is a tool to help describe something, not what is being described. . . . [It] is not made of nylon thread, words or any durable substance but is the trace left behind by some moving agent. You can hang your fish nets to dry, but you can't hang an actor-network: it has to be traced anew by the passage of another vehicle, another circulating entity" (131–32).

occurs in that place. The work of the church therefore exceeds the limitations of all current ideologies, powers, and dominions—the depoliticizations, the dematerializations, the dehumanizations, the commodifications, the atomisms, ghettos, gated communities, and cosmopolises produced by our current democracies, neoliberal economics, and spurious spiritualities. The church is not unaffected by them, but it works a work that cannot be reduced to them and therefore offers spaces for resistance to them. Third, it is vulnerable because so much of what it does cannot be controlled by the church as an institution. The gospel being preached in practices of piety cannot be patrolled—though it can be informed—by a catechism, by preaching, exposition, or admonition from those with spiritual authority and spiritual oversight. The radical submission to Christ—not Protestantism individualism (which would run counter to my communitarian thesis) but submission to Christ in communion with other Christians living sacramentally governed lives, experiencing through suffering the disciplining of their desires by Christ—is exercised so far beyond the precincts of the parish and the priesthood that it is open wide to making mistakes, making compromises, being blemished. This is the risk the church runs in being the church, but then, that is the risk of faith. Even the church cannot save itself, and the operations of grace are not limited to the *ecclesia*. Its vulnerability means that forever there will be need for confession, correction, repentance, and reconciliation. This is what the kenotic life of being the church and what political discipleship entail.

Only as the ecclesial body, so conceived, engages in civic sociality does it negotiate power relations and the flow of objects that maintain and create the circulations of the social. It cannot prevent such an engagement, for it is itself a sociality. It is only in this engagement that the transcendent values of the body of Christ—love, justice, beauty, reconciliation, worship, forgiveness, and so forth—are produced and promulgated. In acting as the ecclesial body, it works to undo, forestall, and correct other activities not conducive to the transcendent values: injustices, inequalities, alienations, prostitutions, hatreds, envyings, idolatries, dominations, and so forth. It is with this church in mind that we turn now to the city as the theater of (and workshop for) political discipleship.[32]

32. To some extent, this ecclesiology maps on to what Pete Ward, *Liquid Church* (Carlisle: Paternoster, 2002), describes as the "liquid church." I agree with his sug-

The City and Transcendence

Heuristically, this book is divided into two sections—the world and the church—and now we have come to see the relation between those two figures: the world with its immanent self-preoccupations, and the church engaged in creating this world anew in the light of its participation in the eschatological remainder. The materiality of the church, the materiality of its actions, communications, and relations, operates within the world as described in the first three chapters: a world again preoccupied with religion, a world in which democratic polity is changing, a world of globalizing, capitalist forces that generate and demand virtual realities, dematerialized realities. The sites where this world is highly focused are our cities, particularly our global cities. It is, then, the confrontation between the ecclesial body and the secular city to which contemporary Christian thinkers need to return, and return continually.

The city, like the ecclesial body, is a metonymic figure. It is a complex and not in the least homogenized figure. Like the body of Christ, it suggests a bounded whole and an image of order. But it is an image for a collective. Being an image does not render it a fiction; that falls into the nominalist trap. It is an image of something that does appear when the body of Christ or the city acts. Some cities were once bounded with a garrisoned wall. This gave them the appearance of isolated facts. But even then, what went on across the river or outside the walls continually encroached on what went on within. It was difficult to know where the city began and ended. It was always a geographical nodal point, expanding and contracting with every incursion and excursion. But when

gestion that "there are different and more cultural expressions of what this corporate body of Christ might look like," and my own ecclesial descriptions affirm his "idea of church [a]s being constantly reformed, transformed, shaped, and reshaped. Relationships, groups, and communication are fundamental, for through the connections made between people the church is formed" (38). But I differ in seeing the networked body of Christ as nothing new. It is the nature of the church as it has always been. And therefore there is no need to develop new forms of church along the lines of consumerist flows. Such networks and flows must be rooted in the traditions of being church. There always remains the need for discipline, catechism, discernment, and belonging that is transgenerational and historical. The institutional church plays an important role in not only encouraging the development of the body of Christ well beyond its borders but regulating such development. The production of good theology is important in this.

that city went to war with another city, then the city made its appearance, although in this appearance not all citizens participated. Troops were often hired from elsewhere to constitute the city's appearance in war. The city is so much more, then, than its housed institutions—institutions that are themselves constantly changing and being modified. People and systems of organization and government are always on the move, and every move brings about a modification and eventually a new building, or an extension, or a refurbishment, or a demolition. Even so the divisions and hierarchies within the city produced zones carved up by labyrinthine ways—ways not always to be taken, ways that were dangerous when they were taken, forbidden ways. The city was always a dense figure of security, of imprisonment, of sanctuary, of riotous freedoms and sexual license.

Today the city walls of Britain have been replaced with ring roads, and the cityscape conforms to lines of communication suggesting openness and freedom: the railway stations, the arterial roads, and the highway to the international airports and other major cities. The city is more than ever a site of flows—of cars, of planes, of people, of entertaining events, of development and regeneration. Its life is dominated by the suffix "trans-": "transport," "transit," "translate," "transpose," "transform," "transmit," "transfer." The zoning remains: the sex shop area, the place for exclusive shopping, the bank and insurance district, the town hall offices, the barristers' chambers clustered around the courts, the university corridor. But zoning by occupation at the center of a contemporary city is much hazier now, for the city is governed by the ideal of interconnected transparency. The darker corners of city life are pushed into the suburban margins. The murk may gather in the alleys behind the expensive shops and restaurants, but it does not constitute a "social problem" because the streets around the alleys are too well surveilled and the people now inhabiting the center of cities are the new urban wealthy. The new zoning is ethnic, religious, and economic; the cosmopolis is a checkerboard of ghettos and gated communities. On the margins (where the economically deprived and the ethnic and religious minorities abide), the gangs fight it out in areas where people do not go at night and where those living there are imprisoned until dawn breaks. From these areas, the golden halo of the city's floodlit illumination and the pinpricks of red light on the roofs of skyscrapers for passing aircraft are still visible. The allure and spectacle of the city are reflected in the wide-eyed staring of marginalized people; its skyline forms the defining horizon for their hopes and aspirations for a better life.

The contemporary city too aspires—to be a global city. For Saskia Sassens, writing in the 1990s, global cities are the centers of international capitalism—London, New York, Tokyo.[33] These are now the first-tier global cities, transcending national boundaries, for, since that time, with the advances in telecommunications and globalization, a race has developed between competing cities for international image and a stake in the global market. Cities in the past were frequently at war with one another, prey to one another. Now competition prevails. What characterizes the second-tier cities is (a) the marketing of their international links (Manchester or Vancouver's bids to hold the Olympic Games and publicize their official links with China, Hong Kong, the European Union, India, or the United States); (b) the marketing of internationally significant cultural heritages; (c) major investments in national communication links with international destinations associated with tourism and in the construction of lavish hotels; and (d) the development of an international look (iconic new buildings designed by internationally recognized architects). Such cities are the product of the processes of globalization examined in chapter 2, above. Globalization is not the context for these cities; rather, these cities are the very hubs of globalization. In many ways, they also imitate the metaphysics, even theologies, with which (we saw) globalization is invested. To explore this metaphysics is to enter the point where the city and the church struggle to win hearts and minds, struggle over the soul of the city.

This struggle is not simply a rivalry between the secular and the sacred; the struggle is much older than the emergence of the secular. In fact, given what archaeologists (e.g., Vere Gordon Childe), anthropologists (e.g., Mary Douglas and Mircea Eliade), and historians (from Numa Denis Fustel de Coulanges to Lewis Mumford) can tell us about the origins and development of the city and given what we find in the myths of the founding of cities (by the Egyptian god Ptah and by Cain, the son of Adam), the city has never been a secular space. So, in order to appreciate the cultural politics

33. See Graham Ward, *Cities of God* (London: Routledge, 2000), 239–41.

involved here as the metaphysics of the contemporary city confront the transcendent values of the church, we have to take a step back to understand the long relationship between the city and the sacred. We have already seen that the eschatological vision that pervades the discourse on globalization is indebted to the Christian tradition and its continuing imaginary. But there is in the lineaments of our contemporary cities an older sacrality that takes on the ideals of the Christian vision for the city of God.

Theologies in the City

Cities are the greatest and most complex of human art forms. They are aesthetic installations of juggernaut proportions, and they are shot through with transcendental aspirations. Lewis Mumford raises an important question. What, he asks, drew people from the comfortable security of villages into the towers, walls, and precincts of the early cities? Cities were not created simply out of large numbers of people coming together; something attracted them into an orbit that fed not their bodies but their desires and imaginations. Mumford pinpoints the catalyst: the figure of the local chieftain merged with the priest and created the king. With the institution of sacral kingship, a new symbolic world order emerged—the city.[34] Only for the gods would human beings exert themselves in the building of citadels and the construction of walls too thick simply to keep out other human and animal invaders. The king became a symbol, a metonymic figure of dazzling ambiguity, incarnating the corporate personality of the community. It is not that the sacred was invented with kingship, for the shrine had always been a focal point for congregating and, before city dwelling for the living, there were always necropoli, cities of the dead. But with the institution of sacral kingship came an urban explosion, for around him grew the scribes, the lawyers, the military, who fostered an intellectual and cultural life. The city thus came to represent "the cosmos, a means of bringing heaven down to earth, the city [as] a symbol of the possible. Utopia was an integral part of its original constitution, and precisely because it took form as an ideal projection, it brought into existence realities that might

34. Mumford, *City in History*, 47–51.

have remained latent for an indefinite time in more soberly governed small communities."[35] The city, then, has always been shot through with references to the transcendent, while simultaneously being the site for the massive extension of what it is to be human, for in cities human capabilities are extended by the aggregate of human beings dwelling there; there is an accumulation of wealth, power, and intellectual ingenuity. Besides being the sites for the sacred, they are the sites for Promethean aspirations, sites for self-assertion. Here lie the origins over the struggle for the soul of the city.

Mumford's conclusions on the origins of cities coincide with other scholars who rake out the intimations of liturgical sacrifice in the founding of cities and their planning. The city is haunted by anthropological longings and theological reasonings older than Christianity. In the Hebrew Bible, the founding of cities follows on the murderer of Abel, the shepherd; a recent theologian of the city, Jacques Ellul, still insists on the association of cities with murderous acts of hubris.[36] Late in the nineteenth century, Fustel de Coulanges, a classical scholar, drew attention to the complicity between religion and the founding of cities: "As soon as the families, the phratries, and the tribes had agreed to unite and have the same worship, they immediately founded the city as a sanctuary for this common worship, and thus the foundation of a city was always a religious act."[37] Furthermore, the ritual of such a foundation frequently began with a sacrifice, and only those partaking in the sacrificial ritual were deemed citizens. Joseph Rykwert famously drew attention to the accounts of rites for the founding of cities among the ancient Greeks, Etruscans, and Romans. Rome itself was built upon the fratricide of Remus.[38] Much historical scholarship has agreed with the work of Fustel de Coulanges and Rykwert.[39]

35. Ibid., 42.

36. Jacques Ellul, *The Meaning of City*, trans. Dennis Pardee (Grand Rapids: Eerdmans, 1970).

37. Numa Denis Fustel de Coulanges, *The Ancient City: A Study of Religion, Laws, and the Institutions of Greece and Rome* (Baltimore: Johns Hopkins University Press, 1980), 126, originally published as *La cité antique: Étude sur le culte, le droit, les institutions de la Grèce et de Rome* (Paris, 1864).

38. Joseph Rykwert, *The Idea of a Town: The Anthropology of Urban Form in Rome, Italy, and the Ancient World* (Princeton, NJ: Princeton University Press, 1976), 27–40.

39. Carolyn Routledge, "Temple as the Center in Ancient Egyptian Urbanism," in *Urbanism in Antiquity: From Mesopotamia to Crete*, ed. Walter Emanuel Au-

Cities, then, are not simply geopolitical systems, nodal points in a functional logic of state economics. Cities, like their inhabitants, have memories, undergo transformations (for better or for worse), respond to circumstances, try to seize perceived opportunities, and bear the scars of defeat and the laurels of triumphs. And just as we have learned from Augustine that human beings are questions to themselves and so much deeper than even the profoundest psychology, sheering off into their eternal origins, so cities are sites of infinite mystery, with origins shrouded in mists and mythologies. Boundaries were drawn here, not there. In tracts of open savannah, the lines of frontiers were inscribed upon virgin land not in any arbitrary manner but with rites and ceremonies, pieties, prayers, and liturgies to transcending powers. At whatever date the city was founded, something was always there before it that signaled an occupation that cannot now be recovered. And so the city was always, among other things, a religious site, and the sacrificial rite confirmed its sacrality. Liturgical violence and utopianism were the foundations for an ideal commonality that aggrandized (and sometimes conflated) both human potential and divine power. The city, as a simulacrum of heaven, was the site for the ascent and descent of the gods. It marked a place of transit between the terrestrial and the celestial.

In the Common Era, and under the influence of Christianity and then of secularism, the myths and actual performance of sacrifice were more closely associated with the logic of renunciation: a libation offering of one's subjectivity. But well into the medieval period and the era of the divine right of kings, the founding of cities was seen as a royal, theological duty. For Aquinas, the builders of cities are imitators of the divine. Toward the end of Aquinas's rather enigmatic treatise *De regimine principum*, after a detailed exposition of the role of sovereign and pope, attention is turned dramatically to the founding of cities. An important theological analogy shapes Aquinas's thinking: as God creates the world, so in the world kings should found cities. "The founding of a city or kingdom must therefore also be considered as falling within the duty of a king."[40]

frecht, Neil Mirau, and Steven Gauley (Sheffield: Sheffield Academic, 1997), 221–35, rehearses many of the same details regarding the organization of the city, centered on the temple, in ancient Egypt.

40. Thomas Aquinas, *Political Writings*, ed. R. W. Dyson (Cambridge: Cambridge University Press, 2002), 37.

The duty is a theological one, its fulfillment, a theological task. Conceived in this way, cities are always sacred spaces.

Why is the founding of a city a theological task? Because human beings are made by God to live in communities; their happiness is possible only within communities. "For men come together so that they may live well in a way that would not be possible for each of them living singly. For the good life is according to virtue, and so the end of human association is a virtuous life," Aquinas adds. The city is conceived as the space within which human beings achieve their happiness, a happiness born of coexistence and living virtuously. To provide the urban context in which such living is possible is to provide the theological conditions for human flourishing as God ordained it. The king must therefore provide for the community a city that guarantees a place (a) "suitable to the preservation of the health of the inhabitants" (Aquinas discusses geographical conditions and buildings facing in the best directions for the circulation of air and for the balance of sunlight and shade because the social life is related to the natural life), (b) fertile enough to provide them with sufficient food," (c) pleasant enough "to give them enjoyment," and (d) "defended enough to afford them protection" and security from enemies. To these four conditions that satisfy the physical, existential, and aesthetic must be added a fifth—"places suitable to worship"—for "the final end of the multitude united in society . . . will not be to live according to virtue, but through virtuous living to attain to the enjoyment of the Divine."[41]

With Aquinas, more so than even Augustine (who was interested in neither urban planning nor urban culture), we can lay down a theological marker for the relationship between the city and the ecclesia. The point at which he begins his theological construction is a common anthropology in which human beings were created to be happy and in which therefore they require conditions that will best facilitate that "living well." But Aquinas, taking his cue from Aristotle, states that they cannot be happy unless they live in political communities. Living well is not living as individual islands, each best seeking to find satisfaction through his or her own consumer decisions. There is a life in common, a good in common. Aquinas was himself a monk who walked the pavements not

41. Ibid., 38, 39, 40–41.

of a cloistered monastery but of cities such as Naples, Paris, and Rome. His work for the church was accomplished not exactly in the streets with respect to citizens but was certainly caught up in complex political affiliations with an aristocratic family allied with the Holy Roman Empire and a religious order closely associated with the pope. He advocates urban conditions that facilitate the virtues necessary for both happiness and the beatification, the vision of God that is the end toward which living virtuously is orientated. The city is, then, a moral landscape, shaping practices and persons, offering opportunities for developing piety. It is a place where the Good can be lived in community; and it is the political responsibility of citizens to seek out, articulate, and practice how the coflourishing may best be achieved. Happiness here is a goal, a telos, toward which human creatures must aspire because it is their deepest and most providential drive.

Enjoyment is inseparable from this transcendent Good and central to the practicing of these virtues. The king must create a city that is "enjoyable" to live in because the ultimate end of being human is the "enjoyment of the Divine." Just as the city accords, in some analogical sense, with the teleological ordering of creation, so the aesthetic enjoyments of an urban environment are related to the spiritual enjoyments of salvation. Both civic beauty and civic virtue serve the same end—participation in the life of God: they capitulate to the transcendent Truth that gives, maintains, and operates in all things. The aesthetics of urban developments, then, have to be conformed to this teleology—to aspire to the truth and to inspire the practice of what is good, what is just. The temporal is orientated always toward the eternal not as something following after the temporal but as something that already indwells the temporal.

Aquinas recognizes that cities are divided. They are primarily divided between two iconic sites: the castle or fortress (that *in concreto* is the offer and symbol of protection and security) and the cathedral (that *in concreto* provides the care and guidance "towards the harbour of eternal salvation").[42] But between these two topoi are other divisions that, for Aquinas, accord with the order of creation: the different locations where people will group together "in their various occupations," the locations where people

42. Ibid., 40.

will dwell, the transport system that will facilitate the flourishing of the city, and so forth. The founder of the city must divide it up "in such a way as to supply all the needs which must be met if the kingdom is to be complete."[43] Division is, then, not seen as a lack but a positive measure facilitating the autonomy and strength of the city. The divisions are hierarchically arranged. *De regimine principum* rehearses the papal line on authority: the king, as a temporal power, must submit to the higher spiritual power of the pope, and the people must submit to both temporal and spiritual powers. The castle, though the residence of the founder and designer of the city, is only a passage to the cathedral as the "harbour of eternal salvation." The orders of occupations and vocations are eschatologically orientated; through them one embarks on a pilgrimage through time and beyond it. The city always looks toward its future.

Although Aquinas leaves off his speculations here (his treatise was finished by the hand of another), if the designer of the city is analogously associated with God as the Creator of the world, then the city too must be analogously associated with the holy city, the heavenly temple-centered Jerusalem, revealed to Ezekiel and waging war with the secular Babylon in the book of Revelation. The secular Babylon, with all its ostentatious magnificence, will fall:

> "Alas, alas, the great city,
>   Babylon, the mighty city!
> For in one hour your judgment has come."
>
> And the merchants of the earth weep and mourn for her, since no one buys their cargo anymore, cargo of gold, silver, jewels and pearls, fine linen, purple, silk and scarlet, all kinds of scented wood, all articles of ivory, all articles of costly wood, bronze, iron, and marble, cinnamon, spice, incense, myrrh, frankincense, wine, olive oil, choice flour and wheat, cattle and sheep, horses and chariots, slaves—and human lives.
>
> "The fruit for which your soul longed
>   has gone from you,
> and all your dainties and your splendor
>   are lost to you,
> never to be found again!"

43. Ibid., 38.

> The merchants of these wares, who gained wealth from her, will stand far off, in fear of her torment, weeping and mourning aloud,
>
> "Alas, alas, the great city,
> clothed in fine linen,
> in purple and scarlet,
> adorned in gold,
> with jewels, and with pearls!
> For in one hour all this wealth has been laid waste!"
>
> And all shipmasters and seafarers, sailors and whose trade is on the sea, stood far off and cried out as they saw the smoke of her burning,
>
> "What city was like the great city?" (Rev. 18:9–18)

The fate of Babylon in this narration, which many scholars take to stand for Rome, is the fate that befell Sumer, Jerusalem, Athens, Assur, and Banaras—all ancient cities and the centers of ancient cultures. The smoke from the fall of Babylon will drift along the streets and boulevards of all cities, reminding them of the seductions and consequences of human hubris. Behind the monumental facades of every city lie two mythic possibilities: the heavenly city of new Jerusalem and the demonic city of Babylon. These are the futures that race ahead of building programs, urban developments, and regeneration schemes, but the "eternal harbouring" that Aquinas's city builder aspires to, like the new Jerusalem in Revelation, is no product of human engineering. It comes "down out of heaven by God, prepared" (Rev. 21:2 RSV). Its coming announces not a continuation but a disruption of the human city. The human city as an entity will pass away (later we will explore what this means for the church).

Time passes, and if you visit most cities in Europe, what you find are the remnants of Aquinas's double-focused city, with its castle and its cathedral. Often the castle is in ruins or only recently rebuilt with money from the Heritage Foundation and open to the public as a museum. The cathedral, with some exceptions, continues but competes now with buildings just as iconic and imposing: banks, hotels, insurance companies, town halls, stock exchanges. Nevertheless, cities remain haunted by the ancient sacrality that expresses itself in their futuristic and utopian outlooks. The modern designers of cities are all utopian even in their concrete attention to material details. We can hear in the writings of architects such as

Le Corbusier and Ludwig Mies van der Rohe the visionary nature of their ambitions.[44] Some—for example, Frank Lloyd Wright in his plans for Broadacres and Le Corbusier in his project for the Radiant City—are explicitly utopian.[45] They are designers not just of buildings and boulevards, parks, pavements, and shopping malls; they are designers of lifestyles. Every city is an expression of the way its citizens sought and still seek to live out their conception of the good life. This is especially so as we witness a massive return to living in city centers in preference to the leafy suburbs. All cities are oriented toward an ideal future—the creation of increasing wealth, power, and well-being. All cities seek a timeless and universal perfection. They seek to show that here is a place where human beings prosper. They seek to make a name for themselves. With the contemporary city, it is as if the metaphysical and political ideals of the Enlightenment—the absolute freedom of the individual, total rational transparency, the promise of the new at the heart of the modern—were now made technologically possible with the advent of steel framework buildings, reinforced concretes, and laminated glass. The towers of our aspiring global cities, the crystal palaces of our atriums and arcades are demands for a city without shadows, whose values are immediate and self-evident. They are constructions of light and space, just as much as the great gothic cathedrals of Europe. They are the homes and workplaces of angels or those aspiring to a humanity without limitations, a humanity perfected. Our contemporary cities are conceived as cities for angels. And angels do not die. Modernity's emphasis on the immediate and self-evident, the present, the "now"—even though all its facades are futuristic—is about forgetting death. Death is the ultimate human limitation; the flight from death drives us toward the future conditions of being human that cities dream of embodying.

Contemporary cities, then, are teleologically driven. They are shot through with echoes of transcendence and, in a more theo-

44. For Le Corbusier, see *The Radiant City*, trans. Pamela Knight (New York: Orion, 1967). For Mies van der Rohe's interest in Aquinas see, Franz Schulze, *Mies van der Rohe: A Critical Biography* (Chicago: University of Chicago Press, 1995), 93–94, 172–73.

45. For a discussion of Frank Lloyd Wright's utopian planning, see Robert C. Twombly, "Undoing the City: Frank Lloyd Wright's Planned Communities," *American Quarterly* 24, no. 4 (October 1972): 538–49.

logical idiom, aspirations for a realized eschatology. They participate, or aspire to participate, fully in the metaphysics and theologies of globalization. Central to this participation is money—money, which is both increasingly dematerialized and a sovereign power (see chap. 2). The new transcendencies that are being written into the fabrics of our global cities are all made possible by the power of money to transcend all boundaries, laws, limits, and norms—moral, political, economic, social, and geographic. The various flows within the city are all basically flows of money, money as the constitutive rule of modernity's transcendental logic,[46] its "reality principle."[47] The future orientation of money—toward the begetting of more money—allies with the utopian yearnings of cities to install the heavenly in geometries that emphasize the infinite. They are cities created for endless happiness and perpetual enjoyment—for those who have—for, to return to Aquinas, these cities are not rooted in a common good. The end they seek is their own aggrandizement. They are rooted in the cultural trends outlined in the first part of this book: depoliticizing hyperindividualism and neoliberal economics that puts property more and more into the hands of fewer and fewer, and a godlessness that places all its hopes in human endeavor and technological advancement. Our contemporary cities are not sites for the development of virtuous citizenship; they are not sites for the development of citizenship at all. City dwellers aspire not to the transcendent moral values of the good and a just distribution of the city's goods but to the transcendent aesthetic values of the beautiful and the sublime. They cultivate lifestyles without conscience, beyond good and evil. And aesthetics without ethics become anaesthetics. The city becomes a compilation of sites where the forgetting mentioned in chapter 2 can be effected, where we can be diverted away from the seedy,

46. The term "constitutive" with respect to transcendental logic refers here to Kant's schema for understanding and knowledge. The constitutive rule replaces the Kantian "regulative principles," i.e., the three principles without which there would be no understanding or knowledge for Kant and that we thus have to accept "as if" they were provable. They are regulative, for Kant, insofar as they are not provable givens as such but only demonstrably needed in the operation of transcendental logic. Money, I am claiming, is a not regulative principle for thinking through modern living but a proven given. There is no "as if" about money; it is what makes modern living possible.

47. I am indebted here to the examination of the metaphysics of money in Philip Goodchild, *Theology of Money* (London: SCM, 2007).

run-down, dysfunctional margins and be gloriously entertained. In ambitious city halls around the world, in our electronic global age, the image they wish to impress on the world is of a city comparable to Oz or some eternal city of glass and halogen uplighting. The contemporary successful city is measured by how close it can approximate to the clean and radiant cities, cities without shadows—transparent, controlled, reliable, efficient, culturally interesting, and diverse.

It is not insignificant that I have been employing the third-person pronoun "they" throughout, as if these cities have corporate personalities utterly detached from the people who inhabit or even help to govern these enterprises. And this is true. But unlike the older cities where the king, prince, or an oligarchy embodied the city's persona, today the city's ego lacks a face. Contemporary cities encapsulate the analysis by Claude Lefort with respect to democracy (see chap. 1), that democracy is fashioned around a void, a space left empty with the disappearance of the king, a space that the sovereignty of "the people" as such cannot fill because "the people" is too ambiguous and nebulous a figure to occupy that space. Similarly, there is no focus for the city's power other than its own image. Cities thus follow the trend described in chapter 2: the brand name is more important, more powerful symbolically, than the product. This is where the global city differs from the modern city.

The modern city, as conceived by Fritz Lang in the film *Metropolis*, is governed from a panopticon position (represented in the film as the tall central building overseeing all the other buildings). This center is (quite literally) manned by Johann "Joh" Fredersen, who, like a secular God, sees all things.[48] But the global city has no panoptic point. It does not even have the illusion of an all-seeing one. Both Jeremy Bentham and Foucault conceived the modern panopticon as an empty surveillance tower that would nevertheless totally control the prisoners' behavior. Similarly, there is a power vacuum in the middle of the contemporary city that is most magnificently disguised. There is the illusion of power as pyramidical in what is actually a circulation of forces that contest, combine, and compete. And these are not ethereal forces; they are people working in institutions, corporations, academies, courts of law, and so forth. Each city

48. For a discussion of *Metropolis*, see Ward, *Cities of God*, 29–32.

has its governing, even elected, council and its various departments and offices. But the city is not identified with this council, which, as again we saw with democratic politics, is increasingly hidden and shielded from personal responsibility by the out-sourcing of its work to private organizations who bid for short-term contracts. The city, then, is impersonal, and this is why there is a struggle for its soul. Its soul should be the collection of its citizens all working toward what best cultural and social conditions might be provided for the common pursuit of human happiness and enjoyment. It is this working that constitutes the political and where the real struggle should take place. But who can represent such a collection today? There are other contenders for that soul—every major international consortium or corporation that wants to exploit the city's cultural and social resources; every major stakeholder, including the city's most prominent university, that wants to increase the volume and value of its stake; the state at the national level, wishing to fulfill its own designs for the region; and every political party vying for seats on the council. In a sense these contenders are not very interested in the soul of the city. They do not believe that either the city or the citizens have souls anyway. What they are interested in is the struggle for control. This is what they understand as the political—a share in the power of dominion. But out of this struggle and out of the various interests jostling for control, the cultural and social life, which is the soul of the city, is forged.

There are two conceptions of being political involved in this struggle: the working on behalf of the common pursuit of human happiness and enjoyment and the contending for dominion. These two conceptions manifest themselves in two different understandings of the struggle itself—the struggle for maximal human flourishing and the struggle for power. To understand the differences in the nature of the political and the character of the struggle is theologically important because, if the church sees itself simply as another possible stakeholder in the city's life, then it will always lose out. It will be working in accord with an understanding of politics and struggle that belong to the market, understandings that are not its own.

I am not saying that cities attain this perfection; I am only pointing to the ways in which transcendence is written into the architectures and layouts of these cities, giving expression to their ambitiousness, their hunger for international recognition and international tourists. The contemporary city's appeal to an aesthetics of transcendence is the city's most recent attempt to make itself an object of worship. As cities become increasingly multicultural and pluralist and as therefore the multiplicity of differences becomes the basis for violences, cities must turn themselves into sites of veneration and cultivate a new form of civic religion.[49] They must make of themselves an image. The aesthetic seductions of its architecture, shopping, and leisure facilities—along with the multiplication of closed-circuit television, the staging of sports and entertainment events, prominently placed giant plasma screens, and heavy, no-tolerance police patrolling—are all attempts at controlling the potential violences out of which the contemporary global city is born.

Mumford, after detailing the rise and splendors of the early cities in Mesopotamia and Egypt, adds a cautionary note: "Even the early civilisations of the East, perhaps *especially* these, suffer from the vice which now threatens to overwhelm our own civilisation in the very midst of its technological advancement: purposeless materialism."[50] The struggle for the soul of the city is a struggle over the shaping and quality of the human culture found there. Our social imaginaries are governed by the cultural possibilities for conceiving how to live the good life. The church, as I have conceived the church, must necessarily be engaged in this struggle. It must affirm all that is good in city living—the opportunities for enriching social life, its diversity, especially religious diversity, since religious diversity enables the church to reflect on its own practices of piety. The church can celebrate the transcendent aspirations expressed in the British city: the construction of iconic buildings and civic magnificence, even the fostering of civic pride (the pride in belonging); its ambitions to host the world, to be a player on the international stage; its desire to make all the different flows through the city easier, cleaner, and more efficient; its ability to generate work, on which so much self-worth is founded; its facilities for leisure; its deep and continuing connectedness to the values and meanings of the past, materialized in the Saxon remnants of

49. See William T. Cavanaugh, "From One City to Two: Christian Reimagining of Political Space," in *Political Theology* 7, no. 3 (2006): 299–321. Developing some Augustinian ideas, Cavanaugh draws attention to "the false religion of the earthly city" (315).

50. Mumford, *City in History*, 134.

its cathedral, the seventeenth- and eighteenth-century hostelries, its nineteenth-century public library, town hall, and hospital; its energies; its creativity; its festivities; its potential for inclusiveness; its freedoms; and its inventiveness. The church can celebrate the visual paradoxes of white Portland stone and monumental prisms of glass, weighty baroque and Shinto simplicity: violent, even visceral contrasts that make possible, continually, new civic discoveries—an ornate window molding here, the back view of a redbrick tenement there; a Doric portico, a reconstructed waterway, a gothic extravagance, and a postmodern fantasy of a seaside exterior created inside a derelict printing business. It can even celebrate the contemporary city as an architectural fairground because, as Aquinas reminds us, human beings were born to be happy and they should also enjoy. But the church must use this cityscape for a very different end.

This new ordering of the British city center—which banishes the primal clutter of poor housing and badly maintained 1960s public housing—creates a new kingdom, but at a cost. Although there is a development of mixed housing "across the river" or "the other side of the rail-track," the center itself is fashioned for the propertied, the landlords with buy-to-rent mortgages, the professionals who need saline swimming pools and gyms in the basements of designer apartment blocks, who gaze at night out of their floor-to-ceiling windows at the network of lights and the floodlit attractions. And we all want to be with them. Some of us find it hard to admit this. But we want to be with them because we, too, have been sold this dream as the good life, which should be available to everyone. So the church has to be alert to the dehumanizing and godless dangers of the cultural trends outlined in the first part of this book—trends that promote alienation and social atomism, dematerialization and virtualities, aesthetic sensibilities divorced from ethical ones, postdemocratic disenfranchisement, and reductions to the "purposeless materialism" about which Mumford wrote. The church must not allow areas of the city to be walled up. Ghettos and gated communities must be entered; the no-go zones riddled with racial and economic tensions and ruled by violence must be penetrated and linked back to the wider civic society; and the Christians in these places must be hospitable, opening the possibilities for transit, for the flow of communications necessary for freedom. The church must work alongside other agencies at every level, from city governance and planning to networks dedicated to helping those newly arrived in the city to establish themselves, helping those who fall beneath the pressures of the city's ambitions, those dwarfed and rendered insignificant by its towering achievements.

In the final part of *Cities of God*, I drew attention to a startling phenomenon on the streets of British cities in the closing years of the twentieth century—the homeless. The homeless continue to proliferate, but to my mind the new global cities of the twenty-first century are creating two immediate social problems besides homelessness: a new class of slaves, laboring for minimum-level wages in the multiplicity of service industries, and a new class of somnambulists surfeited with shopping and anesthetized with entertainment, cultivating their own lifestyle and profoundly forgetful of civic responsibilities and the proliferating needs of the disadvantaged. These are the city dwellers who wish to live (and have the means to live)—in imitation of the pagan gods—beyond good and evil, free to indulge or restrain as they think fit, dizzied by the simulacra and believing only in their own satisfaction. The church needs to be engaged with the politics of resisting the development of such slavery, insisting that the city's glory cannot be built on the sacrifice of human life (as was the glory of certain cities in the past). It must recognize that the dark side of the city's ambition is its collective will to dominate and find ways to expose and counter such domination. It needs to challenge the secular teleologies in the name of its own eschatological remainder—testifying to the kingdom that is yet to come and cannot be built with human hands; preaching the aspirations for a common society, the commonwealth; awaking those (even among its own numbers) who are living without conscience. The church must become the church in every relationship it creates and maintains throughout the city; it must perform Christ in every microcontext; it must recognize and own the politics of its discipleship.

6

The Metaphysics of the Body

> [To] be no part of any body, is to be nothing. . . . At most, the greatest persons, are but wrens, and excrescences; men of wit and delightfull conversation, but as moales for ornament, except they be incorporated into the body of the world, that they contribute something to the sustentation of the world.[1]

This chapter elaborates the ecclesiology outlined in the last chapter. It counters some of the prevailing trends described in the first three chapters and provides the pursuit of postmaterialism with a metaphysics. In particular, this chapter is concerned with constructing a metaphysics of the body (physical, civic, ecclesial, and christological) that runs contrary to the dehumanizing and dematerializing effects of living in a contemporary city that is being swept away on the tides of secular teleologies that are political (the postdemocratic movement toward ever-increasing control of the social), economic (the euphoric eschatologies of the free global market), and cultural (the development of liquid and commercial-

1. John Donne, quoted in John Stubbs, *Donne: The Reformed Soul* (Harmondsworth, UK: Penguin Books, 2007), 229.

ized religiosity). The bodies of each of us and the various bodies with which we are affiliated and in which we participate are the very focus for the circulation of forces and dominions in the global city, for, as Donne observed, our bodies are "incorporated into the body of the world." The profound forgetting that is intrinsic to current civic living—that turns a blind eye to advancing slaveries and the proliferation of new poverties—is associated with a reduction of the body to mere flesh. An eschatological humanism needs to examine this reduction and enable the body's transcendent and intrinsic values to appear. Only with a right understanding of embodiment in its many guises is effective political agency possible. The body as mere flesh is a radically depoliticized body, and a depoliticized body is a body waiting to be controlled, coerced, and manipulated by the political, economic, and cultural powers that play with it.

This metaphysics of the body deepens postmaterialist trends with two rejections. The first is the rejection of the body as an object. There are no naked objects that just exist. All objects are invested with meaning; the body is meaningful, it signifies. A good metaphysics inquires into this meaningfulness—into the investment of meaning, into who or what is making the investment, into the process of meaning making. Second, and as a corollary, there is a rejection of the dualism of the physical and the metaphysical, materiality and spirituality, nature and culture. By "metaphysical" with respect to the body, I mean the system of values pertaining to embodiment and *through which* embodiment is viewed, shaped, and performed. These are the theological values espoused in Aquinas's conception of the good life: the moral value of goodness, the social values of justice and truth, and the aesthetic value of beauty. There is, then, no materiality as such; materiality is always enmeshed within conceptual evaluations. This does not mean that there is no difference between matter and thought, only that they cannot be separated in any inquiry into either. Now "matter *matters*."[2] How matter matters is related to how it is made to speak, how it speaks, and what it speaks. We are reminded that "bodies only speak if and when they are made heavy with meaning."[3] To

2. Judith Butler, *Bodies That Matter: On the Discursive Limits of Sex* (New York: Routledge, 1993), 27–56.

3. Annemarie Mol, *The Body Multiple: Ontology in Medical Practice* (Durham, NC: Duke University Press, 2002), 10. Mol tries to overcome the notion of the body as a single object and even raises the question of what an object is as such.

be made "heavy with meaning" relates to the events in which the body presents itself, announces itself, and performs its meaningfulness. This is a series of operations that enact a metaphysics. While one would have to admit that the dualism of matter and thought, too, announces a certain metaphysics, it does so by creating a false clinical space in which materiality can appear as itself, shorn of any values, naked under the clinician's objective gaze. The body becomes an object, and its nakedness is claimed as the truth, as what is real. These are metaphysical claims because they announce that this is how things are: the furniture of the world is a collection of objects out there that can be subject to various forms of empirical analysis and to the data collecting of positivists. But the creation of such a reductive view of materiality constitutes a bad metaphysics. A good metaphysics is one that avoids such falsehood-creating reductions, acknowledges the complicity of meaning and matter, and recognizes that this complicity is not epiphenomenal or a contamination of one by the other but, rather, points to the necessary cohabitation of the material and the metaphysical.

Why does it seem absolutely critical that we move toward constructing a good metaphysics of the body, of bodies made "heavy with meaning"? Because the cultural devaluation of the body is shockingly ironic given the attention to fitness, the intensifying biopolitics of various governments, the all-too-publicized concerns with obesity and dieting. It is an irony that parallels the plethora of material goods that flood our main streets together with the attention to branding that idealistically elevates the name above any material content. The irony is bold: the greater attention to the physical, the more dematerialized it becomes. Ellis's novel *American Psycho* opens up this contemporary paradox concerning the marketing and production of contemporary embodiment.

This is not a novel for the squeamish, but it is a parable of the reductions brought about by rapacious free-market capitalism. Pat Bateman, Ellis's protagonist (see chap. 2, above), is a high-earning young executive with a perfectly toned body living in New York. He is film-star handsome. He moves among a similar kind—people with what Brett calls "hardbodies," clothed from socks to tie in designer wear, continually on the lookout for new, expensive, and exclusive restaurants; people who look so alike and are so accustomed to using others that they frequently fail to recognize one another. Bateman is also a sadistic killer who carves up and sometimes eats his victims with little show of emotion. "In my locker at Xclusive lie three vaginas I recently sliced out of various women I attacked in the past week. Two of them are washed off, one isn't. There's a barrette clipped to one of them, a blue ribbon from Hermès tied round my favourite."[4]

The novel, written in the 1990s, points to a fascination with embodiment that has emerged with postmodernity and continues up to the present day with the public exhibition of dead bodies in a plastic coating.[5] This fascination could be called "the return of the flesh" with the Pauline understanding of *sarx*: human beings reduced to their sheer physicality.[6] *American Psycho* is a testimony to the hell of such a reduction; indeed, Dante's *Inferno* echoes throughout the text, along with advertisements for *Les Misérables*. Bateman is the dark side of our fascination with the body. What concerns Ellis is that this bourgeois cultural obsession with gyms, cooking, sex, and bodily fluids expresses an unapologetic materiality that is ultimately nihilistic. It is a materiality that cheapens the body. The overproduction of the body not only commodifies it; it dehumanizes and depersonalizes it. And this is what Ellis's novel plays out. The body is just a billboard for an accumulation of brand names. Beneath it there is nothing, a void. Bateman senses that neither he nor anyone else is anything: "Where there was nature and earth, life and water, I saw a desert landscape that was unending, resembling some sort of crater, so devoid of reason and light and spirit that the mind could not grasp it. . . . This was how I lived my life, what I constructed my movement around, how I dealt with the tangible."[7] The action described here is "movement," not purposeful agency; the tangible is only an image from

4. Bret Easton Ellis, *American Psycho* (New York: Vintage, 1991), 370.

5. The program notes of a highly controversial exhibition titled "Bodies" at Earls Court, London, in 2006 announced, "A collection of 22 life-sized, whole human bodies are on display in Bodies The Exhibition, accompanied by 260 assorted organs and body parts. Stripped of their skin and plastinated in various poses, the exhibits are intended to show the science of human biology up close and personal." When it was staged in Berlin, Catholic priests rightly performed an act of political and cultural resistance to this exhibition by staging an equally public requiem mass.

6. Giorgio Agamben examines this reduction in terms of "bare life" and views the creation of "bare life" as endemic to contemporary political living (*Homo Sacer: Sovereign Power and Bare Life*, trans. Daniel Heller-Roazen [Stanford, CA: Stanford University Press, 1998]).

7. Ellis, *American Psycho*, 374–75.

a war zone in Afghanistan, Iraq, Lebanon, or Darfur. Bodies are not persons in Bateman's world, only screens for the commercialized empire of labels. Ellis's novel presents us with the experience of contemporary nominalism.

I want, then, to "humanize" the body by arguing that the body can be valued positively and participate in political agency only when it is viewed metaphysically and made heavy with meaning. Along with an eschatological ecclesiology, I wish to develop an eschatological humanism, for the humanism that emerged with the concerns with civility in the eighteenth century and the liberalism that arose in the nineteenth have led to the situation that Ellis's novel describes. In the theological language of Paul, I want to put the *sōma* back into the *sarx*. The danger is not just mass murder in the name of a no one. The danger is the disintegration of the social into the heartless aesthetics of postmodern culture, and when this happens, we can say good-bye to being political, because people are valued only as long as they are entertaining.[8] Ellis's novel depicts a final stage in an atomism and an alienation that turn the body (as several of Bateman's victims are turned) into a depersonalized shell. Beyond the rampant and competitive individualism of laissez-faire capitalism lies the marketing of people as products; beyond the reduction to materialism lies the omnipresence of the image, the simulacrum, and the virtually real.

In *Cities of God* I examined the Eucharist as a site in Christian theology for rethinking an embodiment that is resistant to material reductiveness and for rethinking Jesus Christ's body and the ecclesial body in terms of displacement and transcorporeality.[9] In more recent work, I have employed phenomenological analyses by thinkers such as Maurice Merleau-Ponty, Michel Henry, and Jean-Louis Chrétien to explore the nature of touch, for touch cannot reduce the body to an object seen, to a visible surface, in the way sight can.[10] But it strikes me that beginning with the human body,

8. The enormous popularity of TV reality shows such as *Big Brother* reveals this tendency. When contestants stop being entertaining, they are voted out and disappear into the vast anonymity from which they had emerged. But there is no lack of people willing to step forward to take their place; being a celebrity is nowadays the only way to get oneself named and one's existence confirmed.

9. Graham Ward, *Cities of God* (London: Routledge, 2000), 81–149.

10. See Graham Ward, *Christ and Culture* (Oxford: Blackwell, 2005), 61–72, 101–4, 120–27.

even if it belongs to Jesus of Nazareth, capitulates, to some extent, to modern individualism. The understanding that the freedom of the individual was the greatest achievement in human integrity has a complex history that travels down a thousand capillary byways from the Protestant Reformation, the personalized mysticism of sixteenth-century saints, Cartesian skepticism, and John Locke's understanding of the human being as a tabula rasa to Stuart Mill on liberty. And paralleling this exaltation of the individual was the loss of an ontologically founded community—that is, a community rooted in a sense of belonging one to another, to a social order, to a cosmic order ordained and sustained by God.[11] To focus, then, simply on Christ isolates once more this body as the object under investigation and prevents an understanding of the body as multiple, the body as belonging to, and participating in, numerous corporations, the body as enacted within a diverse range of scenarios, each of which stages different meanings and values that transcend the modern atomized individual who is set adrift on a sea of choices. In switching attention to the corporations that the body is mapped on to, we can elude some of the neat and stable identifications made about an isolated subject, for the body, as will be shown, is never one.[12]

Think of the body in a hospital, in a mortuary, at prayer, in a gym, in a nightclub, at a political debate, in the act of sleeping, or in the act of making love. In one site it is an object of clinical investigation; in another it is subject to a health and/or beauty regime advocated by various current ideologies; in another it is being social; in another, political; in another, physically intimate; and so forth. In each of these sites, the body speaks differently and enacts embodiment differently—sometimes individually but mostly collectively. Granted, all these practices of being embodied relate back to the same body (if we set aside the fact that internally and externally the body is continually changing chemically, emotionally, and physiologically). But the body's identity is never fixed; its

11. Such a community could be called real as distinct from the imaginary communities—or what one might call nominal communities—that will be discussed later with reference to the work of Benedict Anderson on national communities. Communal belonging in modernity is increasingly fixed on the family; it is biological. Enlightenment thinkers such as Kant and Hume, however, sought to establish a sense of a universal human community.

12. See Mol, *Body Multiple*.

singularity is composed of any number of coordinated practices, and in this way it is incorporated into other larger corporations and corporealities. The body as object "is the new subject of politics. And democracy is born precisely as the assertion and presentation of this 'body': *habeas corpus ad subjiciendum*, 'you will have a body to show.' . . . This new centrality of the 'body' in the sphere of politico-juridical terminology thus coincides with the more general process by which *corpus* is given such a privileged position in the philosophy and science of the Baroque age, from Descartes to Newton, from Leibniz to Spinoza."[13] In this exploration, then, I want to disrupt the privilege of the physical body and develop the metaphysics of the body not from the perspective of one body, Jesus Christ. In fact the body of Christ reveals the densest mode of all embodiment. Rather than from Christology, I want to begin from another perspective entirely that foregrounds the ecclesiology sketched here: the body politic.[14]

The Body Politic and Its Current Crisis

Influenced no doubt by Hellenistic part-and-whole thinking, we have a tendency to understand the word "body" in "body politic" as a metaphor. The physical body is an organized whole made of various interdependent parts, and so we extend this understanding of embodiment to a political organization. And so the body, either physically or politically, is a homogenous entity. Some commentators see this in Paul's use of the body analogy for the church in 1 Corinthians: the body is used properly with respect to the physical and metaphorically with respect to the ecclesial (or political). The assumption here is that the physical body is an object that can be grasped, that can be known—reductive materialism again.

13. Agamben, *Homo Sacer*, 123–24.

14. What associates the physical body with the political body is that both are social bodies. "The body-as-used, the body I am, is a social body that has taken meanings rather than conferred them. My male body does not confer masculinity on me; it receives masculinity (or some fragment thereof) as its social dedication" (R. W. Connell, *Gender and Power: Society, the Person, and Sexual Politics* [Cambridge: Polity, 1987], 83). Although I disagree with Connell that the body is simply a passive recipient in a wider social and sexual politics, he nevertheless allows us to see the extent to which the physical and political body is constructed through designations and always viewed through the rich association of socialized images.

But the body is always an imagined thing. We only ever deal with body images, and so the body as a metaphor or the body as an analogy is only a specific rhetorical employment of the imagined body. Paul plays with imaginative understandings of the body when he extends his use of *sōma* to speak of sin (Rom. 6:6), humiliation (Phil. 3:21), dishonor (1 Cor. 15:43), and death (Rom. 7:24). It is these other uses of the word "body" that can reorientate our thinking about embodiment and open up a repositioning of the human body in terms of the body politic.

In political thought, the body politic has had a long history. How long is still a matter of debate among biblical scholars and historians of late antiquity. Landmarks include John of Salisbury's text *Policraticus* (ca. 1159) and Christine de Pizan's *Book of the Body Politic* (ca. 1407). The medievals, following Plato, recognized an analogical relation between human embodiment and social embodiment. There was an ontological continuity between personal and political corporeality. A great chain of being associated the microcosm of the human body with the macrocosm of the heavenly bodies, establishing a series of analogical resemblances between the ordering and governance of the cosmic, the political, and the physical. Theologically, on the basis of the doctrine of the incarnation, these analogical resemblances led to the development of ecclesial and sacramental understandings of the body. The perfect form of embodiment (of being human) was Jesus Christ and then, after the ascension of Christ into heaven, the church understood as a kingdom of God being present but not yet fully realized.[15]

Hobbes famously describes the state as an "artificial man."[16] He signals a new development in our understanding of the body. The body politic for Hobbes is a machine. It is no coincidence that this conception of the artificial state appears alongside a new

15. Henri de Lubac, *Corpus Mysticum: L'Eucharistie et l'Église au Moyen Âge* (Paris: Aubier-Montaigne, 1944), details the development and complexities of this understanding of the body, although, unfortunately, because his emphasis is on the development of eucharistic theology, he does not relate it to the body politic. *Policratus* and *Book of the Body Politic* could have added a significant layer to the theological nexus he excavates. Ernst H. Kantorowicz, *The King's Two Bodies: A Study in Mediaeval Political Theology* (Princeton, NJ: Princteon University Press, 1957), charts much more of this story.

16. For a more detailed analysis of Hobbes and the community of desire, see Ward, *Cities of God*, 127–31.

model for understanding the physiology of the body. One of the key figures in developing this model was Hobbes's Oxford friend Richard Harvey. It was Harvey who, through experimentation on both humans and animals, mapped out the fluid mechanics of blood circulation, which led to the development of blood transfusions.[17] The mechanical body was, then, both a political and a physiological phenomenon at the same time.

Hobbes, like Harvey, was announcing a radical distinction between the natural and the artificial; this followed what Charles Taylor calls the "great disembedding" and the rise of "the impersonal order."[18] The great disembedding is what took place with the advent of modernity. Previously, "human agents are embedded in society, society in the cosmos, and the cosmos incorporates the divine." But the new attention to the individual, "to have our own opinions, to attain to our own relation to God, our own conversion experience . . . disembeds us from the cosmic sacred . . . disembeds us from the social sacred; and posits a new relation to God, as designer."[19] With God as architect and mechanic, the ontological relations that bound the physical, the political, and the cosmic together no longer hold. Hobbes conceives the state as a human construct based on contracted relations, an artificial machine necessary to rein in the murderous lusts of the natural man. His thinking expresses an enormous shift in how we understand what the political body is founded on. The mechanical body, like the mechanical understanding of the cosmos, impersonalizes the world. The world becomes a place indifferent to human beings, a theater of increasingly calculable forces and counterforces with no meaning beyond their own mathematical operations, with no intrinsic moral meaning such as goodness or beauty or justice. Although there is a hierarchy with an absolute ruler at the apex, there is no longer a controlling sacramental world order analogically related to a transcendent principle. We are now the makers of our world and of any meaning, moral or otherwise, that we might find in it. Corporate living in which, as for Augustine, the private was related to the Latin *privatio*—a sin because it is a lack

17. Locke, who began life as a medical student, participated in these experiments.

18. Charles Taylor, *A Secular Age* (London: Belknap Press of Harvard University Press, 2007), 146–58, 270–95.

19. Ibid., 152, 157.

of something substantial to being human—was now a matter of convention and consensus, for the social is composed of "disengaged, rational agents."[20] The social (from *socius*, friend, relation, associate, fellow human being)—now divorced from a theological account of grace-bound nature—was subjected to the cultural, that which human beings make for themselves.

There is no one more disengaged and rational than Ellis's Bateman, and the bodies in *American Psycho* are merely fleshly envelopes over a mechanics that, through weights and push-ups, is able to reach maximum efficiency. Bateman is the apotheosis of a cultural trajectory to which Hobbes (and Harvey) gives a particular expression. But by the time we arrive at Ellis's novel, what is rational is viewed as subjective, not universal: the more one justifies one's actions to oneself, the more one's rational intelligence can view itself as superior to another's. This shift to the mechanical, impersonal world with its disengaged individualized agents has consequences not only for how nature, ethics, and society are understood, as Taylor's work details; it has consequences for the body politic and, by extension, the understanding of physical embodiment as well. Latour points to one of these consequences that takes us right back to the paradox with which this discussion opened: the greater the attention to the body, the more dematerialized it becomes. "From the myth of the social contract onward, the body politic has always been . . . a *problem*, a ghost always in risk of complete dissolution."[21] In this shift the political body becomes a fiction, a virtual reality, cut off from the substantiality of human embodiment. There remain only an image and a series of actions that point to the enactment of this political body, that make manifest a political body—for example, the televised proceedings of the House of Parliament, or the Chancellor of the Exchequer announcing his budget, or the declaration of war. The body politic itself cannot be seen in the way it was seen previously—in the physical body of the emperor or the king (see the discussion on Lefort in chap. 1). The democratic body politic is an empty cipher waiting for someone arrogant enough to fill the space with his or her body and open to analysis only through tracing of the points at which it acts politically.

20. Ibid., 283.

21. Bruno Latour, *Reassembling the Social: An Introduction to Actor-Network Theory* (Oxford: Oxford University Press, 2005), 162.

The state as such becomes imaginary, in Benedict Anderson's understanding of this process: a voluntary association made up of people who never or rarely meet face-to-face, whose sense of belonging together is constructed through certain cultural vehicles (a map, a museum, a census, a national newspaper) that generate the means for envisaging a collectivity and a homogeneity.[22] And every new wave of migration, every new fold in a culture's pluralism, destabilizes this image of the collective and triggers a new round of questioning: "What is it to be British?" "What is it to be European?" "What is it to be an American?"

But perhaps there is a further turn in this cultural logic that we have been tracing from Hobbes through to Anderson and Ellis. Modernity spawns imaginary communities and reductive understandings of the body as a highly sophisticated biochemical machine. Yet recently Hardt and Negri exposed a suggestive genealogy in which there is a further shift— from the imaginary body of the nation-state to what they term the "contemporary Empire." In the past "the traditional army thus forms an organic fighting body, with generals for its head, lieutenants for its midsection, and the common soldier and sailors for its limbs." But in the move toward Empire, there is a "command shift from a centralized model to a distributed network model."[23] They proceed to examine what this shift entails for the political body.

I want to extend their analysis also to include the personal, physical body. My suggestion is that in this shift toward the motile and the imaginary, bodies become fictions, cultural and social waifs, disposable because their identities are dispersed across networks of symbolic exchanges, enmeshed in the march of metaphors, lost in a forest of brand names and market manipulations. And this situation is a step beyond liberal humanism with its convictions of progress and civilization. In the network society, physicality is diffuse and identity is dissolved into a plethora of user names and log-in codes. Intimate conversations continue across vast distances between people who will probably never meet or do not wish to meet, people whose bodies are reduced to avatars. There are second-

22. Benedict Anderson, *Imagined Communities: Reflections on the Origin and Spread of Nationalism* (London: Verso, 1991).

23. Michael Hardt and Antonio Negri, *Multitude: War and Democracy in the Age of Empire* (New York: Penguin Books, 2005), 56, 59.

life options of living in a virtual community, with a fantasized body shape and body sex. Living increasingly online, to the extent that it is possible—for the computer keyboards and the people behind them are still located somewhere—makes Latour's ghost of the body politic even more phantasmagorical. Bateman's world teeters on this edge of the shift (there are cell phones in the novel but not the telecommunicative possibilities we have today). Nevertheless, one wonders whether this current shift toward networks resists or entrenches a nihilistic metaphysics. Despite all the potential for new forms of political resistance to emerge because of instant access to server lists, resistance is spasmodic and responsive. Are bodies in a network, political and physiological, not further surrendering to the impersonal, the disengaged, and the arbitrary? The fear that this is so makes only more urgent the need to weight the body with meaning.

The Metaphysics of the State

How, then, do we go about examining and therefore producing a good metaphysics of the body politic, a metaphysics of the body that can at least offer an alternative, and a more robust postmaterialism? After all, a postmaterialism that is not centered on the body politic and embodiment more generally is just airy utopianism.

As seen in the first section of this study, the shift toward postmaterialist values points to a new emphasis on well-being and quality of life, but it remains strongly attached to the affluent society and the individual choice of lifestyle. Furthermore, its values—such as freedom of speech, equality, humanism, community, world peace, and a sustainable environment—operate at a consensual level among those who buy into them. It is closely associated with the immanent ordering of things and, as such, responds to economic and political stability where the struggles for survival, food, and security are in the past. The postmaterialism advocated here is theologically and metaphysically rooted. It is only when it is so rooted that postmaterialist values are sustainable above and beyond economic and political trends. Postmaterialism may well be constructing "a new worldview framed by sustainable development and based on altruistic, co-operative individualism, which will give rise to 'deep' democracy (embodied in all aspects of our lives), greater social cohesion, strong communities and families, and so heightened quality of life and wellbeing."[24] But in the context of the trends identified in the first section—among them, postdemocracy, globalization, depoliticization, dematerialization, and hyperindividualism—it needs the gravitas of belonging to a metaphysical and theological worldview.

How can we provide postmaterialism with such a worldview? We could reconstruct the analogical world order, reimagining bodies from a certain Catholic and Eastern Orthodox perspective. I attempted this in *Cities of God*, but I want to take a different approach this time, though with the same aim: to examine the metaphysics of the modern state—the state conceived, after Hobbes, Locke, and Hegel, as a mechanical body politic—and suggest an alternative theological metaphysics that will support, from a scriptural perspective, the analogical worldview proposed in *Cities of God*.

The state is a metaphysical entity, even when conceived as a machine lodged within the clockworks of a universe. The disembedded and impersonalized body politic is still nevertheless embroiled in a metaphysics—that which it believes is the true state of affairs, transcending the views of individuals, a universal condition. I am exploring the metaphysics of the modern state in order to replace that metaphysics. Fascism clearly recognizes its metaphysical investments. Keynes, writing in 1915 about Germany, could speak of "a sort of idealism. The nation will grow into a 'closed unity,'"[25] a monad in which all parts constitute a whole. The fascist state as a collectivist state demands the commitment, even sacrifice, of its members for the good of the fatherland. There is something ultimately Spinozistic about this metaphysics—there are no individuals, only modifications of the transcendent One.[26] The body figures forth this oneness, this closed unity. For Spinoza, that one body is God's; his is the ultimate monotheism, the dissolution of all difference. With the fascist state, the polity of the radical immanence of Spinoza's metaphysics is made plain, but

24. Richard Eckersley, "Challenge of Post-materialism," *Australian Financial Review* (March 2005): 28.

25. Quoted in Friedrich A. Hayek, *The Road to Serfdom* (London: Routledge, 2001), 188–89.

26. For a more detailed examination of Spinoza's body politic, see Ward, *Cities of God*, 131–37.

monotheism has morphed into an imperial *Volksgemeinschaft*: the state is a religion.

But let us not suppose that liberal democracy avoids the metaphysics of the state. Certainly, it does not aspire toward a closed unity; rather, it seeks to be inclusive of difference, embracing plurality positively. The liberal-democratic state is not, then, monistic. But inclusivity is not without its limits. There are boundaries to how inclusive a liberal-democratic society can be. Migrating peoples come face-to-face with these boundaries, which can either exclude them or include them on the basis of some nationality test. But for the majority of people, these boundaries are invisible because they are profoundly internalized. These are boundaries made up of core shared values: freedom, equality, mutual exchange and benefits, and, more recently, human rights, transparency, and accountability. To some extent, these values are protected by law. But the values themselves are abstract, universal principles for coexistence in the liberal-democratic state. Through these values and lofty ideals, such as the maximization of individual liberty, self-rule, and the sovereignty of the people, the state becomes a metaphysical entity. In a postdemocratic condition, some of these values and ideals can seem remote and virtual, with increasing skepticism about the sovereignty of the people and alarm at what appears to be invasions of privacy and the erosion of personal freedom. In fact, the more ethereal the values and ideals, the more metaphysical the state becomes. If the totalitarian and fascist state is grounded metaphysically on the notion of the One, the liberal-democratic state is founded metaphysically on a relationship of the One to the Many. In the history of philosophy, there are several versions of the metaphysics of the One and the Many. But the one that best suits liberal democracy is the emanationist account: from the One there is an overflowing that multiplies through various mediating offices until it produces the Many. Those who are farthest from the power and influence of the One can imagine that they are free although, in truth, their continuing existence depends on the One. At the outer edges of the Many, in the emanationist account, is unformed and chaotic *hylē* (matter)—bare life, disengaged, unregistered as either serf or slave.

It is thinkers of the liberal-democratic artificial state who tend to view as a metaphor the body with respect to the political. Fascists such as Mussolini accepted that political corporatism was the body macro made up of the bodies micro. The metaphysics of Mussolini and Hitler's understanding of corporatism was then wrapped in the pseudoscientism of natural law: *Blut und Boden*. The correlation held between the political and the physiological, for, while the Third Reich was under construction and its mythology was being cultivated, films were produced that presented models of the Aryan body and its healthy physical development. The fatherland was to be composed of sturdy, energetic, well-formed blond-haired and blue-eyed men and women.

Liberal democracy, by contrast, seeks to portray itself as a political machine without a head, not a political organism. And its relationship to being embodied is ghostly, as we have seen. The head of this machine is nominal, a primus inter pares accountable to his or her cabinet and party and the electorate. The head can be removed—impeached, for example, or voted out next time. But there is a headship; hung parliaments and coalition governments are always weak parliaments and weak governments. With the "return of the king" (see chap. 1) comes the increasing demand for stronger leadership given by such a head. The stronger the leadership, the more the complete political vision for the state is realized and the more embodied it becomes as the nation. Strong headship is frequently expressed in terms of spearheading the nation's destiny—a nation's messianic mission. Hayek, in his famous and highly influential 1944 book against socialism, *The Road to Serfdom*, quotes the English political historian Paul Lensch writing in 1918 about German socialism fulfilling "her historic mission of revolutionising the world."[27] The same rhetoric appears in Lenin, as it does in Hitler and Mussolini: it is not just that certain nations have to be the political and economic avant-garde idea of nationhood; this indeed is their destiny. But how frequently have we heard this same rhetoric in recent years in the speeches of prominent liberal-democratic leaders? This direction toward a greater national solidarity runs counter to the dissolution of political and physiological embodiment in both the processes of globalization and the advance of the network society. There is a tension here that is, no doubt, rooted in conflicting metaphysics.

The argument here has been that there is a relationship between how the physical body and the political body are conceived in any

27. Hayek, *Road to Serfdom*, 179.

social and cultural period. The relationship bears on the kind of metaphysics, its governing values and ideals, that the state is enacting. Furthermore, the relationship and its metaphysics correlate with whether the language of embodiment, when viewed politically, is either metaphorical or analogical. The physical body—or the way in which embodiment is understood and fashioned—is, then, directly related to the body politic. This does not mean that one is the cause of the other. The relationship is more subtle than Foucault's notion of biopower, although such biopower is a key aspect in modern methods of governmentality.[28] Instead of "biopower," I prefer the term "state apparatuses," used by Althusser and adapted by Foucault to his own end.[29] The body politic works out its ideology, its metaphysics of physical and political embodiment, through various state-informed practices acting through various state-related institutions—schools, hospitals, universities, religious bodies supportive of state policy, the army, the police force, the courts, and so forth. These apparatuses not only promote certain values and views of the bodies political and physical; they shape them through specific disciplines imbued with specific values (usually held to be moral values). By this means the metaphysics of one kind of body produces the metaphysics of another, and vice versa.

The distributed networks composing the new political "body" of Hardt and Negri's Empire must, then, affect our conceptions of physical embodiment. This is why it is important to read the cues about how this embodiment is construed as they present themselves culturally—in *American Psycho*, for example, or Tracey Emin's installation *My Bed* with its used condoms and blood-stained underwear, shortlisted for the 1999 Turner Prize.

Hegel's Metaphysics of the Body Politic

Since the metaphysics of the state continue to produce dehumanization and dematerialization, where can the resources be found for an alternative metaphysics? If the liberal dreams for humanism are fading fast, then how do we construct humanism in a differ-

28. On Foucault's notion of biopower, see Ward, *Cities of God*, 34.

29. Louis Althusser, *Lenin and Philosophy, and Other Essays*, trans. Ben Brewster (New York: Monthly Review, 2001).

ent way that weights the body, political and physiological, with a meaning that is not arbitrary?

Fascism, liberal democracy, and the distributive body of Empire each deny a theological foundation for political sovereignty; the denial comes with the great "disembedding" and the emergence of a secular public realm. All three polities are implicated in the promotion of complex metaphysics, moral codes, and lofty ideals; it is not immediately evident whether these are good metaphysics or what will happen to these values and ideals with the advent of the postsecular condition, although some scholars have begun to think through what a postsecular state might look like.[30] It is in the space opened by the new visibility of religion that we can examine more closely these metaphysics and their relationship to theology, bearing in mind the rejection of the dualism that pitches the materiality of the body against its spirituality, matter against thought.

Hegel also rejected this dualism (though not the nature/culture distinction): the actual is the rational, the concept and its existence are two aspects of the same thing. Philosophical inquiry, whether regarding individual human bodies or the state itself, seeks to discern "in the semblance of the temporal and transient the substance which is immanent and the eternal which is present."[31] The word "eternal" points to Hegel's conviction that the metaphysics of the body implies a theology of the body (I will develop this later). Hegel begins his treatise on the body politic with an analysis of human embodiment, leading eventually to a study of international law and the World Spirit.

> The concept and its existence [*Existenz*] are two aspects [of the same thing], separate and united, like soul and body. The body is the same life as the soul, and yet the two can be said to lie outside one another. A soul without a body would not be a living thing, and vice versa. The existence [*Dasein*] of the concept is its body, just as the latter obeys the soul which produces it.[32]

30. See Maeve Cooke, "The Secular State for a Postsecular Society? Postmetaphysical Theory and the Place of Religion," *Constellations* 14, no. 2 (June 2007): 224–38.

31. Georg Wilhelm Friedrich Hegel, *Elements of the Philosophy of Right*, trans. H. B. Nisbet (Cambridge: Cambridge University Press, 1991), 20.

32. Ibid., 25.

To some extent, this could have come straight from Aristotle's *De anima*, but Hegel explicitly develops the logic of existence (body), concept (soul), and their interrelationship into an account of the content and form of the state and the operation of reason that governs both: "For *form* in its most concrete significance is reason as conceptual cognition, and *content* is reason as the substantial essence of both ethical and natural actuality."[33] For Hegel, then, the political body can be understood only in terms of a *thinking about* and a *reasoning concerning* the body.[34] The body politic is, for Hegel, inseparable from "concepts of truth and the laws of ethics"; the state is a metaphysical entity. Furthermore, it is an "inherently rational entity"; that is, its form and content, its soul and body, participate in the great dialectical reasoning of *Geist* as it moves toward the actualization of the Absolute.[35]

> The states, nations [*Völker*], and individuals involved in this business of the world spirit emerge with their own *particular and determinate principle*, which has its interpretation and actuality in their *constitution* and throughout the whole *extent* of their *condition*. In their consciousness of this actuality and in their preoccupation with its interests, they are at the same time the unconscious instruments and organs of that inner activity in which the shapes which they themselves assume pass away, while the spirit in and for itself prepares and works its way towards the transition to its next and higher stage.[36]

A nation, when composed of individuals in families, a civil society organized into corporations, and a governing class of professional civil servants, becomes a state. A group of individualized states, freely consenting to an international law code and under the sov-

33. Ibid., 22.

34. In the preface to *Elements of the Philosophy of Right*, Hegel argues polemically for the role that philosophy has to play in understanding the state and the political. He counters contemporary suggestions about the secularity of the state and the denigration of metaphysics in political science, advocating the need to establish any thinking about the state in terms of "universal principles" (18). For those opposing the metaphysics of the state, "the claims of the concept constitute an embarrassment," but, Hegel adds, this is an embarrassment "from which they are nevertheless unable to escape" (19).

35. Ibid., 19, 21.

36. Ibid., 373.

ereignty not of any single ruler but governed by the dialectic of the "universal spirit, the spirit of the world,"[37] gives way to the final state, which is the actualization of that universal Spirit. In terms of feeling and the ethical life, this final state is the embodiment of faith, love, and hope.

This is where the metaphysics of the body becomes inseparable from a theology of the body, for the final embodiment of faith, love, and hope, a triad Hegel takes from 1 Corinthians (13:13), is the Christian kingdom of God, Christianity being the highest expression of the spiritual and the rational: "Heaven [is brought] down to earth in this world, to the ordinary secularity of actuality and representational thought."[38] This is the end of history, though not the end of time.

Fukuyama is right, then, to read Hegel as announcing a final consummation, although Fukuyama emphasizes that the key virtue of such a realm is individual freedom—rather than faith, love, and hope—expressed in a universal democratic condition.[39] He misunderstands the nature of freedom for Hegel because Hegel would not concur with Fukuyama's individualism; he is no liberal. The individual, as Hegel makes plain, loses his or her identity as such. An individual's freedom is sublated to the freedom of the whole in the actualization of the freedom of the Absolute Spirit. The only true freedom is the "free infinite personality."[40] The state is the end in itself; everything else, everyone else, is sacrificed to the logic of the state. This is hardly Fukuyama's apotheosis of free-market liberal democracy. In fact, although Hegel's account is evidently communitarian, there is a question whether it is democratic at all. Numerous commentators have believed that he provides the philosophical basis for totalitarianism, and we can see some reflection of the Spinozistic monism of the fascist state. But the metaphysics of Hegel's state is not totalitarian. Hegel positively endorses constitutional monarchy—"the achievement of the modern world, in which the substantial Idea has attained infinite form."[41] This is as far as

37. Ibid., 371.

38. Ibid., 380.

39. Francis Fukuyama, *The End of History and the Last Man* (Harmondsworth, UK: Penguin Books, 1992).

40. Georg Wilhelm Friedrich Hegel, *Phenomenology of Spirit*, trans. A. V. Miller (Oxford: Oxford University Press, 1977), 20.

41. Hegel, *Elements of the Philosophy of Right*, 308.

he goes in his last major work, but in view of Hegel's theology and the working of the Universal Spirit beyond the particularities of nationhood, constitutional monarchy would find its consummation in a messianic rule. "The usual sense in which the term 'popular sovereignty' has begun to be used in recent times is to denote *the opposite of that sovereignty which exists in the monarch*. In this oppositional sense, popular sovereignty is one of those confused thoughts which are based on a *garbled* notion [*Vorstellung*] of the people. *Without* its monarch and that *articulation* of the whole which is necessarily and immediately associated with monarchy, *the* people is a formless mass. The latter is no longer a state."[42] The constitutional monarchs of nations must give way, in the final actualization of *Geist*, to the absolute monarch; the realization of the kingdom of God is the realization of the rule of Christ, whose Spirit was given totally to the world after the death of God on the cross. I will return to the "formlessness" of popular sovereignty at the end of this chapter. Here it is important to understand that Hegel cannot easily be secularized in the way Fukuyama, after Alexandre Kojève,[43] secularizes him. In fact, secularization is the final achievement of the coming down of heaven to earth, of the laboring of faith, love, and hope; only then is the transcendent principle made fully immanent.

In one sense, that Fukuyama reads Hegel badly is not the point. It is, rather, that Hegel's state as the body politic is a thoroughly metaphysical and theological notion, and the individuals whose wills and desires are sublated to the logic of the state's development participate in a spirituality that refuses the sheer materialism and its consequent irrationalism announced in Ellis's novel. It is because bodies are spiritual that they are free and must be political. In *American Psycho* there is no scope for political action when all action and agency are reduced to the anonymity and moral anesthesia of "movement" in an infinite Sierra Nevada. "Hardbodies" are consumers, customers, or clients; they are not citizens.

Nevertheless, there is a certain symmetry between Bateman's world and Hegel's that can lead to the conclusion that Hegel's is

42. Ibid., 319.

43. For Alexandre Kojève's famous Marxist/Heideggerian reading of Hegel, see his *Introduction to the Reading of Hegel*, trans. James H. Nichols Jr. (New York: Basic Books, 1969).

a bad metaphysics. Both worldviews are governed by immanent processes, although, for Bateman, these processes are blind and arbitrary. With Hegel, the language of the infinite, the truth, the eternal, the universal, and the absolute is articulated within the dialectical circles of the immanent that has a teleology, a goal. His speculative philosophy is a metaphysics, announcing, in Kantian terms, a transcendental logic, but it has nothing to do with transcendence itself. For Hegel, this logic is founded on a theological and historical conception of the Trinity in its working in the world. Christ on the cross dissolved the transcendence of God the Father into the immanent operations of the Spirit of Christ within the world. Two important corollaries issue from this philosophical theology.

First, there is no ulterior standpoint exterior to and transcending the dialectics of this world. Salvation is a product of a relation between the mental (*geistliche*) contemplation that goes on within this world, such as the philosopher's speculative logic, and the movement of Absolute Mind (*Geist*). The relation does not admit alterity, a fundamental and unsublatable difference such as might be possible in the analogical worldview, where difference remains difference even though in relation.[44] Instead there is a univocal relationship between the spiritual (*geistliche*) operations within human beings and the Absolute Spirit (*Geist*).

Second, the theological dynamic for the dialectic of history is the way of the cross. The work of the Spirit is a work of negation. The trajectory along which the politics of the state moves toward the ultimate kingdom is constituted by negativity. Hegel analyzes this work of negation in terms of the will and desire in determining the particularity of the "I." There are two moments in this particularization. In the first moment is the I's emergence from "the element of *pure indeterminacy*," from a negative freedom that Hegel describes as "the freedom of the void, which is raised to the status of an actual shape and passion."[45] At this point, what is posited to the I in its self-contemplation is a representation, an abstraction. But Hegel is not content, in this analysis of

44. On analogy, see Ward, *Cities of God*, 129–30; and, more extensively, Ward, "Speaking Otherwise: Postmodern Analogy," in *Rethinking Philosophy of Religion: Approaches from Continental Philosophy*, ed. Philip Goodchild (New York: Fordham University Press, 2002), 187–211.

45. Hegel, *Elements of the Philosophy of Right*, 38.

the I, to restrict himself to psychology. There can be a collective I, a corporate personality. Hegel then immediately adds, "If it turns to actuality, it becomes in the realm of politics or religion the fanaticism of destruction, demolishing the whole existing social order, eliminating all individuals regarded as suspect by a given order, and annihilating any organisation which attempts to rise up anew."[46] What we glimpse here is Hegel's positive evaluation of the French Revolution as it appears more clearly in his letters: the pure destructiveness and iconoclasm that characterized the Reign of Terror. This is Hegel's account of a negative or, we might say, apophatic body politic.

But the second moment in the determination of the I is not a cataphatic reversal. The actual *positing* of this determinacy and differentiation "is just as much *negativity* and cancellation [*Aufheben*] as the first—for it is the cancellation of the first abstract negativity. Just as the particular is in general contained within the universal, so in consequence is this second moment already contained within the first and is merely the *positing* of what the first already is *in itself*."[47] Indeterminacy is negated to become the determined, and the determined then is overreached in a further dialectical sublation, and so on. Speculative philosophy, then, as a political science must "apprehend the negativity which is immanent within the universal."[48]

What are the consequences of this radical immanence, driven by the universal laboring of negativity, for a metaphysics of the body politic? First, we are not treating monism as anything like the way it appears in Spinoza—exactly because Hegelian metaphysics is dynamic and differentiation is not epiphenomenal. If the fascist state can be associated with Spinoza's metaphysics, then with Hegel we approach something similar to Leon Trotsky's notion of the permanent revolution.[49] The World Spirit, working in and as the human spirit, continually transforms the cultural given. Hegel notes that modern society and its prevailing polity is an outworking of the Reformation and the French Revolution. But as we saw, this modern politics will, too, give way to what has yet to appear,

46. Ibid.
47. Ibid., 39.
48. Ibid., 40.
49. Leon Trotsky, *The Permanent Revolution, and Results and Prospects* (New York: Pathfinder, 1969).

although it remains concealed in the present as a potential. If there is one overriding polity, it is a theocracy, except that there is no direct rule by God; the operations of the Absolute are always and only mediations through concrete circumstance. Although Hegel's own representation of the state comes closest to being oligarchic—since the monarch is only a figurehead and the actual governing proceeds through bureaucratic leaders—the content of the state is never fixed. Its essential form is not liberal-democratic, communist, monarchic, fascist, or oligarchic, and yet potentially it is all these polities and more. Hegel did not celebrate the French Revolution because it was a move from absolute monarchy to democracy. He celebrated it because "the human spirit has outgrown like the shoes of a child" the ancien régime.[50] Although any state has specific content, then, it is continually subject to indeterminacy. There is always a body image, if you like, that gives shape to the body itself, but the image is governed by a prevailing iconoclasm, a political and theological apophaticism. This forestalls idolatry, in a manner similar to the way the apophatic safeguards the mystery and transcendence of the divine for the mystic theologian. But it is with the mention of "transcendence" that we have to recall the immanentism of Hegel's thinking on the body politic. The working of the negative in Hegel is a continual reminder of limitations, of finitude, but it is also, because it is an operation of *Geist*, a continual reminder of the infinite. One might suggest that Hegel has transposed the mystic's cosmological notion of transcendence into a historical one. But history cannot be infinitely open for Hegel; he would then fall victim to his own analysis of the nihilism of the "bad infinite." A final state, an end of history, is presupposed. The system has a closure, and Hegel does not view the immanent development and exposition of *Geist* as a circle that endlessly repeats itself—what Nietzsche would call eternal reoccurrence.[51]

50. Hegel, *Elements of the Philosophy of Right*, 397.

51. Walter Kaufman quotes Heinrich Heine as Nietzsche's source for the idea of "eternal reoccurrence." Heine sums this idea up in Nietzsche's famous words: "Time is infinite, but the things in time, the concrete bodies are finite. . . . Now, however long a time may pass, according to the eternal laws governing the combinations of this eternal play of repetition, all configurations that have previously existed on this earth must yet meet, attract, repulse, kiss, and corrupt each other again" (cited in Walter Kaufmann, *Nietzsche: Philosopher, Psychologist, Antichrist* [Princeton: Princeton University Press, 1959], 276).

As with the mystic's apophasis, Hegel's negativity announces a limited understanding, the lack of a panoptic view. But Hegel is convinced that we develop an increasingly greater understanding and discernment of the Absolute—that is what thought and rationalization is concerned with bringing about. The body (political or otherwise) does not understand itself fully, cannot grasp itself as an object. It is on a journey, collectively, through a long crucifixion, to an eternal salvation: a final disenchantment, an ultimate enlightenment that is a grand demystification. The laboring of the negative requires an ascesis, just as it requires a teleology, but does it not also require a continual suffering? Is this why, for Hegel, war is seen as both inevitable and necessary? Why peace is viewed as stasis as "people become stuck in their ways"?[52] Why, in the closing sections of his analysis, the descriptor is that most foregrounded "sacrifice"? In the Gospels the ascesis of the body also demands a health, a glorification, a delight; the eschatological remainder is both a futural and a present excess. The kingdom is not just to come; part of the irreducibility of its meaning is that it is already here, that it "remains" (in Agamben's language). I can see how Hegel would concur with this eschatology, but I wonder whether his anthropology (and, by extension, political science) remains too Lutheran, too orientated to the working of the crucifixion. And my question is whether this negative, immanent, and sacrificial metaphysics of the body can adequately sustain a postmaterialist conception of embodiment, whether a sustainable metaphysics requires an exteriority, a threshold of transcendence, a God otherwise than being, that is not one with the operations of sublation. Does Hegel need a more adequate doctrine of analogy that would announce a sacramental politics of the body and a participation in the divine that was not simply negative? How would this sacramental and participatory understanding of the body (political and otherwise) revise Hegel's thought?

These questions can best be sharpened when one compares Hegel's metaphysics of the body politic with those of St. Paul. Although Paul is strictly examining the nature of the church, the corollary of Hegel's argument is that the state is the church.[53]

52. Hegel, *Elements of the Philosophy of Right*, 362.

53. For Hegel's exposition of the relations between church and state, see ibid., 291–304. His views are based on the premise that "since religion is that moment

St. Paul's Metaphysics of the Body Politic

In recent years much critical attention has been paid to St. Paul and the political. This has only partly come from the New Testament critical industry itself—through the work of Richard Horsley, Neil Elliot, and Bruno Blumenfeld.[54] It has also come from philosophico-political voices concerned with examining and responding to where we are culturally situated today—for example, Badiou, Agamben, and Žižek (see chap. 4, above).[55] But there remains a reticence in both New Testament cultural historians and interpreters about examining the major model organizing Pauline ecclesiology—the body. Blumenfeld, who recognizes "the critical, foundational role that the body of Jesus plays," comes closest to breaking through this reticence when, in his exposition of the political subtext of Paul's Letter to the Philippians, he observes Paul's "wide body-language register" and concludes, "The *polis* reaches the depths of physicality."[56] The *ekklēsia* is, for Blumenfeld, the heart of the new political community (the *polis*) that Paul is committed to forging. But he adds little more to these observations, given how critical and foundational the body is, in his detailed analysis of the Letter to the Romans (one of the four major texts employing the body analogy). We are told again that "the idea of Christ as the body of which the people are members, connects again with the idea of the *polis*," that Paul is abandoning the older "*polis-psuche* similarity" (of Plato and Aristotle), and that this "could have been mediated by the Hellenistic Pythagorean pseudepigrapha, which used both

---

which integrates the state at the deepest level of the disposition [of the citizens], the state ought even to require all its citizens to belong to such a [religious] community" (295).

54. Richard Horsley, ed., *Paul and Empire: Religion and Power in Roman Imperial Society* (Harrisburg, PA: Trinity International, 1997), Horsley, ed., *Paul and Politics: Ekklesia, Israel, Imperium, Interpretation* (Harrisburg, PA: Trinity International, 2000); Neil Elliot, "Paul and the Politics of Empire," in Horsley, *Paul and Politics*, 15–39; Elliot, *Liberating Paul: The Justice of God and the Politics of the Apostle* (Minneapolis: Fortress, 2005); Bruno Blumenfeld, *The Political Paul: Justice, Democracy, and Kingship in a Hellenistic Framework* (Sheffield: Sheffield Academic, 2001).

55. See Alain Badiou, *Saint Paul: The Foundation of Universalism*, trans. Ray Brassier (Stanford, CA: Stanford University Press, 2003); Giorgio Agamben, *The Time That Remains: A Commentary on the Letter to the Romans*, trans. Patricia Dailey (Stanford, CA: Stanford University Press, 2005); Slavoj Žižek, *The Puppet and the Dwarf: The Perverse Core of Christianity* (Cambridge, MA: MIT Press, 2003).

56. Blumenfeld, *Political Paul*, 383, 299–300.

political similes" (e.g., Pseudo-Archytas).[57] But Blumenfeld goes no further.

Where these new analyses of the political Paul by both New Testament scholars and cultural theorists leave us is very unclear. For Badiou, Agamben, and Žižek, in quite different ways and with different agendas, Paul is a revolutionary, a left-wing radical *avant la lettre*, able to offer us victims of both modernity and liberal democracy a way forward. To Blumenfeld, Paul is a conservative supporter of Roman imperialism (a precursor to Josephus, the famous example of Jewish accommodationist policy) and a defender of the *Pax Romana*. For Elliot, Paul is a pragmatic thinker whom we should not expect to find having "a clear, consistent, univocal 'pro-Roman' or 'anti-Roman' posture."[58]

To this celebrated collection of critics excavating the political Paul should be added a second group of New Testament commentators working with *traditionsgeschichtlich* interests in the Pauline body, going back to at least 1919.[59] From this scholarship, two theologies of the body as a *societas* are evident, the first found paradigmatically in 1 Corinthians and the second in Ephesians. The latter has Christ as "the head of the church, his body" (Eph. 5:23 RSV); the former has the church as an ancephalous body. Critical opinion is divided on whether these two theologies cohere; much of the argument centers on whether Paul can be recognized as the author of Ephesians. On the basis of the undoubted Pauline authorship of the Letter to Philemon and the Letter to the Colossians and the profound relationship between these two letters and Ephesians, I accept Ephesians as Pauline and view the two theologies as constituting one coherent line of thought.

57. Ibid., 383. Earlier in his study, Blumenfeld goes exhaustively through every one of these political pieces of pseudepigrapha.

58. Elliot, *Liberating Paul*, 13.

59. The literature is expansive, but a chain of inquiry often begins with Traugott Schmidt, *Der Leib Christi* (Leipzig: A. Deichert, 1919), and continues through Ernst Käsemann, *Leib und Leib Christi* (Tübingen: Mohr, 1933), to class studies in English such as John A. T. Robinson, *The Body: A Study in Pauline Theology* (London: SCM, 1952); and Ernst Best, *One Body in Christ* (London: SCM, 1955). More recent studies include Gosnell L. O. R. Yorke, *The Church as the Body of Christ in the Pauline Corpus* (Lanham, MD: University Press of America, 1991); Dale Martin, *The Corinthian Body* (New Haven, CT: Yale University Press, 1995); and Michelle V. Lee, *Paul, the Stoics, and the Body of Christ* (Cambridge: Cambridge University Press, 2006).

The central text for Paul's understanding of the body politic is found in 1 Corinthians 12:12–27:

> For just as [*kathaper*] the body is one and has many members, and all the members of the body, though many, are one body [*onta hen estin sōma*], so it is with Christ. For by [*en*] one Spirit we were all baptized into one body—Jews or Greeks, slaves or free—and all were made to drink of [*en*] one Spirit. For [*kai gar*] the body does not consist of one member but of many. If the foot should say, "Because I am not a hand, I do not belong to [*estin ek*] the body," that would not make it any less a part of the body. And if the ear should say, "Because I am not an eye, I do not belong to the body," that would not make it any less part of the body. If the whole body were an eye, where would be the hearing? If the whole body were an ear, where would be the sense of smell? But as it is, God arranged the organs in the body [*etheto ta melē*], each one of them, as he chose. If all were a single organ, where would the body be? As it is, there are many parts, yet one body. The eye cannot say to the hand, "I have no need of you," nor again the head to the feet, "I have no need of you." On the contrary, the parts of the body which seem to be weaker are indispensable, and those parts of the body which we think less honorable we invest with greater honor, and our unpresentable parts are treated with greater modesty, which our more presentable parts do not require. But God has so composed [*synekerasen*] the body, giving greater honor to the inferior part, that there may be no discord [*schisma*] in the body, but that the members may have the same care for one another. If one member suffers, all suffer together; if one member is honored, all rejoice together. Now you are the body of Christ and individually members of it [*kai melē ek merous*]. (1 Cor. 12:12–27 RSV)

There are several points to observe about this passage from a letter written to a church in the highly politicized Roman colony of Corinth. The first is its predominantly ontological tenor—the repeated use of *estin* and *onta*.[60] The body is a condition of being. The verb "to be" is not merely used as a copulative; it is employed emphatically in the sense of "to participate," as the prepositions *en* and *ek* emphasize, and hence the translation "belong to" in this

60. Lee, *Paul,* notes the ontological order of Paul's understanding of the body and relates it back to a similar emphasis on the role of the spirit (*pneuma*) in the Stoics, who "based their ethical philosophy upon an ontological system" (75; see also 131). The Spirit ontologically roots the ecclesial body in the Christic body.

quotation from the Revised Standard Version (the King James Version translates more literally). But the ontology announced here is not one that is concurrent with the natural order. We do not grow into becoming members of this body; we are initiated into it through baptism. By inference, then (this is the second point), this body "which is also Christ" is both related to and yet different from other physical bodies. *Kathaper* introduces a similitude, but the similitude does not have the grammatical logic of a simile, where the predicate intrinsically and ontologically belongs to the substantive ("as white as snow").[61] *Kathaper* has, rather, the grammatical logic of analogy, where two substantives (in this case, the human body and the body of Christ) share properties but in a way that does not admit of their being intrinsically related or extrinsically associated. "Paul uses the analogy of the human body to elucidate his teaching that Christians form Christ's body. But the analogy holds because they are in literal fact the risen organism of Christ's person in all its concrete reality. . . . It is almost impossible to exaggerate the materialism and crudity of Paul's doctrine of the church as literally now the resurrected *body* of Christ."[62] The body of Christ becomes the governing body and the condition for the possibility of a new ordering of the human body.[63] In an analogous manner, the Eucharist as the given body of Christ nurtures and nourishes the life of this new ordering of the human body.

61. Lee (ibid., 9) refers to the famous fable by Dionysius of Halicarnassus, *Roman Antiquities* 6.83.2, in which the body is likened to a commonwealth, and Livy, *History of Rome* 2.328–412, where it is likened to the state. But this is very different from the Pauline emphasis that the kingdom of God *is* a body. As Lee points out, Paul's use is much closer to Stoics such as Seneca and Cicero, who also employ the body analogy politically to speak of a universal humanity.

62. Robinson, *Body*, 51. See also Herbert Gale, *The Use of Analogy in the Letter of Paul* (Philadelphia: Westminster, 1964), 117: the "Christian community . . . is not *like* a body; it *is* a body." This contentious thesis is critiqued by Best, *One Body in Christ*, 16, who insists that it is only a metaphor. It is attacked more vigorously by Robert Gundry, *"Sōma" in Biblical Theology* (Cambridge: Cambridge University Press, 1976), 228, because, for him, Paul would then be identifying the church with the physically resurrected body of Christ whereas elsewhere Paul takes pains to emphasize the pastness of Christ's resurrection and point to the future in which the faithful are resurrected. Gundry, however, takes insufficient account of an eschatological understanding of time that folds the past into the present and the future—the eschatological remainder. Lee, *Paul*, 130, interprets 1 Cor. 12 as both a comparison with a body and an identification as a body.

63. Ward, *Cities of God*, 97–116.

Granted, this is a theological rather than a philosophical argument. In the grammar of analogy, the attribution of properties proceeds from the primary to the secondary analogue. The transcendent body of Christ, the resurrected body, redefines the human body from a more exalted, indeed, glorified position, so that the properties of coabiding in Christ's body are communicated to the human body and to the church through the Spirit. This does not merely boil down to the idea that I do not naturally, as a human body, belong to the body of Christ. Baptism "by [*en*] the one Spirit" marks an ontological shift from being in the world to being *en Christō* (a favorite use by Paul of the dative of location).[64] But neither members nor even Christ are translated out of this world; the use of *en* suggests, rather, another level of ontological intensity available in this world but not concurrent with it. There is an incorporation effected by baptism—an incorporation maintained through the Eucharist—and this incorporation does not leave the human body, as such, unchanged. The incorporation is made possible because an analogical relation is created and maintained in the eschatological remainder.

The return to the world and the new relation in Christ that is made with it bring us back to the ecclesiology located amid the politics of the city (chap. 5). The body was a favored political metaphor for the state or the cosmic city. Paul's letter was written to a Roman city, and so, in extending the analogy of this term and incorporating it into the resurrected body of Christ, Paul is announcing a new ecclesial politics. The incorporation into Christ brings about two changes that seem to be antithetical to life in the global city and yet offer valuable possibilities for a common human flourishing.[65] The first change concerns social and racial

64. Baptism functions as a liturgical practice signifying what Paul elsewhere calls "adoption" (Gal. 4:5): by nature we are not children of God. This adoption marks a difference between teleology (as in Aristotle and Hegel), in which an efficient cause moves a final cause—that for which it was created—and eschatology, in which there is a shift to another order of being, wrought by divine grace.

65. Earlier in 1 Cor. 12, discussing the gifts of the Spirit, Paul teaches that the gifts are distributed "for the common good" (*pros to sympheron*). The noun *sympheron* is the political term at the heart of Aristotle's politics and ethics (see Aristotle, *Nicomachean Ethics* 8.9.4–5; *Politics* 3.4.7–5.1). Again, Paul's explicit use of a political vocabulary underlines his awareness of the politics of discipleship. For analysis of the political overtones in Paul's rhetoric in 1 Cor. 12, see Margaret M. Mitchell, *Paul and the Rhetoric of Reconciliation* (Louisville: Westminster John Knox, 1991),

differences: Jews, Greeks, slaves, and the free are indicators of social tensions and hierarchies. In Galatians, Paul adds a second change, concerning "male and female" (Gal. 3:28), that characterizes sociosexual tensions and hierarchies. Each of these social identities was embedded within value systems concerning the human body—class notions of embodiment, ethnic and sexual ideologies, and so forth. But with incorporation *en heni pneumati* and *en Christō*, a new social order is announced. The christocentric body politic constitutes this order. It is not an order where difference is elided; the body is not one organ but many different functions. This is not, then, Spinoza's monism and the metaphysics of the fascist state. The differences, functioning as such, live out this polity. Paul equates this body with a group of people, the church in Corinth ("you are the body of Christ"), although the body is not restricted to that one location. But location is important, because only by being located somewhere can the body of Christ be made visible, even while simultaneously affirming the greater invisibility of the church that transcends the local while being rooted in it. The body of Christ is both a collection of people and a coordination of operations. The body is made manifest in the events in which these people are seen to be working. Its location in Christ and in the Spirit is, then, both specific to and transcending of any spatial or temporal coordinates that can be mapped. "Transcending," here, has to be understood not as attaining a level of abstraction above the spatial and temporal but as an intensification and multiplication of times and spaces.[66] Church institutional order issues from this mediation of the particular and the universal with the church as an institution presenting a representation of the performances that constitute "church." (How else would the people learn about the church, its meaning, and its values?) But Paul is emphatic that

35–39, 157–64; Richard A. Horsley, "Rhetoric and Empire—1 Corinthians," and N. T. Wright, "Paul's Gospel and Caesar's Empire," in Horsley, *Paul and Politics*, 72–102, 160–83, respectively.

66. Taylor observes in *A Secular Age* that sacred or "higher" time operates very differently from secular or "ordinary" time. "The church, in its liturgical year, remembers and reenacts what happened in *illo tempore* when Christ was on earth. Which is why this year's Good Friday can be closer to the Crucifixion than last year's midsummer day" (58). We could extend this analysis of time with a similar analysis of space. Sitting in church on Sunday gives one a geographical proximity to those sitting in churches in other parts of the world.

the governance of this body politic is through an inner composition (*synekerasen*) effected by God.

The word *synekerasen* is the aorist active of the verb *synkerannumi*, a highly unusual word for Paul. Although it is found in Plato, the verb does not occur in the Septuagint at all and is found only twice in the New Testament, here and in Hebrews 4:2. In both cases, it means "mix, temper, be united with," although in the passive it can describe very close relationships between people. It is related to the verbs *parakoloutheō* (follow closely, follow beside), as in discipleship, and *syzeugnumi* (yoke), likewise used in the Gospels regarding discipleship.

The tense and the voice here in the Pauline text suggest that God put together this body at some definite point in the past and that this action continues until now. Commentators seem to fight shy of this verse, but I suggest that what Paul is referring to here is the making of the primal human being. We have to read this verse, then, in the context of Paul's wider theological interests in the first and last Adam (1 Cor. 15). The verse shifts its reference from the ecclesial body of Christ to the physical body itself. The body, human and divine, does not issue from Bateman's void and so be without meaning. It is created by an act of God and preeminently significant, "heavy with meaning." The politics of incorporation in the body of Christ fashions an understanding of the body as God first created it, an original humanity now restored. Again, the Christic body becomes the model for understanding all embodiment. The act of discipleship, which is the operation of a Christic politics, realizes these coterminous bodies—the human and the divine.

Let us take this further. Mention was made earlier of Althusser's notion of state apparatuses that fashion ideologies that we live out, often unconsciously—ideologies that have value systems implicit within them. And as noted, Foucault examined such apparatuses in terms of "technologies," particularly technologies of the self. Asad examined these technologies in terms of medieval monastic institutions, extending, for example, Foucault's analyses of confession.[67] But we go further here, on the basis of the relation exposited by

67. Talal Asad, "Pain and Truth in Mediaeval Christian Ritual" and "On Discipline and Humility in Mediaeval Christian Monasticism," in *Genealogies of Religion: Disciplines and Reasons of Power in Christianity and Islam* (Baltimore: Johns Hopkins University Press, 1993), 83–124, 125–68, respectively.

Paul. The human bodies constituting the ecclesial community at Corinth would be fashioned by specific institutional and cultural practices, and indeed, later in this letter and in others, Paul would outline several of these practices. Dale Martin, among others, has helped us to see the understanding of the human body with respect to these practices and their context.[68] Martin enables us to see the human body as a cultural product. Here we will try to glimpse the human body as a product of the Christic polity, the product of a fundamental realignment that goes on in that incorporation into the body of Christ. For no doubt also the Greek, the Jew, the slave, and the freeborn would each be fashioned by the dominant practices defining his or her own cultural situation. The Greek would live out her Greekness and all that this culturally entailed; the Jew would live out his Jewishness with all that this entailed. The slave would live out his slavery, and the freeborn will live out what was then valued and expected of one who was born free. But institutions or state apparatuses aside, when the Greek, the Jew, the slave, and the freeborn were incorporated into the body of Christ, these fashionings are transposed by a further working of the Spirit. Paul's language plays on what would normally be scandalous. For the Greek, the abrupt contrast between the things of the soul (*psychikos*) and the things of the spirit (*pneumatikos*) in 1 Corinthians 2:14–15 and the phrase "the mind of flesh" (*tou noos tēs sarkos*) in 2:18 are nonsense. For the Jew, the phrase "in the flesh" (*en* [*tē*] *sarki*) in Romans 7:5 and 8:9 brings confusion because human beings *are* flesh; they are not *in* a domain that is fleshly. The language of "freedom" and "bondage" equally overturns what either of these terms might mean to one born free and another born into slavery. *En Christō*, Greek, Jew, slave, and freeborn become something else. They live out and become produced as hands, feet, eyes, ears, honored parts, inferior parts, weaker parts, and stronger parts within this new body. They become incorporated and transformed into other forms of behavior.

We can observe this transformation in the very language Paul employs. The final image in the body picture that Paul creates is of the genitals: "and our unpresentable parts are treated with greater modesty." The Stoic political body was always hierarchized with the head as the summit of power, but there is something of

68. Martin, *Corinthian Body*.

an inversion of such hierarchies here. Even so the final image of "our unpresentable parts" does not suggest that they are the most important parts of the body but only that they are a focus for particular attention. The body that Paul pictures is both sexed, because of this image, and sexless, for it is neither a male nor a female body, just as in Christ there is neither male nor female, according to the Letter to the Galatians. The Greek of 1 Corinthians 12:23 reads, *kai ta aschēmona hēmōn euschēmosynēn perissoteran echei*. The key word transformed in this clause is *schēma* (behavior, manner, dress, dignity). The verse tracks the movement, then, from the parts "which behave in an undignified manner" (*aschēmona*) to the same parts "behaving in a dignified manner" (*euschēmosynēn*). *Schēma* can also mean "form," and so we can read this verse cosmologically: the parts of the body that have the potential to generate the chaotic and formless are transformed into parts that are well ordered.[69] In Christ, the body is transformed into other value systems, another ordering with other conceptions of embodiment and pneumatic movements that fashion bodies anew, in accordance with the living—that is, the operational—body of Christ; hence Paul's elliptical phrase "the Lord for the body" (*ho kyrios tō sōmati*, 1 Cor. 6:13), where "Lord" is the political title for that which is sovereign. The human body is fashioned by the politics of the body of Christ and the position of that body with respect to other cultural corporations that make up the world, the city. What does this signify?

Any possible democratization in terms of equality—as individual members within one body, ruled over by one Spirit, equally valued before God, and so forth—does not occur necessarily in terms of social, sexual, or racial status. It occurs through the new politics of living in Christ and being governed by a command to love one

69. According to the Stoic metaphysics of the "cosmological Eros," there is an Eros that is irrational and transgressive of order, an Eros closely associated with our "unpresentable parts," but there is also the work of a cosmological Eros, which bears a close relation to Paul's understanding of agape. "For the internal harmony of a city must be dependent quite specifically on harmonious relationships existing between all its citizens, and to this extent on the love that the citizens have for each other. And this love is precisely the love of the cosmological Eros: it is the love by which the disparate elements of chaos were brought together into the harmonious arrangement of the cosmos" (George Boys-Stones, "Eros in Government: Zeno and the Virtuous City," *Classical Quarterly* 48 [1998]: 168–74, quoted in Lee, *Paul*, 170).

another. Love in 1 Corinthians 13 constitutes the great erasure of statuses of any kind because it "bears all things, believes all things, hopes all things, endures all things" (13:7). What being a member of the body of Christ entails, in other words, is a political discipleship that does not readily translate into institutions or even modes of political activity in this world. Granted, this discipleship and the politics it enacts take place in, and with respect to, this world, but as seen in the discussion on the nature of a Christian act in the last chapter, its import lies in the operations of God with respect to salvation understood as becoming truly human, truly embodied. This is important for understanding the apophaticism of the body of Christ. The New Testament scholar John A. T. Robinson sums up why, commenting on 1 Corinthians 13–20: "It is in their [Christians'] 'bodies' (v. 15)—as *sōmata* and not merely 'spirit'—that Christians are members of Christ . . . so there is no real line between the body of His [Christ's] resurrection and the flesh-bodies of those who are risen with Him."[70] *Sarx*, or mere flesh, dies; it is mortal, weak, corruptible, and prey to sin. But since there is only one body, *sōma*, composed of many bodies, *sōmata*, and that body is a glorified and resurrected body, *sōma* is immortal, eternal. This "body is not among the things that are seen (*ta blepomena*, i.e., the *sarx*) and belong to this age only (*proskaira*), but it is *aionion* [eternal], belonging to the age to come."[71]

The human body participating in the risen, eschatological body politic of Christ lives in a transpositional state. It has only liminal identity. It lives physically in this world, offering politically what N. T. Wright has called a "pagan challenge";[72] it lives, equally as physically, in the world to come. We can observe this liminal condition in the verbal tenses of Paul's description in Ephesians: God "raised us up with him [*synēgeiren*—aorist active], and made us to sit with him [*synekathisen*—aorist active] in the heavenly places in [*en*] Christ Jesus" (Eph. 2:6 RSV). The verbs are newly coined by Paul to emphasize our con-formity in the one body at a punctiliar moment in the past. Just as, in Paul, there is a continuity between the physical and historical body of Jesus the Christ and his resurrected body, so there "is therefore no ultimate distinction between the individual

70. Robinson, *Body*, 53.

71. Ibid., 76.

72. Wright, "Paul's Gospel and Caesar's Empire," 168.

resurrection and the one resurrection Body."[73] The cataphatic body, that which is visible (after the Greek *kataphasis*, affirmation), that which is and can be spoken about, is also, in Christ, apophatic (after the Greek *apophasis*, denial, negation), that which is beyond the powers of human beings to conceive or think. *Phasis* is often in Greek associated with *phainomai* (appear).[74] Hence Paul has to invent a new language in which to sketch his theological conception of this body.[75] What individual *sōma* can say, "I am a hand . . . or a foot . . . or an eye . . . or an ear"? No one can identify one's function. And if one cannot identify one's function, then one's functioning is hidden from one also. Perhaps it is not hidden entirely insofar as one has a sense of vocation, but the events in which one enacts the church as a "foot" or a "hand" or an "ear"—the events in which one is identified as the operative body of Christ—are only graspable as acts of faith. One's identity within the body of Christ is worked out in Christian terms of practices of faith, hope, and love that go beyond the naming and labeling of the churches, fellowships, and denominations in this world. While remaining a Greek, a Jew, a male, a female, a slave, or a freeborn, one is also and more significantly a member of the body of Christ. It is a body that is "heavy with meaning" that is not possible to translate. One condition or identity is not necessarily effaced in the other, but it is transformed in ways beyond telling. One discovers one's somatic nature in the tranquillity of recollection; it is not self-evident. It is discovered not discretely but by continuing to work within the body of Christ, a new polity, with new relationships and new distributions of power that can never find their full realization in any political system in this world and that therefore resist accommodation with the politics of this world and offer possibilities for an alternative politics. The altar on which Paul asks the Roman Christians to present their bodies as a living sacrifice can never be identified with a particular throne. The body is continually being given, continually moving out and being enacted elsewhere, and so it continually transcends strict identifications that it imposes on itself or are imposed on it. The body is never there as such (as if a static object in a freeze-framed still photo); the body is there only

73. Robinson, *Body*, 79.

74. H. G. Liddell, R. Scott, and H. S. Jones, *A Greek-English Lexicon*, 9th ed. with revised supplement (Oxford: Oxford University Press, 1996), 1918.

75. Robinson, *Body*, 63.

because it moves, it circulates, it acts, it disseminates its knowledges, rejecting, absorbing, and adapting itself to new knowledges. It is in this way that it can be deemed apophatic.

It is because *sōma* is apophatic that it is, for Paul, always and only a theological and metaphysical entity. Hence there are also two other bodies: one of sin and one of death. These are metaphysical conditions of embodiment affecting *sarx*, conditions of which *sarx* has little or no understanding because *sarx* is the secularized, demystified body. This is the body that can be viewed as a physical and politically artificial machine for Hobbes and, for Bateman, a worthless, political nonentity dressed in designer labels that bears no relation to the products that label it. *Sarx*, even though it possesses, for Paul, a psychic nature (the "fleshly mind" of Col. 2:18 KJV), is a materialist reduction of embodiment—not necessarily bad in itself, for it is the purely natural condition for humanity. But to be human is have a body, not just be flesh. *Sarx* cannot inherit the kingdom of God (1 Cor. 15:50), and it is the body, not the flesh, that is redeemed. The bodies of sin and death are, like the body of Christ, realms, but they are realms of enslavement. They too are metaphysical and operate transcendentally in this world, but they constitute a bad metaphysics. The good metaphysics is arrived at only through enacting the body in and through the body of Christ, through the politics of discipleship, through the eternal life of the Spirit. And this returns us to Hegel.

What is immediately apparent is that the working of the negative in Hegel is quite different from the operation of the living Spirit in Paul. For Hegel, God has given himself entirely to this world through the death of Jesus Christ on the cross. Through the work of the "inwardness of this principle is the . . . reconciliation and resolution of all opposition."[76] For Paul, the immanent logics of this world have to bow to the power not of the death of God but of the resurrected Christ. There are no reconciliation and resolution of all opposition for Paul; those not participating in the body of Christ are sundered from the life of God. Any reconciliation and resolution are on the basis of total commitment to a new covenant between God and human beings. Paul speaks of an end to "discord [*schisma*] in the body . . . [when] the members . . . have the same care for one another" (1 Cor. 12:25 RSV), that is, when

76. Hegel, *Elements of the Philosophy of Right*, 380.

they are enmeshed within a network of eros/agapeic relations.[77] But opposition, for Hegel, is the dialectical encounter with the other, and resolution is the sublation of that otherness, an incorporation. The body politic, like the human body, is caught up in temporality, desiring and willing an eternal condition of rest beyond representation in the absoluteness of the idea. There is something gnostic in this desiring, a yearning to be beyond the materiality of state institutions, religions, and sciences in an unbounded universalism. And yet it is never so simple with Hegel, who to the end affirms the concrete and the actual in what can only be the development of this world into the kingdom of God. The Christian body politic, for Paul, is already constituted in the risen Christ; it can never be, then, a development from within this world. Furthermore, in the incorporation into Christ, otherness and difference remain and are unsublatable. The Greek will continue Greek; the Jew, Jew. The hand will not be the eye; the ear will never be the foot. The difference and materiality of *sōmata* are guaranteed by the one transcendent *sōma*. Not being of this world and yet enabling the world to participate in it, this body can be truly metaphysical in a way that greatly enriches a postmaterialist condition and resists the depoliticization and virtualities of current city living. We have been observing how the liberal-democratic state is never there as such, that it is present only in its performances—in parliament, in the staging of elections. Its sovereignty of the people is nebulous if not vacuous. But belonging in Christ enables a true apophasis of the body that guarantees its mystery, its sovereignty, and its sanctity through a politics of redemption.

Enacting the Body of Christ

What are the implications of the metaphysics of the body politic for ecclesiology, for the church in the city? Chapter 5 spoke about the church as an institution and a eucharistic community and about functions that might operate far from such institutional contexts.

77. I write eros/agapeic because I do not accept a dualistic relation between eros and agape. We can distinguish between human love as eros and divine love as agape only as long as we see an analogical relationship between these two loves. A doctrine of incarnation and participation in Christ does not allow us to draw a neat distinction in Christian loving between eros and agape.

Here I have been developing an understanding of the apophatic nature of the body of Christ: it appears only in the recollection of events in which it was enacted; it resists the neat and static labels and identities that render it readily understandable. To avoid becoming too abstract, too amorphous, too liquid, we need to return to specifics. Let us develop this further and clarify some important differences between a previously noted observation by Hardt and Negri and the open, relational operations of church being defined here. Hardt and Negri observed, "The traditional army thus forms an organic fighting body, with generals for its head, lieutenants for its midsection, and the common soldier and sailors for its limbs." But in the move toward Empire, there is a "command shift from a centralized model to a distributed network model."[78] I suggested that this political conception of the body would have important cultural analogues in the way the physical body is understood and valued—or, rather, misunderstood and not valued at all—for discourses on the physical body correlate with discourses on the political body. The difficulty with Negri and Hardt's observation that the current Empire is a decentralized, desubjectivized, deobjectivized "distributed network model" is that if this is a correct observation, then the concrete becomes dispersed across an extensive horizontal plane. Thus flattened, the body can disappear from view. But this occurs only at the level of abstract, theoretical description. The Empire is one such abstraction, and to concentrate on the abstraction is to miss the actual trees in an idealized forest. All writing tends toward such abstraction, but this is the apophatic body of Christ in action:

> When the Son of man comes in his glory, and all the angels with him. . . . Then the king will say to those at his right hand, "Come, you that are blessed by my Father, inherit the kingdom prepared for you from the foundation of the world; for I was hungry and you gave me food, I was thirsty and you gave me something to drink, I was a stranger and you welcomed me, I was naked and you gave me clothing, I was sick and you took care of me, I was in prison and you visited me." Then the righteous will answer him, "Lord, when was it that we saw you hungry and gave you food, or thirsty and gave you something to drink? And when was it that we saw you a stranger and welcomed you, or naked and gave you clothing? And

78. Hardt and Negri, *Multitude*, 56, 59.

> when was it that we saw you sick or in prison and visited you?" And the king will answer them, "Truly I tell you, just as you did it to one of the least of these who are members of my family, you did it to me." (Matt. 25:31–40)

Granted, there is no mention here of an institution such as the church coordinating these actions undertaken as Christians. The words of Jesus precede the founding of the church. But what Charles Taylor has called "a network of ever different relations of agape"[79] characterizes this activity done in the name and the Spirit of Christ that is prior to and more fundamental than the church order to which such relations give rise. Concrete practices restore the body, and the bodies of those enacting them. The concrete practices are strung out along an eschatological trajectory—a movement oscillating between "when" and "then." When these things are done belongs to the eschatological remainder. The acts undertaken in these exchanges constitute the body of Christ, the church, as such. They are social, political, and ethical interventions in the fabric of the world that incarnate Christ and are oriented toward him. Such interventions constitute "transformative practices of hope."[80] Hope is not the same as optimism. Optimism is a mood, an emotion that arises when circumstances seem favorable. It looks to the future, but its affectivity is all in the present and depends on that present. Hope is an act that disregards circumstance and does not know what it will achieve. There is an agnosticism and a questionability about hope: "When was it that we saw you hungry . . . when was it that we saw you a stranger . . . sick or in prison?" Hope looks not to the present but to the unknowability of the future; this is why it is related theologically to faith. And if here it might seem that such acts are self-interested because the church appears to look after its own—"these who are members of my family" (more accurately translated "those who are my brethren")—then we have to recall the apophasis that makes it impossible for the church to know who and who are not part of its composition and therefore who are and who are not included in "family." Perhaps this is why,

79. Taylor, *A Secular Age*, 282, where Taylor speaks about the church as "a quintessentially network society, even though of an utterly unparalleled kind, in that these relations are not mediated by any of the historical forms of relatedness."

80. Graham Ward, *Cultural Transformation and Religious Practice* (Cambridge: Cambridge University Press, 2005), 168–74.

in the verses that follow, when Jesus reverses the story in dealing with those who did not perform such acts, he says, "I tell you, just as you did not do it to one of the least of these [the hungry, thirsty, or unclothed one, the one in prison, the stranger], you did not do it to me" (Matt. 25:45). The church is not inward-looking here: "one of these" makes no reference to whether they are "members." They are neither designated insiders nor outsiders—they are simply there as hungry, thirsty, naked, imprisoned, and far from home.

Indeed this could be taken further: there is no insider or outsider in Christ and therefore in the operations of the body of Christ. Those who act and those who are the recipients of such action are all incorporated into Christ, in an eternal reciprocity of giver and given that begins with the asymmetrical sacrifice of Christ himself and sheers off into the intratrinitarian nature of God's own being. Those who do not act become those who are excluded because they could not receive the gift of Christ that was given, just as the refusal of food, drink, clothing, a prison visit, or hospitality prohibits the performance of the body of Christ. Political discipleship thus begins with being able to receive the gift.[81]

81. This observation invokes the other side of a question that has dominated some of the best contemporary philosophical and theological minds, each taking its cue from Marcel Mauss's anthropological study *The Gift* (New York: Norton, 1954). "Can the gift be given?" preoccupied Derrida as it would later preoccupy Jean-Luc Marion and John Milbank. Salvation (however we picture it) hangs not only on whether the gift can be given but also on whether it can be received.

7

The Politics of Election and of Following

> We need a form of self-referential politics, which would aim at strengthening capacities for political action itself, and at reigning in an uncontrolled economic dynamic both within and beyond what still counts as the authoritative level of nation-states.[1]

The last two chapters have been developing two accounts based on a central Christian teaching on eschatology: an eschatological humanism in the context of the global city, and an eschatological ecclesiology. The eschatological humanism focused on developing an account of what it was for a Christian to act, since to act is fundamental to being political. The global city was understood as the public space in which the three trajectories—political, economic, and cultural—described in the first three chapters dominated, a

1. Eduardo Mendieta in conversation with Jürgen Habermas, in Habermas, *Religion and Rationality: Essays on Reason, God, and Modernity* (Cambridge: Polity, 2002), 153.

space in which the church contended in a struggle for the soul of the city. The eschatological ecclesiology of chapter 5 was a development of this civic struggle and arose especially from a concern to develop a metaphysics of the body that could resist the prevalent dehumanizing and dematerializing trends in politics, economics, and culture and root political postmaterialism. Examining first the correlation between the body politic and the physical body, their meanings and their values, I argued that all political accounts of the social were implicated in metaphysics. These metaphysics could be either good (fostering human flourishing and the commonwealth) or bad (deleterious for, or reductive of, the human condition). Lacking a theological appeal or foundation, these metaphysics of the social I viewed as inadequate to resist a prevailing dehumanization and dematerialization. These metaphysics were then contrasted with two accounts of theologically informed construals of the body politic—Hegel's and St. Paul's—and concluded that Paul's account of the body provided the physical and social body of the church with a weight of meaning that adequately supported a postmaterialism, resisting current dematerialization and dehumanization. This final chapter draws the consequences of this eschatological humanism, inseparable from an eschatological ecclesiology, for discipleship. Discipleship empowers us to overcome the key issue: depoliticization. If we cannot act politically, then we cannot counter the enemies either of dehumanization or of dematerialization.

But first a word of warning: my account of Christian political discipleship will not inform you how Jesus wants you to vote. Such accounts may be rendered in certain fundamentalist churches, but it is most certainly not my gospel. And from what we have already seen, I am not going to tell you that Jesus loves democracy, or that Jesus and Che Guevara shared the same political vision, or that the Christian gospel advocates the political need for hierarchy and dictatorship. At particular points in the history of Christianity, all these political positions have been declared biblical: the confederacy of the twelve tribes of Israel was read as a protodemocratic manifesto; the description, in Acts of the Apostles, of members of the early church sharing their accumulated wealth was read as the gospel's preference for socialism, even communism; and dictatorships from Constantine the Great to Mussolini have viewed the Christian religion as support for their imperial regimes. Throughout Western history, the Bible has been used to justify societies of free love, Calvin's theocracy in Geneva, absolute monarchy, and cells of anarchic radicalism. As seventeenth-century divines were fond of saying, Scripture is a nose of wax; it can be shaped at will into whatever form is desired. There is always a politics of interpretation. We are not given in the Bible a political blueprint that would make deciding between Republicans and Democrats, Old Labour, New Labour, Liberals, Conservatives, or the Green Party for that matter any easier. But this must not be taken to mean that the Scriptures are indifferent to politics; they are not, as we shall continue to see. And this awareness of the political dimensions of human life is very important particularly in the complex societies within which we are embedded today.

Why is politics an important dimension in practiced religion today? In brief, great shifts in international sensibilities are increasingly changing the older relationships between religion and politics, the private and the public (see section 1). As already noted, the birth of the modern secular state followed closely on the demise of the older religious state, in which, from the Reformation onward, the principle of *cuius regio, eius religio* was enshrined, in which the religion of the country was that which was declared by the ruler of that country. The moment Queen Elizabeth I came to the throne in 1558, she instructed her jurists to formulate the laws of religion that would operate throughout her reign; these would be ratified by Parliament and published as the Act of Supremacy and the Act of Uniformity. But even while Elizabeth was embarking on such a task, Western Europe was heading into what were later called the "wars of religion." "Religion" here did not mean what it came to mean in the nineteenth century: specific sets of beliefs and cultic practices that distinguished Hindus from Muslims and Jews from Jansenists and that all came under the genre "religion." "Religion" meant either Catholic or Protestant. To view the wars of religion as a battle for the true faith is misleading; the swords, the pikes, and the lances that the German princes wielded for Luther and Protestantism may well have been heated in the coals of religious conviction, but they were certainly hammered and sharpened through, and wielded by, political opportunism. Religion was a thoroughly political matter, as it had been under the Romans and as again today in Pakistan, for example, or modern Egypt, Syria, Iran, and so on. Religion was an arm of the state.

For much of Western Europe, however, this situation changed with the birth of the modern secular state and the promulgation of acts of tolerance from the late seventeenth century on. The price paid was the separation of religion from politics; there was private conviction, on the one hand, and public debate, on the other. But with the new public visibility of religion (see chap. 3) and further erosions of the boundaries separating the private from the public—the ubiquitous use of closed-circuit television, the introduction of identity cards, the collection of DNA for national data banks, and the technologies employed by various "homeland securities"—religion can no longer be a matter of private conviction, for it wears an increasingly public face. We must recognize, then, as believers in erstwhile liberal democracies in the West (whether we are Jewish, Hindu, Buddhist, Christian, or Islamic), a new political situation. And it is the Christian who is probably in the worst position here, for two reasons.

First, the depoliticization of religion was an inter-Christian affair, a way of diminishing conflicts of conviction in the public realm. It was Christian thinkers and politicians who ushered in secularism and pushed God to the margins of what mattered socially, culturally, and scientifically. God became at best a hidden hand, a concealed clockmaker, and at worst an irrelevance, a lingering superstition. Western Europe as the showcase for Enlightenment secularism became the beacon in the universal progress toward rationalization that would occur everywhere. And so Christians in Western Europe have centuries of depoliticization that they have to conquer mentally and an inner resistance to recognizing the politics of their faith.

The Jewish people are not embroiled in this tradition to the same extent, mainly because they were denied a presence at the debating table when the process began and, when later they were invited, it had to be on the basis not of their piety but of the contributions they could make as those assimilated to western European secularism. Then, after such assimilation, their political wakeup call came with the violences of *Krystallnacht* and all that followed. There had been pogroms before, but the grand orchestration of the German genocide put an end to the Enlightenment dreams of thinkers such as Moses Mendelssohn and those of liberal Jewry. Some had already seen the dream as exactly that; enlightened idealism had to be seen within what was a history of brutal European anti-Semitism. These Jews canvassed support for the establishment of a homeland (not necessarily in Palestine, for Theodor Herzl, the founder of Zionism, considered tracts of territory in Argentina, Mauritius, and Uganda). This homeland was granted them by the United Nations in 1947 after the return of the British mandate, and Palestine was partitioned to create it. Because of the history of anti-Semitism and the continuing conflicts over the establishment of a Jewish homeland through the partition of Palestine, Jewish believers cannot be politically naive. History has and still is teaching them otherwise.

The same could be said of the Muslim. Because, like Christianity, Islam is an expansionist religion, a proselytizing religion, it has been profoundly political from the establishment and then the decline of the Ottoman Empire onward. In the twentieth century, despite the secularizing policies of Kemal Atatürk in Turkey (perhaps even because of these policies), Islamic identity and Islamic resistance have made themselves a political force out of the sheer carving up of their territories by the world's power players after the First and Second World Wars. The carving up after the First World War politicized Muslims right throughout the Middle East and the African Mediterranean coast. The carving up after the Second World War politicized Muslims (and Hindus) across India, Pakistan, and Bangladesh. In subsequent waves of migration, these Muslims came to Western Europe; the very forces that enforced these migrations made the Islamic people political. To be political does not mean that they eschew peace; this is not true. But the hardships they have borne have made them political whereas the seductive comforts of bourgeois living have greatly softened the political edge of so many Christian believers in the West. Continuing anti-Semitism, continuing racism, the failure of state policies for the assimilation of differences into homogenous national identities, and the development of ghettoes in our global cities have all helped to maintain the inseparability of religion from politics for the Jew, the Muslim, and the Hindu. The Christians' wakeup call, on a level that effects everyone, probably came only with 9/11, although one has to recognize continuing traditions of Christian (often Catholic) political theology and liberation theology in the second half of the twentieth century.

The second reason Christianity has been profoundly affected by depoliticization concerns the nature of capitalism itself. Between the establishment of the division between religion and politics, from the late seventeenth century, and the current demise of such a division lie the development and advance of democracy (see chap. 1) and globalization (see chap. 2), both profoundly associated with capitalism. Capitalism encourages apolitical attitudes and depoliticization more generally. From the beginning in the words of Jesus, wealth has been viewed as inimical to piety. However much today we might catalog a variety of powers—symbolic, cultural, social, economic, biological, and psychological[2]—Jesus divides power according to two forms: the power of mammon and the power of the true God (Matt. 6:24). It is perhaps not wealth itself that is a stumbling block to grace, for Jesus accepted the hospitality of men with wealth, but what is done with the wealth. Even so, the rich man does not fair well in the parables of Jesus, perhaps because wealth creates certain accumulative, greedy, self-orientated habits that are difficult to overcome; the temptation to hoard is too great. Neither the rich man in Luke's parable (Luke 16:19–31) nor the rich young ruler (Luke 18:18–23) can get the better of their riches; it is easier for a camel to pass through the eye of a needle than for a rich man to enter the kingdom of heaven. So, "Woe to you who are rich! You get all the comforts [*paraklēsin*, 'comforting'] you will ever get [*apechete*, 'you have your share']. Woe to you who have your fill [*empeplēsmenoi*, 'you who are satiated'] today," Jesus warns (Luke 6:24–25 Moffat translation). Grace requires a hunger, a sense of what one lacks, a recognition of vulnerability, weakness, the need for redemption. Salvation cannot operate where there is nothing needed or where there is satisfaction with what one has. And wealth can satisfy so many wants and wishes. It can entertain. It can divert. And we have seen the proliferation of such practices in the global city. Wealth always requires new satisfactions, and this is why the power of wealth utterly corrupts Bateman of *American Psycho* in his Manhattan apartment (in a block he shares with the likes of Tom Cruise). Without the ability to see what more is needed not just for oneself but for the common good to be realized, there will be no political action.

2. Other than "biological" (a person's strength and stamina) and "psychological" (a person's charisma and ability to persuade others), these forms of power are adapted from Pierre Bourdieu's typology of different forms of capital. See Pierre Bourdieu, "The Field of Cultural Production," in *The Field of Cultural Production*, trans. Richard Nice (New York: Columbia University Press, 1993), 29–73.

We can go further. As Weber with respect to Protestantism, Tawney with respect to religion more widely, and Werner Sombart[3] with respect to Judaism have shown, nascent capitalism has a religious dynamic that, over the years, has been secularized. Frequently, in its secularization, as noted in chapter 2, the religious aspiration still remains—for infinite freedom, infinite choice, total immersing satisfaction, and so forth. The power of wealth can seem deifying. It runs absolutely counter to the Christian conception of salvation as *theōsis* in that it sets up a false god, an idol, a fetish. We examined this with respect to Marx's descriptions of gold. The pursuit of wealth for its own sake is a deep and powerfully religious undertaking. The power that money has is locked intimately into the nature of being human itself. We are creatures who desire,[4] and money not only provides the means for the satisfaction of our infinite desiring but also produces ever more forms that such desiring can take.[5] As both instrument and object of modern desire, money facilitates the ultimate principle governing selfhood in both Freud and Jacques Lacan: desire that does not seek its consummation but, rather, seeks the prolongation of desiring itself. It envelops the subject in a self-perpetuating economy. Thus the temptation of wealth is self-worship.

Three interrelated practices—capitalism, depoliticization, and secularism—have, then, continued to exert a most profound impact on Christianity because the countries of the world that are most

3. Max Weber, *The Protestant Ethic and the Spirit of Capitalism* (London: Routledge, 2001); R. H. Tawney, *Religion and the Rise of Capitalism* (New York: Harcourt, Brace, 1926); Werner Sombart, *The Jews and Modern Capitalism*, trans. M. Epstein (New Brunswick, NJ: Transaction Books, 2006).

4. This study has deliberately said little about the nature of desire as it relates to both human beings and God's desire for us. My theology and theological anthropology of desire are worked out in more detail in Graham Ward, "The Analogical World-View," part 2 in *Cities of God* (London: Routledge, 2000), and *Christ and Culture* (Oxford: Blackwell, 2005), 183–218.

5. "As the universal mediator, money substitutes its own desire as the secret essence of every heart's desire" (Philip Goodchild, *Theology of Money* [London: SCM, 2007], 66). I am not saying quite the same thing, since the desire for money can be seen not as a "substitute" but as an alternative. Jesus recognized being in service to mammon as an alternative, not a substitute, for worshiping the true God. Such dedication cannot deliver salvation, it cannot save the soul, but it is not pathological either. The seductions of money are very real and form the basis for the second of Christ's temptations in the wilderness. Ultimately the power of money in the New Testament is demonic.

secularist and most capitalist (and perhaps most depoliticized) are also those dominated by the Christian tradition. How best can we encourage and affirm the necessary repoliticization of Christianity, given both the long history of its increasing depoliticization and its entrenchment in capitalism's secular teleologies? The parable of the prodigal son in Luke's Gospel narrates not only the practices that led to depoliticized Christianity; in it can be read also the economic history of that depoliticization between the public separation of religion from politics and the erosion of such a separation in recent years.[6] During this period of time and through these interrelated practices, the Christian, like the prodigal son, has made a journey into a far country. And central to the argument of this chapter is the need for Christians, again like the prodigal son, to "come to ourselves," to a recognition of how alien and dangerous a separation between religion and politics is. Election itself is not just a theological matter; it is a political one.

The Politics of Election

We begin in the *oikos*, an embryonic *polis*, with two sons, a father, and a demand, "Give me the share of the property that will belong to me" (Luke 15:12). In the history of the Jewish people, nationhood begins in domestic scenes such as this—with Abram and Sara, with Isaac and Rebecca, with Jacob and Rachel. The younger son begins his alienation here, an alienation that, before becoming spatial, is economic, based in property. The property does not belong to him; it is a future inheritance, a promise he wants to cash in now. The separation from the father that began rhetorically with the demand is deepened by what the son de-

6. Evidently my "anachronistic" reading of this text can draw little from historico-critical approaches for its interpretation, nor can it find support at the level of authorial intention (if this can ever be more than a postulate). Nevertheless, my reading, though no doubt controversial, is not without textual evidence, for the movement of the narrative unveils a structural and spiritual rule. The rule is that the more one becomes satisfied with the goods of this world and therefore the more one becomes secularized, the more one becomes depoliticized. Repoliticization, then, means a reversal of the logic of this rule. Read historically, in terms of modernity and its concurrence with the secular age, the separation of religion from the political inevitably encourages depoliticization. In fact, the more secular we are, the more depoliticized we will become.

mands: the division of the estate now. In effect, this disregard for the authority and governance of the elder is parricide, for only the father's death would legitimately give him a share of the property. From the state of harmony and order, we are plunged into a civil war—the younger son challenging the father as Absalom rose up against *his* father, David. But what starts as an act of rebellion, a political act, soon turns into something more prosaic, even banal: "A few days later the younger son gathered all he had and traveled to a distant country, and there he squandered his property in dissolute living" (15:13). Unlike Absalom, who raised the people of Israel against his father, this younger son is seduced by his wealth and retreats into self-indulgence. He forgets everything except the pleasures that his spending can purchase. There is a kind of desperation in the completely senseless, meaningless squandering of his money. The Greek verb here for "squandered" is the aorist tense of *diaskorpizo*, which means "scatter throughout." It is more emphatic than the action of sowing seed, *skorpizō*. This is a wasteful, irrational, arbitrary act—aimless and pointless. It suggests a mad lust, an unfettered desire—*asōtōs* (dissolutely)—a gluttonous hunger. This is the state of depoliticization; the son is a subject given up to the privacy of satisfying his many different cravings. There is a freedom here—to choose one's delights, to have control over one's gratifications—but it is a solipsistic freedom, a profound autoaffection. It is the freedom only to be enslaved to one's own desires. This is a scriptural picture of a laissez-faire liberalism that is ultimately antisocial and isolating.

When the famine comes and the younger son has spent all he has, there is no one to help him: "no one gave him anything" (15:16). In that "distant country," he belongs to no society; he is not a citizen of any city. The final moment of this journey into depoliticization is when he, out of necessity, "hired himself out to one of the citizens of that country" (15:15). The Greek verb is the passive form of *kollaō* (attach oneself to). The action has none of the sense of contract that "hiring" might suggest. The prodigal is a hanger-on—less even than a servant. Later, when Luke speaks of the father's "hired hands," the Greek is *misthioi*, the technical term for salaried servants. The younger son's depoliticization is complete when he has to linger around a citizen's property, waiting for work. The very use of political language by Luke sets up the contrast between one who is a participant in the *polis* and one who is not. For Aristotle, a human being was defined as a social and political animal. Outside human society, the prodigal is a *homo sacer*, someone without rights, beyond the law, someone subhuman and therefore to be housed with the animals.

But then, in that plight of utter alienation, "he came to himself" (*eis heauton de elthōn*,15:17). The Greek verb translated "came" (*elthōn*) is complex and rich in meaning. Here the aorist active participle is used of the deponent verb *erchomai*. The deponent is a middle voice, which means that at the turning point in this narrative the protagonist is neither active nor passive. Actively, the son realizes something about his condition; passively, the son receives enlightenment about his condition. A movement is involved, but the verb plays with whether that movement comes from the son or is part of a divine providence that will return him to the father. So, at the turning point, the origin of the dynamic behind the shift is mysterious. The prodigal is brought to see things as they really are, but given his own blindness and lack of reason, by whom is he brought to see these things? There is a moment of illumination, the passage of grace, by means of which he is set free to act. He recalls his former homeland, its hierarchical order, and the rewards of laboring under obedience: "bread enough and to spare" (15:17). The memory provokes a decision and an act of penitence: "I will get up and go to my father, and I will say to him, 'Father, I have sinned'" (15:18). The use of the future tense returns us to the future inheritance that he usurped in his demand to have his property and have it now. In a way, after all the immediate gratification of spending, the prodigal reestablishes the future with these words. The Greek is resonant with meaning. "I will get up" is *anastas*, from the verb *anistēmi*, a word that can have a political resonance associated with "to rise up, rebel"; it is also a theological word related to resurrection (*anastasis*) and the eschatological remainder. The former rebellion against the father is now overturned by this new uprising, this renewed politicization. It is a politicization that comes from accepting a position within an established order; the prodigal's sin is both political and theological. His admission and acceptance of that sinning is an act of imaginatively placing himself back in obedience to the father, not as a son but in an even more inferior role within the hierarchy, a salaried servant.

"So he set off [*anastas*] and went to his father" (15:20). The order of the good, the true, and the just is attuned to humility but cannot accommodate humiliation. The son remains the son (the father, the father; the salaried servants, salaried servants) even in his sin. He must be restored to his sonship. The parable is delivered in a political context. Jesus is speaking, after all, to the Pharisees and the doctors of the law after their accusations that this messiah is not separating himself from the sinners but is embracing them. The Jewish code of holiness, in Luke's narrative, demanded a complete distinction between the pure and the impure; it established a sacral order. But Jesus is fueling an insurrection against such an order by revealing a deeper, more just, order altogether. The prodigal is not chastised, offers no atoning sacrifice, and receives no outward cleansing. He is simply taken into the arms of the father, and only by this means is the order restored. Through love, not law, is the just order established; through love is the alienated citizen once more called to play his or her part. The politics of election is a politics of love. And yet how strange this sounds—that love is political.

But love *is* political; this is the fundamental insight of Christianity and of this parable in particular. Personal ethics cannot be divorced from social ethics, and both are implicated in actions that affect the community. Love orientates desire, and desire animates the intention to act. In Luke's parable, the father's demonstration of love toward the younger and reprobate stirs up the politics of the *oikos*. It is not an irrational and temperate love; it is a love that, in doing good, acts most justly. But this display of justice toward one son, and him the younger, provokes the question of injustice in the heart of the older son: "Lo, these many years I have been serving you; I never transgressed your commandment at any time; and yet you never gave me a young goat, that I might make merry with my friends. But as soon as this son of yours came, who has devoured your livelihood with harlots, you killed the fatted calf for him" (15:29–30 NKJV). The elder son initiates his own rebellion from the order of the household by rejecting his relation to his brother ("this son of yours") despite earlier being told by the servant that the merrymaking celebrates "your brother." The elder brother's refusal to go into the house requires the father to go out a second time to receive one of his sons back into the household. Politics always concerns relations, just as depoliticization always concerns the denial of relations and social atomism. To be political, to act politically, is always to be implicated in a field of relations in which there is an uneven distribution of power (seen here in the hierarchy of the father and the elder son). The younger son's return to this field of power relations is an indication of his willingness to accept his political function in the *oikos*. The elder son's questioning of the hidden laws of justice (hidden because it is dependent on the unwritten laws of love) is an indication of his own understanding of the political situation and his inseparability from it. It is a real questioning arising from a real set of circumstances, actions, and responses. Without the elder son's reaction, then, the justice of the *oikos* is questionable, and the father's rule would appear arbitrary, even tyrannical—that is, suppressing the political nature of the power relations. If the elder son persisted in his rebellion, however, it would bring about a repetition of the violence of the younger son's earlier alienation. The elder son is in danger of such an action, as his spatial separation outside the feast and the denial of a relation to his brother ("this son of yours") signify. But the point of the parable is not that such penetrating questions cannot be asked of the order of the household or the governance of the *polis*. The point of the parable is that the *oikos* is a political arena where such questions can and must arise for justice to be seen publicly to be done and love to be seen not to be arbitrary. The father cannot act unjustly. This is at the heart of his answer to the elder son: "Son, you are always with me, and all that I have is yours. It was right that we should make merry and be glad, for your brother was dead and is alive again, and was lost and is found" (15:31–32 NKJV). For "It was right," Luke employs *edei*, the imperfect of the Greek impersonal verb *dei*, derived from *deō* (bind or put under obligation). It has not simply the moral force of "It is the proper thing to do in the circumstances" but the force of which has been decreed by God. Later (24:44) Luke employs the verb to indicate that everything written about Christ in Scripture must be fulfilled, including the destiny of Christ in undergoing his suffering on the cross, his death, and his resurrection. The term connotes a predetermination, even providence, and as such it translates the father's action from a personal and social ethic into the cosmic one by invoking an order of being, a universal law.

This just law of love has two corollaries. First, the elder son's position as now the father's sole heir is made clear; "all that I have is yours" shows that there is no restitution of what the younger son wasted. Second, the elder son's relation to the younger is that of "your brother." These corollaries establish and make manifest the political hierarchy of the *oikos*—a hierarchy founded on acts of love that incarnate the operation of the good, the true, and the just.

The parable records no further response from the elder son; the narration is suspended with the father's answer. We do not know whether the elder son's anger persists, whether his rebellion will force him to undertake the same depoliticization from which the younger son has been redeemed. The reader is confronted with an imaginative choice, although we have seen and understood the trajectory of choosing wrongly. If the elder son goes in and reconciles himself to the situation—he himself has said that he has never transgressed the father's command (*oudepote entolēn sou parēlthon*, 15:29)—then the parable ends on a restoration of the political order. This order is liturgically enshrined in eating—a theme throughout the parable. Feasting in all the parables is an eschatological symbol for the true satisfactions of salvation. It was the lack of food that provoked the younger son into thinking through his alienation. It is to these two polarized forms of consumption, a wrong one and a right one, that the elder son draws attention when he tells his father that his son "devoured your living with prostitutes" (15:30). *Kataphagōn* (devoured) here is in direct contrast to the father's use of *phagontes* (eating) in 15:23 when he asks the servant to prepare a feast. The prefix *kata-* connotes a destructive form of consumption. The family meal around the fatted calf looks back to the Jewish Passover and forward to Luke's account of the Last Supper, the institution of the eucharistic feasting, and eschatologically to the heavenly banqueting.

That the right order of things is enshrined in such a routine and daily activity underlines that this is a lived political order, organically related to a cosmos that is nonhuman, human, and divine, not a constituted, mechanical, and contracted order. It is lived through a politics of election announced in the recognition of the realm to which one belongs in Christ (seen in terms of the younger son's return from self-imposed exile). It demands a politics of responsible following (seen in terms of the elder son's continuing faithfulness ["you are always with me"]) and a liturgical politics of celebration (the father's doxology for the son's return). The freedoms of depoliticization—freedoms profoundly associated with the ability to spend money, consume destructively, and be seduced by the goods on offer in the market; freedoms also profoundly related to an intemperate libido or sexual excess—are understood as dehumanizing. The younger son is turned away from himself and forced to dwell with the nonhuman. It is not that the order of the father rejects property or economics. The elder son will inherit. But love is excessive to such property owning and the rationale of the market. The fatted calf will be sacrificed because the son's return to the politics of the *oikos* is more important than either property or the market. The father's just excesses redeem the excesses of the prodigal son.

Political Discipleship

As mentioned in the opening remarks of this chapter, we can map the historical trajectory, with its present depoliticization and its present preoccupation with customer satisfaction and the freedoms of the marketplace, on to the narrative trajectory of this parable. This is done to emphasize the need for Christian believers to take seriously the politics of election regarding the consequences of capitalist and secular freedoms, and the politics of following. It is the living out of these two politics in the context of the Christian kingdom that constitutes the politics of discipleship.

The language of discipleship (*mathētēs*, disciple) is the language of pedagogy. There is no disciple without a teacher. In the ancient world, as in the medieval, the teacher attracted pupils who would follow him or her, and the educational program was one in which the transfer of knowledge included moral and metaphysical instruction. It was a hierarchical relation in which the disciple submitted to, and was in obedience to, the teacher. Two of the central questions Aquinas takes up in his compendious *De veritate* concern the teacher and the nature of the mind. For Aquinas, these questions are inseparable not only because teaching is concerned with the transfer of knowledge and understanding and minds both facilitate and maintain this knowledge and understanding but also and principally because the mind contains the image of the Trinity; the mind is the *imago Dei* mentioned in the creation of human beings in Genesis. For Aquinas, God communicates interiorly to human beings through the mind. Hence arises the question whether God is the first and perfect teacher. Aquinas answers in his inimitable *sic et nunc* manner, claiming that although God is the first cause of true knowledge, reason is the efficient cause and teachers can act as external cooperators with God. The final cause, as throughout Aquinas, is communion with God. He concludes his analysis of teaching by making a significant distinction: "The insight of the teacher is a source of teaching, but teaching itself consists more in the communication of the things seen than in the vision of them."[7] Human teachers, then, stand in some analogical relationship to God as teacher in the same way sight stands analogically related to vision. There is similarity but there is also difference. This is important regarding discipleship, for the primary teacher here is Christ himself. Aquinas has nothing to say about Christ as teacher in his analysis. But what is significant about Christ as teacher is the manner in which he both communicates "the things seen" (as the parables demonstrate) and "the vision of them." Furthermore, whereas, for Aquinas, the teacher is always superior to the pupil as the doctor to the patient (he frequently relates teaching to healing), the sovereignty of Christ has the capacity to subvert this hierarchy: "No longer do I call you servants . . . but . . . friends" (John 15:15 RSV). Christian pedagogy and Christian following both begin and end with the commandment to love; true service is loving. And love, as seen above, is political, that is, always implicated in a field of differential power relations.

The connections between teaching, following, and love are ancient. From Plato is the tradition that knowledge is a remembrance of a truth known outside time and corporeality, a truth about whence we came and whither we will return. From Plato also is a tradition that what we desire is that which is true and beautiful and beyond (again) time and corporeality. Both Plato's understandings of truth and beauty are inseparable from his teaching on the Good, the Good beyond being. It is this Good that draws us, dragging us like prisoners from the depths of the cave into the natural light in the parable that Socrates relates in *The Republic*.[8] There is a reason for following—not just blind obedience. Education, for Plato, was the disciplining of desire, the orientation of desire toward that which was truly desirable. Augustine, as an exemplary Christian

7. Thomas Aquinas, "The Teacher and Mind," questions 10 and 11 in *Truth* [*De veritate*], trans. James V. McGlynn, SJ (Chicago: Henry Regnery, 1953), 2:57.

8. Plato, *The Republic*, trans. Benjamin Jowett (London: Vintage, 1991), 253–61.

teacher, advocates a similar disciplining of desire, orientating the soul toward a greater and greater attunement with God through love. But he differs from Plato not least in that his teaching is not his but Christ's. Furthermore, Christ is both teacher and what is being taught. Christians *may* follow Augustine's wise counsel but *must* follow Christ's. The politics of Christian discipleship, then, may bear some analogical relation to the model of teacher/pupil, and Mary attests to this in the garden on Easter Sunday when she calls Christ *Rhabbouni* (John 20:16), but there are important differences. Jesus instructs Simon and his brother Andrew to "follow *me*," not simply to follow his teaching.

The language of Christian discipleship is the language of pedagogy with a difference: it is to be taught the true understanding of God by God himself through the Spirit, who "will guide [*hodēgēsei*] you into all the truth" (John 16:13). *Hodēgeō* is related to *hodeuō* (to travel or journey) and *hodoō* (lead the right way). The Spirit of truth travels alongside, guides in moving the disciple forward, onward, into truth. As with all good teaching, the discipleship is fostered in a relationship with the teacher, but the Christian relationship to Christ is more profound. Discipleship is participation in God's own self-expression, rooted in the economy of God's grace toward creation. The disciple's love and desire, which govern the profundity of the relationship with the teacher, are not just orientated toward but created and sustained by the love and desire of God. Jesus prays "that the love with which you have loved me may be in them, and I in them [*kagō en autois*]" (John 17:26) (see chap. 4, above, on the character of this coabiding). The politics of Christian discipleship has one goal, con-formity with Christ. There may be other by-products—salvation, the forgiveness of sin; the coming of the kingdom; the acting out of justice, truth, goodness, and beauty in and through the body of Christ; the preaching of the gospel—but these are all effects of a more profound operation: "I am in my father, and you in me, and I in you" (John 14:20). This operation and the following it enjoins go far beyond the teacher/pupil relation.

The operation of God's grace that brings about this con-formity with Christ involves each Christian in a journey toward a personhood yet to be fully unveiled—an eschatological personhood, an eschatological humanity. "Beloved, we are God's children now; what we will be has not yet been revealed. What we do know is this:

when he is revealed, we will be like him, for we will see him as he is" (1 John 3:2). We can observe again the chiasmus, the crossing over from one subject to another: what *we* will be has not been revealed, but the revelation is what *he* is, not what we are. It is the same logic as "you in me, and I in you." Eschatological humanism that stands in excess of what Taylor defines as the "exclusive humanism" of the secular age is worked out in the following.

But how do we follow? For the first disciples, it was literally a matter of getting up and moving to the places to which Jesus traveled. But on another level, their following also entailed coming to a clearer understanding of what it was that Jesus had come to do and what they would have to do when he was no longer there. This second following included listening and seeing. They were encouraged to hear the parables carefully, and they were encouraged to observe the signs of the times—the miracles, the attention of the crowds, and the demonstrations of power in quelling the tides and withering the fig tree. The Gospel accounts themselves bear witness that although the disciples did not understand Jesus at the time and neither listened nor observed the times well, eventually they were brought to understand. The account of Peter's first public speech, after the day of Pentecost, in the Acts of the Apostles (2:14–26) is a narrative aimed at making clear how much had been understood in the wake of events following the resurrection. In the light of the resurrection and the baptism in the Spirit, what they had listened to and observed while Jesus lived was illuminated, so that a coherent picture emerged. This picture became the gospel that was preached.

John 10:1–6 provides us with a parable about following in which the Greek verb *akoloutheō* (follow) is closely associated with *akouō* (hear, obey, know) and *oidasin* (to know). The sheep of Christ's fold will hear his voice (John 10:3) and will follow that voice obediently (John 10:4), because they know the one they hear and obey (John 10:4). The followers were transformed by the knowledge of Christ that they entered into through their engagement in, and then continuation of, his ministry. Mark's Gospel, in particular, portrays the ignorance and stupidity of the early disciples and their misguided expectations of the messianic mission, and the church would not exist had such ignorance not been overcome. Although theologically we understand our participation in Christ through the sacraments, the only Jesus we can identify, this political Jesus, is the Jesus created for us by those who followed him. It is out of their stories, their images, and their representations, as we interpret them in our own times, that we construct our Christologies and our patterns of imitation. The church that grew up in the decades following the death of Jesus maintained a strong notion of imitating Christ quite literally. Paul exhorts the church to "imitate (*mimētai*) me, then, just as I imitate Christ" (1 Cor. 11:1 GNT)," for as 1 John 4:17 puts it, "because as he is [*ekeinos estin*] so are we [*hēmeis esmen*] in this world" (RSV). The ontological language of John's first letter is scandalous in the same way as Jesus's use of the verb "to be" in its present tense when, at the Last Supper, he holds up a piece of bread and states, "This is my body" (*touto estin to sōma mou*, Mark 14:22 NRSV, RSV).[9] Imitation of Christ here is not copying; it is not an imperfect repetition of the same act. It is not an echo. It is a reperformance albeit in another key and on another instrument. It is scandalous that we walk down our Market Streets, our Seventh Avenues, and our Tottenham Court Roads as Christ walked. But this is the corollary of our eschatological humanism and the ecclesiology outlined here. It is the corollary of our political discipleship. Following is a mimetic practice, a practice of obedience, and a practice of faith.[10] Faith is the character of living in the zone of indistinction that messianic time announces (see chap. 4, including Agamben's insights). This faith is not the same as "belief" in our contemporary world. Philip Goodchild has drawn attention to the way the dematerializations and virtual realities that capitalism breeds leads to a culture in which belief and desire abound.[11] Contemporary believing is cheap, in fact lazy, almost passive. Faith, on the other hand, is an act of entrustment, the entrustment necessary if one is to continue following. Finally, following is a movement forward, beyond oneself, beyond even the community within which the self is constituted. To live beyond oneself is to live the way of the cross and the resurrection, and it

9. For a more detailed examination of this ontological scandal, see Ward, *Cities of God*, 81–96.

10. For a detailed elaboration of this notion, see Ward, "Christology and Mimesis," in *Christ and Culture*, 29–59.

11. Almost a refrain throughout Goodchild, *Theology of Money*, an analysis of contemporary capitalism, is the phrase "belief and desire"; these are the pillars on which our culture now rests—not facts but imagination, aspiration, and need.

is in this living, this participation in the cross and the resurrection, that we deepen that primary relation to Christ.[12]

Our following differs circumstantially from that of the early disciples, but not substantially. The following still entails a listening and a watching; the engagement is one of trusting, of entrusting oneself to the future promise of what has yet to be revealed—the eschatological remainder. We each are shaped by the practices we engage in, by the other people and the institutions that facilitate these practices, even legitimate them. This is what it means to be a social animal. This does not mean that we are completely socially determined, for we come to judgments and make choices. Nevertheless, our sense of self issues from the way we interact with our environment and the way this environment interacts with us. The eschatological personhood that issues from following Christ situates Christians in a place beyond the times and spaces of a particular environment. Christians live out, for example, in the practices of faith and hope, a temporality that does not conform to what has passed and what now is. We can be neither victims of history nor condemned to the present. As noted earlier, globalization and advanced consumerism are obsessed with the present—the pseudo-eternity of the present. To seize the day is to live the present moment to its fullest, to be satisfied. But the temporality of Christian discipleship always recognizes a remainder: where Christ is not fully revealed, then the present remains incomplete. To live, to act out this remainder in a culture that glorifies the buzz and adrenalin rushes of living in the present is not simply an act of resistance but a testimony to an alternative understanding of what is true. Christians are continually called on to live in and beyond their cultural conditions, whether these are dominated by consumer markets or by climates of fear that can whip up, for example, racism and xenophobia. The eschatological character of the personhood that Christians are working out involves them in practices that cut across, or run counter to, some of the ideas and ideologies in their immediate contexts. In this way, following is political because con-formity to Christ necessitates the cultiva-

12. See Hans Joachim Schoeps, "Von der Imitatio Dei zur Nachfolge Christi," in *Aus frühchristlicher Zeit* (Tübingen: Mohr, 1950), 286–301, who views following as a messianic claim, although it must be recognized that following the way or path (Hebrew *derekh*) of righteousness is a profoundly Jewish idea. In Hegel's politics we live out only the cross.

tion of attitudes and actions that can align themselves only to the things of this world with an eschatological remainder.

At the very cutting edge of the practice of following is prayer, for it is only in prayer that the discipline of listening is developed. The *via activa* is rooted in the *via contemplativa*.[13] An examination of prayer will help us to understand something further about eschatological personhood as con-formity to Christ. Although in the last three chapters we saw that discipleship and following are not concerned primarily with the individual person—with the working out of my calling, my vocation, and my response to God's grace—the examples of visiting the sick and the imprisoned, of feeding and clothing the poor can appear to exalt outward activity by an undescribed agent.[14] Attention here to prayer as an inward activity will correct any misapprehensions. Fundamental to prayer is recognizing that, as a Christian act, it is not locked into any post-Cartesian and Pietist subjectivity. Prayer differs from much of New Age religion that finds its focus in self-development and self-advancement—to become better equipped to take advantage of what is around us.[15] It is both I and the Spirit within me who pray. As mentioned above, personal salvation is a by-product, an effect of the operations of God's grace. Christ in me disrupts the atomized individual, unseats him or her from being in command, opens the self to the infinity of what is God. None of the acts of following, outwardly or inwardly, can be reduced to the exertion of an individual's will. Every act is folded into the orientation of the self toward what endlessly transcends it, what Maximus the Confessor describes as "the divine, universal infinity . . . of his greatness there is no end . . . that boundless abyss of goodness, too great for astonishment."[16] What we bring in prayer to this enfold-

13. See Thomas Aquinas, *De veritate*, question 10, where he discusses the active and the contemplative life with respect to teaching.

14. Having rejected the dualism of mind/body, I do not like the dichotomy that "outward" and "inward" suggests, but I can think of no better way of putting this. The relation between inner mental activity and outer physical activity is a continuum. Aristotle understood this and contemporary neuroscience confirms it. See the popular works of Antonio Damasio, e.g., *The Feeling of What Happens: Body, Emotion, and the Making of Consciousness* (London: Vintage, 2000).

15. See Slavoj Žižek, *On Belief* (London: Rougledge, 2001), 63–68, on Western Buddhism.

16. Maximus the Confessor, *The Ascetic Life: Four Centuries on Charity*, trans. Polycarp Sherwood (London: Longmans, 1955), 192.

ing is the world itself—not simply ourselves but the whole world we are caught up in, that vast network of relationships of which we are a part, the complex corporations onto which our bodies are mapped. As Christians, we bring to God all the concerns and connections we have with the contemporary world (see chaps. 1–3): the crisis of democracy, the reduction of life to economics and consumption, and the various roles that religion is playing and being forced to play in the public sphere. Praying is thus the most political act any Christian can engage in—richly layered, nuanced, and continuous.

Prayer is not just intercession, and prayer need not be vocalized at all. Being in the world in Christ, being in the world as Christ, as a living organism, we are continually being called on to respond to the environment that envelops us. We respond physically, emotionally, and mentally. Indeed, we cannot apprehend all the levels on which we are responding: "The brain knows more than the conscious mind reveals."[17] And the body has a knowledge into which we have only oblique insight.[18] There is prayer at conscious, verbalized levels—public prayer, the solitary confession, thanksgiving, the Ave or Our Father, for example. But dwelling as we are in Christ, there is a praying at somatic and mental levels over which we have no control. There is a praying that goes on within us as the Spirit breathes and the soul communes. The world's events as they come to our attention from various sources—the media, present circumstances, the hearing of other people's stories, and so forth—are filtered through our ensouled flesh. They are registered within and they modify within as we attune ourselves to the world. That miraculous escape we read about in the newspaper that caused us joy, those gangs of teenage girls and boys congregating at the corner shop late at night that cause us to fear and move us to pity, those scenes of carnage on the news in the wake of a bomb attack that cause us to shudder at the violence and grieve with the shell-shocked—all these events pass through us and change us. And as we dwell in Christ and Christ in us, then they pass through Christ also. This is what I mean by praying: that deep inhabitation of the world, its flesh and its spirit, that stirs a contemplation and a reading of the signs of the times that is more profound than we

17. Damasio, *Feeling of What Happens*, 42.
18. Ward, *Christ and Culture*, 95–96.

can ever apprehend or appreciate. This is what in German can be described as the *Urgrund* of Christian discipleship: we live and act as transistors for the transformation of the world through Christ. It is not just the individual who is being conformed to Christ; it is the whole of creation. Indeed, it is only as individuals give back to Christ the world in which they subsist that they themselves are transformed. In an observation on Aquinas, Kathryn Tanner notes, "One perfects oneself in imitation of the self-diffusing goodness of God by perfecting others."[19] I take the act of prayer as the root practice by which such perfection is given and received. All things are brought before the feet of the cosmic King, brought to confess the lordship of Christ, through prayer as deep inhabitation of the world and through the contemplation that necessarily issues from this inhabitation.[20] This is the logic of following and the politics of discipleship.

In our inhabitation of the world, we are continually listening. For what? Maximus the Confessor can again assist us here: part of what we listen to is our yearning, the reaching out of our desire for communion with Christ. There may be a thousand petitions, requests, voiced frustrations, and cries of hurt in prayer, but fundamentally what we are articulating is our yearning. In this yearning we glimpse the yearning of the church itself, glimpse ourselves as part of the body of Christ extended through time and across space. And since Christ is that which is most interior to us, as the "I in you," then part of what we listen to is Christ's yearning, that yeaning in the heart of Christ to heal and transform. This desire to transform will always be restless with the status quo; it can never accommodate the world on the world's terms. The healing that Christ wants can come only after recognition of the conflict of values, of understanding; it can follow only the judgment of sin, of hubris. Our conformity to Christ will necessitate sharing in this yearning for the healing and transformation of the world—and sharing also in the conflict and the judgment. Prayer is thus

19. Kathryn Tanner, *Economy of Grace* (Minneapolis: Fortress, 2005), 27.

20. The New Testament warns about not hardening one's heart. Hardening of the heart is the exact opposite of the openness to the world that discipleship requires. To harden one's heart is to become locked into the fury of one's pain, anger, bitterness, resentment, hatred, etc. There is no redemption from this position, no healing possible, without surrendering once again to what is given. This hardening is the deepest sin, which only repentance and confession can transfigure.

always concerned with ushering in the kingdom of God, even though what this kingdom is has yet to be revealed. Every prayer reaches out toward some inchoate understanding of, even present participation in, another order—a true, just, and good order being prepared, waiting to be revealed. For us who are created, prayer is the primordial participation in the eschatological remainder. It is the very fact that the kingdom has not yet been revealed and cannot now be delineated and defined that distinguishes such a notion from utopian dreaming. For "utopia" etymologically means "nowhere" (*ou* + *topos*); it has no place and therefore is not a real alternative. Utopian thinking can function critically regarding current political scenarios; it is not, then, without importance, for it challenges the imagination to conceive differently.[21] But the Christian kingdom is not utopian at all because, in faith and hope and in the practices of prayer and following, it has a substance, even if this substance remains incomplete. Every act of Christian living is testimony to the reality of the kingdom as a new social and political realm. It is not the stuff of dreams because it makes possible, is the condition for the possibility of, the experienced renewal of, hope.

The kingdom operates as a horizon to all Christian acting and believing, like the hills in Psalm 121 that are constantly looked to for the advent of salvation. The Christian is thus continually engaged in practices of hope, making claims in a faith at odds with what is visible. And so the church operates and maintains a virtual existence quite distinct from the pursuit and generation of simulacra, one of the consequences of globalization (see chap. 2). This is the church as the apophatic body (see chap. 6). It is important to examine this difference to appreciate how another understanding of virtual reality can operate, antithetical to that produced and disseminated by advanced capitalism. For if the most political act for a Christian lies in the act of prayer, drawing what issues from the politics of election and of following into a communion of mutual yearning with God, then the political arena within which such political acts are empowered is the kingdom.

21. See Paul Ricoeur, "L'idéologie et l'utopie: deux expressions de l'imaginaire social," in *Du texte à l'action: Essais d' herméneutique* (Paris: Éditions du Seuil, 1986), 379–92.

Discipleship, then, is political in two related senses. First, it is implicated in a field of relations.[22] The "you in me, and I in you" relation is primary, but this is given substance in the relations that this relation fosters with other disciples—the coworkers, the differential ministries, the callings of those who also responded, albeit in a different manner, to the politics of election. Second, discipleship is political because it is explicitly engaged in ushering in a kingdom. The political nature of Jesus's life, death, and resurrection is signaled throughout the New Testament by references to the messiah, to the new lawgiver, and to the new Joshua. The Gospel of Luke is particularly sensitive to this politics. He frames his narrative with reference to Herod of Judea, the emperor Augustus, and Quirinius, the governor of Syria, and Jesus's ministry with reference to Emperor Tiberius and Pontius Pilate, the governor of Judea. Mary heralds the birth of her son in a Magnificat that sings of a great social revolution: the scattering of the proud, the bringing down of thrones and dominions, the exaltation of the lowly, and the filling of the hungry. Jesus begins his preaching of the gospel by reading from a scroll that tells of his anointing to bring good news to the poor, proclaim release to captives, recover sight to the blind, and free the oppressed. The language of kingdom and kingship reverberates throughout, culminating in the scenes before Pilate. Discipleship is political because it is implicated in a messianic reversal of established values and in a challenge to received authorities and principalities. It is not simply anarchic and iconoclastic; rather, Christian discipleship is political because it demands to know in what relation to Christ stands any other sovereignty. This discipleship began with the ministry of John the Baptist, already caught up in a political battle with Herod, and continues with Christ.[23] The first disciples may have been tax collectors and fishermen, but the last words of Jesus in Matthew's Gospel present a phenomenal political challenge: "All authority in heaven and earth has been given to me" (Matt. 28:18). It is a statement in line with the call to arms: "Do not think that I have

22. This concurs with, e.g., Karl Barth and Stanley Hauerwas. Hauerwas sees that "the 'self' names not a thing, but a relation. I know who I am only in relation to others, and, indeed, who I am in relation with others" (Stanley Hauerwas, *The Peaceable Kingdom* [Notre Dame, IN: University of Notre Dame Press, 1983], 97).

23. See John Howard Yoder, *The Politics of Jesus* (Grand Rapids: Eerdmans, 1972), 27–29.

come to bring peace to the earth; I have not come to bring peace, but a sword" (Matt. 10:34); "The one who has no sword must sell his cloak and buy one" (Luke 22:36). All this and the language of servanthood![24]

As stated at the beginning of this chapter, Scripture can be, and has been, used for any number of political agendas. Discipleship has always been a political matter because it concerns the commission to preach and enact the kingdom of God. It entails choices, judgments, commitments, values, and actions informed always by that ruling con-formity with Christ. It also entails defeats and overcomings, and these are not at all just metaphorical; the rejection of property by St. Francis, the stand of Luther before the emperor Charles V at the Diet of Worms, the decision by Bonhoeffer to be linked with a plot to assassinate Hitler, and the call made by Archbishop Oscar Romero to the Salvadorian army to mutiny were not metaphorical acts. They challenged authority even within the church itself, and it is always important that the space for this remains open because the church is not coextensive with the kingdom. Each one of these decisions and acts was done in the name of Christ, in the faith that these were Spirit-led actions in accordance with Christ. The same is true of other less dramatic, but no less effective, initiatives: the establishment of Oxfam by a Jew, an Anglican, and a Catholic; the founding of one of the largest nongovernmental organizations, CARE, by Quakers after the Second World War, and the work of the Christian Democrats in Europe on behalf of the European Union.

The Kingdom

If the church is not coextensive with the kingdom, how does discipleship (which the church fosters and facilitates) relate to the kingdom? The kingdom of God is far older than the church historically, but it contained the church eschatologically. The idea is

24. Oscar Cullmann suggests that up to half the disciples were Zealots (*The State in the New Testament* [New York: Scribner, 1956], 8). Although this assertion can be challenged, the association between Jesus's teaching, the sedition for which he was crucified, and the work of the Zealots is the center of two significant accounts of the Zealot movement: Martin Hengel, *Die Zeloten* (Leiden: Brill, 1961); S. G. F. Brandon, *Jesus and the Zealots* (New York: Scribner, 1967).

found throughout the Hebrew Scriptures, from the writings of the Deuteronomist through the Psalms and into both the Major Prophets (e.g., Isa. 33:17–19) and the Minor Prophets (e.g., Mic. 4:6–13). Indeed, Zechariah 9:9 provides the intertext for Jesus's triumphal entry into Jerusalem on the back of a colt: "Lo, your king comes to you; triumphant and victorious is he, humble and riding on a donkey, on a colt, the foal of a donkey." As Oliver O'Donovan reminds us, a Christian political theology must concern itself with the history of Israel and with history as providence, as the history of God's salvation.[25] For political theology, as O'Donovan observes, rests on the one who has the authority—or, as Carl Schmitt points out, sovereignty and monotheism.[26]

The Gospel of John provides the most elaborate account of the kingdom—although the Synoptic Gospels treat it also[27]—through the story of Jesus's confrontation with Pilate regarding the nature of sovereignty.[28] The context of this confrontation is that already in the Passion Narrative Jesus has had to confront the authority of Annas and Caiaphas (John 18:12–24) before submitting to Roman rule. "Are you the King of the Jews?" Pilate asks. "Jesus answered,

25. See Oliver O'Donovan, *The Desire of the Nations: Rediscovering the Roots of Political Theology* (Cambridge: Cambridge University Press, 1996), esp. 30–192, which provide an exegetical account of "Israel's political tradition as normative" (74).

26. See Carl Schmitt, *Political Theology: Four Chapters on the Concept of Sovereignty*, trans. George Schwab (Cambridge, MA: MIT Press, 1985), and Schmitt, *Political Theology II*, trans. Michael Hoelzl and Graham Ward (Cambridge: Polity, 2008).

27. Despite Luke's political theme, his Gospel has no discussion about kingship.

28. I am crossing a hermeneutical line here concerning the relationship between the Gospel narration and the historical Jesus, but Yoder—a better theologian than I—has crossed it before me: "It should not be thought that by failing to deal at length with such historical-critical problems, the present paper makes any neo-fundamentalist assumptions about the composition of the Gospel text, or about the diversities within the development of the early churches and during the formation of the canonical texts" (Yoder, *Politics of Jesus*, 24). A substantial treatment of the old quest or the new quest for the historical Jesus would not be at all irrelevant, but it would blunt the message here, which is not only that the situation Jesus faced was a highly political one (which means that he was self-consciously a political actor) but also that the Gospels were themselves part of the ongoing politics of the situation opened by Jesus, as all Christian theology continues to be. Apologetics is the stock-in-trade of demagogues—as George W. Bush and Blair remind us—and *euangelion* was a political and public proclamation. The fact that many New Testament scholars might angrily wish to challenge my exegesis is all to the point: theology is political—indeed, perhaps politics at its most raw—because we are treating ultimate power, authority, and jurisdiction.

'Do you ask this on your own, or did others tell you about me?'" (18:33–34). And so begins this strange exchange—strange because of Pilate's dramatic profile (he is not simply a villain or an indifferent Roman functionary), the simple directness of his questions, and his complex response to the figure before him. Two kingdoms confront each other like the forces arraigned on either side of a chessboard.[29] Earlier Jesus had fled from a crowd, discerning that they wanted to make him king. Now the challenge of defining the truth of the situation is to be faced head-on. The ignorance, even naiveté, of Pilate's opening question is countered by a two-part question from Jesus aimed at clarifying the motivation behind Pilate's question: does he ask because he himself wishes to know the truth, or is he merely repeating the accusation against Jesus brought by the leaders of the synagogue? What is astonishing about this scene is that they speak to each other as equals. Pilate's opening move for control of the situation is countered, just as later, after he has had Jesus flogged and finds him silent before his questions, Pilate will state, "Do you not know that I have power [*exousian echō*] to release you, and power to crucify you?" only to be answered by Jesus, "You would have no power over me [*Ouk eiches exousian kat' emou*] unless it had been given you from above" (19:10–11). Between these two exchanges lies the heart of the matter:

> "My kingdom [*basileia*] is not from this world. If my kingdom were from this world, my followers would be fighting to keep me from being handed over to the Jews. But as it is, my kingdom is not from here." Pilate asked him, "So you are a king [*basileus*]?" Jesus answered, "You say I am a king. For [*eis*] this I was born, and for [*eis*] this I came into [*eis*] the world, to testify to the truth." (18:36–37)

Several observations can be made on the basis of this passage. First, there are, it seems, two types of kingdom and two types of king—those of this world and those "not from [*ek*] this world," "not from here [*enteuthen*]." The phrases "kingdom of God" and "kingdom of heaven" are not found in the Hebrew Bible, although, given the economic realignment often associated with the coming of

29. In the background lies another of Jesus's titles, "Son of man," which refers back to the messianic figure in the book of Daniel, which, as O'Donovan notes, is anti-imperialist throughout (*Desire of the Nations*, 87–88).

the messiah (the exaltation of the poor over the rich), some scholars point to the account of the Jubilee Year in Leviticus 25:8–12 as a prophetic model.[30] Mark 11:10 speaks of the "kingdom of our ancestor David." Whatever the place to which Jesus will go after his death—the place, announced to his disciples, that he goes to prepare (John 14:2–4)—it cannot be circumscribed either geographically or historically. It can be located only negatively with respect to the "world." It is another place, an alternative place, and it preexists the founding of the church. "The church is not the kingdom but the foretaste of the kingdom. For it is in the church that the narrative of God is lived in a way that makes the kingdom visible."[31] The importance of this truth for the church itself and for the world cannot be overestimated. The church has no control or monopoly over the kingdom; God will act where God wishes to act. The work of Christ is not restricted to the church and in all likelihood is not always done in and through that church. The kingdom, then, is more like Augustine's conception of the *civitas Dei*, which Augustine, too, never identified with the church visible and institutional. The church thus cannot boast of any sovereignty or jurisdiction of its own, for it has none. The sovereignty and jurisdiction belong to the kingdom that "is not from here." And so the church has to exist in humility and patience, submitting all its judgments to an agnosticism that will not be removed before the day when the truth of all judgments is revealed. The church cannot dictate when, how, and where Christ will work. It cannot itself circumscribe the kingdom and say what is in and what is out. The boundaries of the kingdom are hidden in God, just as the life of the church is hidden in God. The church, like the disciples who make up the church, lives with the eschatological remainder (see chap. 4).

Second, Jesus will speak about a kingdom (*basileia*) but appears reluctant to designate himself king (*basileus*); the word is Pilate's, not Jesus's. Twice Pilate attempts to make Jesus to use the word and confess his kingship, and twice Jesus thwarts his desire. Con-

30. See André Trocmé, *Jésus-Christ et la révolution non-violente* (Geneva: Labor et Fides, 1961). More recently, see Michael S. Horton, *The Lord and Servant: A Covenant Christology* (Louisville: Westminster John Knox, 2005), 245–48. Horton also reminds us that messianic kingship is related to Christ's fulfillment of two other offices, prophet and priest.

31. Hauerwas, *Peaceable Kingdom*, 97.

tinually Jesus distances himself: the kingdom is elsewhere and he has come into this world. The repetition of *eis* in the final sentence emphasizes both a dynamic and a purpose to the actions of being born and entering into creation. But the repetition leaves Jesus a figure set apart from other human beings—both in the world and not of the world. This is the situation, he announces before his arrest, that his disciples will occupy (15:18–19). With Jesus and with his disciples, the kingdom is, then, both in the world and not of the world; it is a kingdom operating in the world but drawing its citizens out of the world. It is a kingdom in which sovereignty is exercised, but in a way that does not map easily on to terms for such a sovereign ("king") in this world or to terms related to governance as we know it ("nation," "state").[32] Indeed, throughout Jesus's Farewell Discourses in John, exemplified most clearly in his act of washing the disciples' feet, sovereignty (and teaching) in the kingdom is a sovereignty (and pedagogy) of service (13:12–17).

Nevertheless, Pilate continues to refer to Jesus as a king in a manner that becomes increasingly complex. He asks the Jews, "Do you want me to release for you the King of the Jews?" (John 18:39). This can only be ironic. Given the understanding that any king not established by the emperor was a threat to the *imperium*, a fact of which the Jews themselves remind Pilate, this question sounds like an attempt to test the loyalty of the Jewish community itself. When the Roman soldiers then dress Jesus up in a purple robe and a crown of thorns, the title "King of the Jews" is downright cynical. Something has changed in Pilate by John 19:8, when for the first time he hears the charge that Jesus claimed to be the Son of God: "he was more afraid than ever" (*mallon ephobēthē*). "Son of God" was a term used of the emperor himself; the confrontation between Christ and Caesar is starkly defined. It is not now Pilate's authority that the presence of Jesus is challenging. The former equality between the two protagonists, each facing the other, is

32. Jesus might have avoided the title "king" because kings—Herod Antipas, for example—held only figurehead titles under imperial jurisdiction. They had little power as such; the sovereign power was Caesar's. They helped facilitate the gathering of taxes as the country's tribute to Caesar. Pilate seems nonchalant about giving Jesus the title "King of the Jews," perhaps because this meant nothing to him, although he may be making a cynical remark to the Jewish authorities. The courts of the kings of Roman-occupied Palestine were, if the New Testament is to be believed, places of corruption and self-indulgence.

now under review, and it is at this moment that Pilate speaks of his own power. Now Jesus reminds him of a fundamental difference that ranks himself above Pilate. The power Pilate has is on loan, from Caesar, from above (*anōthen*, 19:11)—the same term Jesus uses when telling Nicodemus, "no one can see the kingdom of God without being born from above" (3:3). The power that Jesus is claiming is his own. When Pilate returns to the Jews, he speaks of Jesus's kingship in a different tone: "Here [*Ide*] is your King. . . . Shall I crucify your King?" (19:14–15).

Critics have made much of the possible anti-Semitism of John's Gospel, emphasizing the politics of storytelling within a certain *Sitz im Leben*. This is, then, according to such critics, a politics within a politics—a politics of kingship within a politics of possible racial discrimination. For us, the importance of Pilate's question to the Jewish crowd is that he appears to accept the title on Jesus's behalf, employing a word he supposes Jesus himself should have used although he did not. Indeed, to preface the statement "your King" with *Ide* is remarkable because this was how emperors and kings were heralded when making a public appearance.[33] The Jewish answer returns us to the central confrontation between Christ and Caesar: "We have no king but the emperor" (19:15).[34] This confrontation is finally played out on the cross itself with the contestation about the plaque Pilate places above Jesus's head. The Jewish leaders object, "Do not write, 'The King of the Jews,' but, 'This man said, "I am King of the Jews."'" But Pilate answers, "What I have written I have written" (*Ho gegrapha, gegrapha*) (19:21–22). Pilate's simple but rhetorical repetition emphasizes a personal involvement, a testimony—rather like the Roman centurion's statement in Mark's Gospel when he sees the crucified Christ die: "Truly this was [a] Son of God" (Mark 15:39 RSV).

Third, revealed through this trialogue on kingship are shifts in power. Jesus, powerless as his power and dominion lie elsewhere, is finally championed by the representative of Caesar, whose very empire Jesus is confronting. The seemingly powerful Pilate acts

33. See Peter Oakes, "Re-mapping the Universe: Paul and the Emperor in 1 Thessalonians and Philippians," *Journal for the Study of the New Testament* 27, no. 3 (2005): 301–22.

34. The Gospel of Luke adds another dimension to this confrontation by describing Barabbas as an insurrectionist: the opposition between the revolutionary politics of Christ and that of the Zealots.

as an instrument no longer of Rome but of the Jewish officials. And the Jews, who seemed to control the action throughout, have now subjugated themselves to the emperor. There is a victory for Christ's kingdom even while he undergoes a seemingly ultimate defeat. The power of the kingdom of God, not of this world, is establishing itself in the very crucifixion itself as Jesus had predicted in his earlier teaching in the Gospel about being "lifted up"—simultaneously crucified and exalted. The cross is the scepter and the sword of this newly established kingdom.

We might read the events that lead up to the crucifixion as Jesus's deliberate drawing out of the political powers of the world. Earlier in the Gospel, Jesus slips away before the (Jewish) powers that be can take further action. After his entry into Jerusalem on a colt, there is a public unmasking of the powers that reign, whether they be the Pharisees and Sadducees, the kingship of Herod (mentioned in the Synoptic Gospels), the proconsul's vicarious sovereignty, the authority of the *Pax Romana*, or the "prince [*archōn*, ruler, leader] of this world" (John 12:31 KJV). What begins as a story of micropolitics ends on the macropolitical stage.[35] It is as if, before the freedoms won by Christ through cross and resurrection can be participated in and before the Spirit can empower this participation for the working out of salvation, human beings have to recognize the forms of slavery in which all are bound. And such a recognition can come about only if the powers ruling this world are made manifest in the unjust killing of this most just man. Making manifest the powers that operate in this world and their limitations allows judgment to be passed upon them, a judgment that history enacts. This exchange, then, with Pilate concerning power is part of this necessary unmasking and judging before the disarming of that last power, death, with the resurrection. This is a most dangerous political action. Pilate warns Jesus that he is playing with the big boys. To push this political action any further will lead to his death both as an insurrectionist and as one accursed (under Jewish law). But Jesus knew this was going to happen anyway; he had predicted it from the start.

Insofar as the church continues this political work of Christ and his kingdom, then its politics too are concerned with unmasking

35. In Luke's Gospel, however, the macropolitical context of Jesus's birth and Herod's slaughter of the children reveals, from the start, the international stakes of the messiah's coming.

the powers that operate in the world, revealing the levels of bondage under which people are living (even if in this bondage the world speaks loudly of freedom and equality). Indeed, "the world has no way of knowing it is world without the church pointing to the reality of God's kingdom."[36] In a similar way, Pilate learns the nature and limits of his own power through this confrontation with Jesus. The nature of this power is arbitrary and pragmatic because, unlike Jesus's power, it considers the question of truth as irrelevant to ruling. "What is truth?" Pilate asks. The limits of this power are evident in that although he himself has his doubts of this man's guilt and tries to find a means to release him, he nevertheless is forced to capitulate to what the Jewish leaders demand, and the Jewish leaders, for their part, are made to attest to their own subservience to Caesar.

There are two common words in Greek for power: *exousia* (authority, government, right) and *dynamis* (ability, capacity, strength, might). Both words have political connotations. The discussion of power between Jesus and Pilate is not about who has the physical might to effect change. Jesus refuses angelic help; he stands naked of the physical power to change his circumstances. Pilate has the physical power but does not refer to it because it is a power being trumped by the arbitrary will of the Jewish crowd, whom he does not wish to incite, for incitement might cost him his employment with Caesar. The power is not his own anyway: the power to command his soldiers is the vicarious use of Caesar's authority; it is the power of an office. It is the question of authority over which they both contend, and, indeed, John throughout speaks only of *exousia*.[37] Jesus then confronts Pilate with a distinction between two kingdoms, two notions of kingship, and two sources of authority and, in doing so, demonstrates who is really the most powerful. But there are not necessarily two different forms of authority, since the same word is used for both. Pilate's power is vicarious and belongs to the imperial orders of this world. Jesus's words to him

36. Hauerwas, *Peaceable Kingdom*, 100.

37. *Dynamis* does not appear in John's Gospel. The Gospels of Matthew, Mark, and Luke, however, do use *dynamis*, which is frequently translated as "miracle" or "miraculous power" and is related to God the Father, whose kingdom will come with "power" (*dynamis*) and glory, as Jesus narrates it in teaching the disciples to pray the Pater Noster. Although John shows Jesus performing the miraculous, John speaks of "signs" rather than miracles and castigates faith that relies on miraculous power (John 4:48).

are fraught with irony. His reply in Greek begins emphatically on a negative (*ouk,* no): "You would have no [*oudemian*] power over me unless it had been given to you from above [*anōthen*]" (John 19:11 RSV). This can be read as a simple reminder to Pilate that his authority to act comes from his superior, Caesar. But there is a famous use of the Greek *anōthen* early in the Gospel when Jesus tells Nicodemus that he must be born "from above" (3:7). *Oudemian* is a hinge word here, often untranslated because it reiterates the negative, and it carries the idea of "useless," "worthless" here. So this reply could be read as, "You have no power over me, and what power you have is worthless if it is not authorized from above." The Greek is deliberately vague, speaking of a power transcending the provisional ebb and flow of human government just as the kingdom announced is located elsewhere—the power of a rule beyond even Caesar's rule. Nevertheless, that the same word, *exousia*, is used by both Pilate and Christ suggests perhaps that, eschatologically, there is only one authority, one power, and that the rule and power of this authority orchestrate all things providentially. The sovereignty of God's kingdom enters into the history and histrionics of what it is to be human, finite, and fallible, guiding and transforming it from within. Athanasius reminds us, "The Word can not be confined to his body; nor was he there and nowhere else; he did not activate that body and leave the universe emptied of his activity and guidance. . . . So also when he was in the human body he himself gave that body life; and at the same time he was of course giving life to the whole universe, and was present in all things; and yet distinct from and outside the universe. And while being recognized from his body, through his actions in the body, he was also manifest in his working in the universe."[38] Athanasius repeatedly refers to Jesus Christ as "All-Sovereign." There is ultimately only one authority and therefore only one kingdom. Other kingdoms may be established and may exercise governance, but there is a final ruling operating within and beyond such kingdoms, bringing all things into submission to its authority. The politics of discipleship belong to this kingdom now come, in Christ, bringing about in this world what is in heaven. "Heaven," we might say, is this kingdom "not from here" and now among us.

38. Athanasius, *De incarnatione*, trans. *On the Incarnation* (Crestwood, NY: St. Vladimir Seminary Press, 1989), 17.

So Just What Is Wrong with Theocracy?

Why is Jesus so wary of the title "king"?[39] The people refer to him as a king when he enters Jerusalem riding on a colt, but only in the Gospels of Luke and John. It is not a title that he ever ascribes to himself. The attempt to understand his wariness takes us into the thickets of a perennial difficulty in the history of the relationship between religion and politics from a Judeo-Christian perspective. We have to return to the Hebrew Scriptures and the appointment of Saul as the first king of Israel, for it was not an uncontested appointment. First Samuel 8–12 retells the story, in which kingship is not God's choice but the people's desire, a desire that God, with warnings, graciously allows them. God wishes to rule over them directly, through his judges-cum-cultic-priests, of whom Samuel is the last (his sons did not follow in his ways). The "word of the Lord" would come to these people, who exercised the sovereign rule of God. God's own political preference seems to have been some form of theocracy, although the Christian tradition has employed 1 Samuel 8–12 on kingship to sanction such totally different notions as papal sovereignty (by Pope Gelasius I),[40] the limitation of papal sovereignty (by Dante),[41] the divine right of kings (by James VI of Scotland/I of England),[42] and the overthrow of monarchic absolutism and the establishment of democracy (by Thomas Paine).[43] In Jesus's own time, kings were understood either as Herodian tyrants, who heavily taxed the people to furnish the wherewithal for magnificent building programs, or as adjuncts in the pay of Rome (as were Herod Antipas and his two brothers). Luke's portrayal of Herod Antipas is far from being a flattering

39. If we accept the account of the ascension in the Acts of the Apostles as Jesus taking up the throne in heaven—if we accept, that is, the ascension as a coronation—then we can understand why O'Donovan sees the "Ascension [as] of great importance to political theology" (*Desire of the Nations*, 144). The *carmen Christi* of the Letter to the Philippians bears out such an interpretation of the ascension with its reference to God raising Jesus to the heights, bestowing on him a name above all names, and placing all things in heaven, earth, and the depths at his feet (Phil. 2:9–11). Jesus finally accepts the title when it is given to him by the only one who can give it to him, the Father.

40. See Michael Hoelzl and Graham Ward, eds., *Religion and Political Thought* (London: Continuum, 2006), 21.

41. Ibid., 49–63.

42. Ibid., 89–101.

43. Ibid., 137–48.

account of kingship. The Zealots and Maccabean nationalists may well have cultivated the notion of Davidic kingship associated with the messiah, but they were committed to violent terrorist warfare. If Yoder is right, Jesus was tempted by such a potentiality in establishing his kingdom but consistently resisted it. The word "king," then, even if there was a quite certain sense of a "kingdom," is too equivocal a term.

With Jesus's reluctance to use the word "king," however, perhaps we have to turn back to 1 Samuel once more and again take theocracy seriously. Despite the origins of the word "theocracy" in Greek—where the word means the rule of God—theocracy is not a Greek political idea. For example, it is not one of Aristotle's forms of polity. The first-century Jewish historian and apologist Josephus coined the word in his polemic against the anti-Semite Apion.[44] He used it positively, even apologetically, to describe the Jewish people living under the law of God, and no doubt, by employing a Greek composite noun, he wished to give the concept Hellenistic clout. He was writing in Rome and in the context of imperial Rome, a Rome that held under its sway both Judea and Egypt (where Apion was). Theocracy was a legitimate form of polity, Josephus announced; this was polity under the sovereignty of God.

The word did not catch on. Although historians look back on Calvin's Geneva as a theocracy, it was never called this. The French *théocratie* is first registered in 1679, where it is used to describe, objectively, ancient Jewish society and the cult of ministers and agents associated with the temple. From there it was taken up into Italian, as *teocrazia*, around 1700, and eventually it found its way into German, as *Theokratie*, in 1728. In the earliest use of the term in English, John Donne, in a sermon of 1622, when he was dean of Saint Paul's in London, spoke of the Jewish people living directly under the mandate of God as a "theocracy." In the context, it was a word used positively. Donne's patron, George Villiers, was the infamous favorite of King James VI/I. It was King James in his own political writings (particularly *Basilikon Doron* and *The Trew Law of a Free Monarchy*) who developed the medieval notion of the divine right of kings in a theocratic direction, always careful to distinguish true sovereignty from tyranny. The Puritan

44. Josephus, *Against Apion* 2.16.

dictator Oliver Cromwell, in the commonwealth and protectorate years of the seventeenth century, put what was becoming a political concept into practice by trying to accommodate English law to biblical precedents and thereby banning Christmas, the theater, and maypole dancing because they were not prescribed in the Bible. The history of theocracy therefore merges into the history of monarchy and absolutism. And these three terms, in their various times, were affirmative.

In our contemporary political climate, theocracy is not a concept in season; in fact, it is set in opposition to democracy. It gained public, and negative, currency in 1979 after the Islamic revolution in Iran and the deposition of the shah. Among those endorsing liberal freedoms and egalitarianism, "theocracy" is now found mainly alongside the adjective "Islamic," and a finger points with moral indignation at countries manifesting forms of Islamic hegemony. But according to a Christian biblical theology (on which James VI/I and Oliver Cromwell drew), the kingdom of God *is* a theocracy and theocratic politics is what Christians are about. Metaphors and apocalyptic narratives apart, the goal of God's covenant—which is eschatological from beginning to end—is a new heaven, a new earth, and a "holy city, the new Jerusalem, coming down out of heaven from God" (Rev. 21:2). The political relations in this city are unique:

> I saw no temple in the city, for its temple is the Lord God the Almighty and the Lamb. And the city has no need of sun or moon to shine on it, for the glory of God is its light, and its lamp is the Lamb. The nations will walk by its light, and the kings of the earth will bring their glory into it. Its gates will never be shut by day—and there will be no night there. People will bring into it the glory and the honor of the nations. (Rev. 21:22–26)

This passage contains three important features. First, three orders—the Lord God and the Lamb, the kings, and the people—are hierarchically arranged. No doubt the arrangement owes much to premodern notions of social order. Second, although kings bring their own glory and the people bring the glory and honor of the nations to which they belong, both kings and people come in adoration. They come as servants to the one Lord and this Lord's coequal Lamb. And third, the church is nowhere on the scene. In the kingdom there is no hieratic order mediating between absolute sovereignty and the masses.[45]

Theocracy is not only the social and political condition to which Christians aspire; it is inseparable from the covenant God made with creation. Humankind is to have dominion over all living creatures—fishes, birds, cattle, wild animals, and every creeping thing (Gen. 1:26)—but the Creator God has ultimate governorship. To the extent that this ordering reflects the hierarchical relation between suzerain and vassal, it also presents a nonhierarchical relation between human beings themselves: all are equal before God, each being made in God's image and likeness. These vertical and horizontal lines of power are again reflected in the Israel-Yahweh relationship. There was the theocratic polity of Israel, mediated through the tabernacle and an ordained priesthood (the Levites) and the establishment of a federation among the twelve tribes; Joseph's line being divided between Ephraim and Manasseh. On the death of Moses, this federation is eventually headed by a judge and obedience was then due Joshua. Even so, these judges (prophets, lawmakers and law defenders, distributors of justice and wisdom) were appointed by God: "the Lord spoke to Joshua son of Nun" (Josh. 1:1). So both the theocratic rule and the federal constitution were maintained. That all did not go well within the federation is a story well told. The judges did not fulfill their role, which was not to rule but to pass judgment, keep the peace, and, like the priesthood, offer intercession. Only God ruled over the people. Indeed, judgment, it seems, was dealt out annually at the cultic sites: "Samuel judged Israel all the days of his life. He went on a circuit year by year to Bethel, Gilgal, and Mizpah; and he judged Israel in all these places. Then he would come back to Ramah, for his home was there; he administered justice there to Israel, and built there an altar to the Lord" (1 Sam. 7:15–17). The people of Israel had no ruler until God granted them their request for a king; part of the request was for "a king to govern us, like other nations" (8:5), and when God spoke to Samuel, God explicitly told him that the people "have not rejected you, but they have rejected me from being king over them" (8:7). In the history of Western political thought,

45. The understanding of the church as a moment in the coming of the kingdom saves the church from "theocratic tyranny" (O'Donovan, *Desire of the Nations*, 27).

1 Samuel has been cited by promonarchists and antimonarchists alike. But with the appointment of kings, as the books of Kings and Chronicles recall, there was an end to the united Israel and the confederation of tribes. Even so the prophets kept alive the theocratic desire, along with a horizontal confraternity, through a developing messianism and apocalypticism. The passage above from Revelation is heir to both these theological trajectories.

The emphasis on the theocratic remains evident in the New Testament. Although the church, as a social organization in the world, must "render unto Caesar the things which are Caesar's" (Jesus's phrase, Matt. 22:21 KJV) or be "subject to the governing authorities" (Paul's phrase, Rom. 13:1), there is the consistent recognition that "there is no authority except from God" (13:1). Jesus Christ is Lord of heaven and earth, even though there seems to be a difference between Jesus's call to a division of responsibility (both to God and to Caesar) and Paul's calls to an affirmation of "those authorities that exist [because they] have been instituted by God" (13:1). This is highly fertile ground for debate among Western political theorists. But the notion of the kingdom of God is a theopolitical one, and it announces the continuing double axis: absolute submission to God, on the one hand, and equality with respect to all neighbors, on the other. If we prefer to call the second axis protosocialist ("All who believed were together and had all things in common" [Acts 2:44]), the former remains unambivalently theocratic or aristocratic. It was the interpretations of Jesus's and Paul's political positions that led, on the one hand, to the danger Rousseau saw to the social contract in a Christian's higher allegiance to God[46] and, on the other, to Tocqueville's reassurances that Catholics were not only good democratic citizens but also fostered democratic values.[47] For both Rousseau and Tocqueville, the answer lay, as it had in the Treaty of Westphalia, in a division between the private and the public: religion should have no political platform.

But as we have seen, we now live on the other side of this convenient dualism of private and public. "The Westphalian separation

46. See "Civil Religion" book 4.8, in *The Social Contract*, trans. Maurice Cranston (Harmondsworth: Penguin Books, 1968).

47. Alexis de Tocqueville, *Democracy in America*, trans. Harvey C. Mansfield and Delba Winthrop (Chicago: University of Chicago Press, 2002), 276–77.

of religion and international politics, an idiosyncratic product of Western civilization, is coming to an end."[48] So where stands theocracy now? As I said at the beginning of this study, this is not a polite book; it is a political book. If the rejection of theocratic language came with the acceptance of liberal-democratic polity and secularism, then, in a time of postdemocracy and postsecularity, should we not revisit this form of polity? Or, rather, should Christians not be honest that this is the polity to which they have committed themselves in becoming followers of Christ? Let us put aside the all-too-evident weakness and limitations of the visible church in its various forms and the all-too-evident weakness and limitations of those of us who follow; we are all swimming in seas of faith where there are zealous thrashing to little avail, undermining hypocrisies, and nauseating lukewarmness. Where we are is not the point, and as I said (without pointing a finger), not all of us in the church are of the church anyway. The culminating political act is Christ's when judgment is delivered. But in principle if not always in fact, every act, every intuition, every emotional response, every thought is to be submitted to God, to be ruled by God—terrifying and liberating as this inevitably is. So, as a people of God, we are theocratic.

Acknowledging our theocratic condition and the theocratic resonance that governs the eschatological remainder sharpens the distinctions, so that contestation becomes inevitable. But contestation is a manifestation of the liveliness of civil society and a refusal of the zero degree dialectic that depoliticization encourages. Furthermore, contestation is not war; it can be honest talk that sets out practices of coexistence and common values. For too long have practitioners of faith suffered under the myths and accusations of those sixteenth- and seventeenth-century wars of religion, and the likes of Dawkins and Hitchens stir up stories of past violences, blending them into the present with vitriolic panache.[49] That they have nothing positive to say about religion

48. Samuel P. Huntington, *The Clash of Civilizations and the Remaking of World Order* (New York: Simon & Schuster, 1996), 54.

49. Richard Dawkins, *The God Delusion* (London: Transworld, 2006), 23, 351; Christopher Hitchens, *God Is Not Great: How Religion Poisons Everything* (New York: Atlantic Books, 2007). I am grateful for the vigorous critiques particularly of Dawkins's work by Terry Eagleton (see his review of *The God Delusion* in *London Review of Books*, October 19, 2006, available at www.lrb.co.uk/v28/n20/eagl01_

betrays a not-just-remarkable ignorance; to reduce religion to its negative impact on civilization is notably trite and astonishingly ungrateful. Is it not time to take a stand? Cowardice is the cost we pay for comforts that may not last long, for not rocking the boat. But we cannot shout "peace, peace" out of fear of being hurt, fear that we are unable to take the initiative, and fear of getting it wrong. Fear rules so much Christian accommodationism—fear that is sugar-watered down to speak of love. We cannot close our eyes to what we see around us; we cannot allow ourselves to be aesthetically seduced into a profound forgetfulness. The forces of dehumanization, dematerialization, and depoliticization are strong and hegemonic; new poverties and new slaveries proliferate; and we are sleepwalking into a future that threatens to overwhelm if grace and a transcendent goodness cannot prevail. There is a time for being apocalyptic if what we are threatened with as a world is making itself manifest, as the writers of the books of Daniel and Revelation understood. Apocalyptic, we recall, is first a genre of writing that is concerned with an unveiling, a revealing of what yet remains hidden (from the Greek *apokalypsis*, revelation). As a form of writing, it does not necessarily pronounce doom but, rather, radical change, the end of something once thought invulnerable, a state of affairs once considered the truth about the way things are in the world. If I am being apocalyptic, it is in this manner, since all the indications are that the future does not fly toward us on the wings of angels—not angels of peace anyway.[50] Today the streetlights still come on in many of our towns as darkness falls, the steaks being marinated for the barbeque lie covered on the kitchen surface, the lime juice drips over the ice as the gin is poured, the beers are cooling in the fridge, and the hot water runs

.html) and John Cornwell (see his *Darwin's Angel: An Angelic Response to "The God Delusion"* [London: Profile Books, 2007]).

50. This study has said nothing about the consequences of climate change and the diminishment of fossil fuel and water resources. Other scholars have performed the research and drawn attention to the challenges that face us here. The issues of immigration across Europe alone beggar belief, and the struggle for control of the land that remains inhabitable is not going to be negotiated quietly or behind closed doors. See Michael Northcott, *The Environment and Christian Ethics* (Cambridge: Cambridge University Press, 1996); Northcott, *The Moral Climate: The Ethics of Global Warming* (London: Darton, Longman & Todd, 2007); Philip Goodchild, *Capitalism and Religion: The Price of Piety* (London: Routledge, 2002); Goodchild, *Theology of Money*, 47–52.

for the children's baths—today. And probably tomorrow. And even during the next year. But for the next decade? For the next generation? The buzzword is "sustainability," and it is loudly voiced in the midst of a rising tide of skepticism about how sustainable the present modes of living in the West really are.

Finally, there are global religions that have the potential to work internationally and in alliance (see chap. 2). They have enormous resources for moral value and the authority to legitimate such value. The Holy See therefore deserves to have a representative in the United Nations, not just an observer. Faith-based diplomacy and faith-based aid have already accomplished much—for example, Muslims giving sanctuary to Christians fleeing the Rwanda massacre, Archbishop Tutu heading the Truth and Reconciliation Commission in the new South Africa, the Quaker body shields in the bombing of Iraq by the United States and British governments, the Catholics at Tantur mediating between the Palestinians and Israelis, and the social aid undertaken by Hezbollah following the Israeli bombing of Lebanon. Religion will not go away; it will not be repressed; it will not succumb to instrumental reasoning. There will be no new Enlightenment.[51] So let us herald the next stage: the advent of the postsecular state.

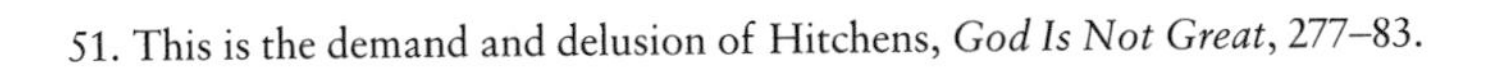

51. This is the demand and delusion of Hitchens, *God Is Not Great*, 277–83.

Author Index

Subject Index